PRESIDENT KENNEDY HAS BEEN SHOT

PRESIDENT KENNEDY HAS BEEN SHOT

Experience the Moment-to-Moment Account of the Four Days That Changed America

by the

NEWSEUM

with Cathy Trost
& Susan Bennett

narrated by
Dan Rather

sourcebooks
mediaFusion

An Imprint of Sourcebooks, Inc.®
Naperville, Illinois

Published by Sourcebooks, Inc.
P.O. Box 4410
Naperville, Illinois 60567-4410
(630) 961-3900
FAX: (630) 961-2168
www.sourcebooks.com

Library of Congress Cataloging-in-Publication Data

President Kennedy has been shot / by the Newseum with Cathy Trost and
Susan Bennett.
p. cm.
Includes bibliographical references and index.
1. Kennedy, John F. (John Fitzgerald), 1917–1963—Assassination. 2.
Kennedy, John F. (John Fitzgerald), 1917–1963—Assassination—Sources.
I. Trost, Cathy II. Bennett, Susan Lewis. III. Newseum.
E842.9 .P74 2003
364.15'24'097309046—dc22
2003015512

Printed and bound in the United States of America
VP 10   9   8   7   6   5   4   3   2

TABLE OF CONTENTS

CD TRACK LIST

1. INTRODUCTION—DAN RATHER

2. FRIDAY MORNING IN FORT WORTH
Kennedy speaks to the Chamber of Commerce.

3. ARRIVING IN DALLAS
Dallas radio station KLIF describes the president's arrival.

4. THE MOTORCADE
Lady Bird Johnson recalls hearing gunfire.
Dallas Police Chief Jesse Curry orders officers to Parkland Memorial Hospital.

5. ARRIVING AT PARKLAND HOSPITAL
Lady Bird Johnson recalls their arrival.

6. FIRST NEWS BROADCASTS OF SHOOTING
ABC News' Don Gardiner broadcasts first national report.
CBS News' Walter Cronkite brings the news to national television.
NBC News' Robert MacNeil reports more details.
ABC News' Bob Clark reports from the hospital.

7. AT THE TEXAS SCHOOL BOOK DEPOSITORY
Dallas police radio calls all squads to the scene of the shooting.
A Dallas reporter describes the police activity in the Texas School Book Depository.
An eyewitness tells what she saw to WBAP-TV in Dallas.

8. THE WHITE HOUSE AND ADMINISTRATION PLANES
The White House relays the news to press secretary Pierre Salinger aboard the Cabinet plane.
Secretary of State Dean Rusk is told to direct the flight to Washington instead of Dallas.

9. POSSIBLE SUSPECT DESCRIBED ON POLICE RADIO
Dallas police radio crackles with the description of a possible suspect.
Officer J.D. Tippit checks in with Dallas police dispatch.

21. LADY BIRD JOHNSON REMEMBERS JACQUELINE KENNEDY ON AIR FORCE ONE
Lady Bird Johnson recalls trying to console Mrs. Kennedy while en route to Washington.

22. PRESIDENT JOHNSON SPEAKS WITH ROSE KENNEDY
From Air Force One, President Johnson calls John F. Kennedy's mother, Rose Kennedy.

23. PRESIDENT AND MRS. JOHNSON SPEAK WITH NELLIE CONNALLY
The Johnsons call Nellie Connally, the wife of wounded Texas governor John Connally.

24. NEWS BROADCAST OF SUSPECT'S BACKGROUND
ABC News' broadcasts information about Lee Harvey Oswald's background.

25. RETURNING TO WASHINGTON
ABC News' Dick Bates describes the eerie scene as Air Force One returns home.

26. A NATION COMES TO A STANDSTILL
ABC News' chronicles several canceled sports events and displays of mourning on Broadway.

27. ANNOUNCEMENT OF OSWALD'S ARREST
ABC News' Walter Porges reports that Oswald is charged with the president's murder.

28. CASKET ARRIVES AT THE WHITE HOUSE
Westinghouse's Sid Davis creates a solemn picture of Kennedy's return.
Davis weeps as he closes his report with one of Kennedy's favorite poems.

29. OSWALD PROCLAIMS HIS INNOCENCE
Oswald tells reporters at the Dallas police station that he is innocent.

30. A FALLEN LEADER LIES IN STATE
ABC News' Edward P. Morgan describes Kennedy family members mourning at the White House.

31. POLICE CAPTAIN FRITZ PROCLAIMS OSWALD'S GUILT
ABC broadcasts Dallas police captain Will Fritz telling reporters that Oswald is guilty.

32. PRESIDENT JOHNSON SPEAKS WITH EDWARD KENNEDY
At the end of his first full day in office, President Johnson phones Senator Edward Kennedy.

33. OSWALD IS MURDERED
NBC News' Tom Pettit is reporting as Oswald is shot, live on television. WNEW Radio's Ike Pappas reports the news simultaneously, with strains of Pettit's report heard in the background.

34. REACTION TO THE SHOOTING OF OSWALD
ABC News' Robert Sharp interviews people in Dallas for reactions to Oswald's shooting.

35. CASKET IS REMOVED FROM THE WHITE HOUSE
ABC News' Bill Downs speaks of the grief and tension in Washington.

36. ANNOUNCEMENT OF OSWALD'S DEATH
NBC News' Frank McGee announces that Oswald is dead.

37. MOURNERS PAY RESPECTS TO KENNEDY
CBS News' Roger Mudd describes the staggering number of mourners.

38. PRESIDENT JOHNSON SPEAKS WITH GOVERNMENT AND CIVIC LEADERS
President Johnson seeks J. Edgar Hoover's help.
President Johnson and Martin Luther King Jr. discuss the challenges that await Johnson.

39. FUNERAL PROCESSION BEGINS IN WASHINGTON
ABC News' Norm Craft whispers his report of the Kennedy family kneeling at the casket and other mournful details of the procession.

40. MEMORIAL SERVICE AT ST. MATTHEW'S CATHEDRAL
Kennedy's memorial service takes place inside St. Matthew's Cathedral in Washington.

41. OSWALD'S BURIAL IN FORT WORTH
A reporter describes the starkly different funeral service for Oswald in Fort Worth.

42. PROCESSION ARRIVES AT ARLINGTON NATIONAL CEMETERY
ABC News' Bill Downs conveys the details of the procession's arrival at Arlington National Cemetery.
Cardinal Cushing's prayer for the fallen president is followed by a twenty-one gun salute.

We all seem to know exactly where we were and what we were doing when we learned that President John F. Kennedy had been shot. It was a moment seared into memories for a lifetime. For those who reported the shooting and subsequent events to the nation and the world, it was a profoundly transforming experience. This is the story of those who were there, the first witnesses to this infamous piece of history, and how they brought the tragedy to a nation in shock. Here, more than sixty journalistic witnesses describe what they saw, what they learned, and how they reported it. Some would go on to legendary careers—others, indelibly affected, would leave journalism, never to return.

The Kennedy assassination story remains so vivid in the national consciousness, however, because of the work those men and women did under the intense pressure of deadline and the trauma of the tragedy. They left us with words and images so sharp and powerful that remain with us as if we saw and heard it all yesterday—a pained Walter Cronkite choking on the news that the president is dead; the haunting images of the Zapruder film; the crumpling body of Lee Harvey Oswald as he is felled by Jack Ruby's bullet.

The programs, exhibitions, and publications of the Newseum, the world's first interactive museum of news (soon to be reopening on Pennsylvania Avenue in Washington, D.C.) take readers and visitors behind the scenes to explain the news process—the how and why of what journalists do. In this book you will see both the competitive and the compassionate sides of reporters doing a difficult job under difficult circumstances. Journalists typically are forward-looking, anticipating the next story, preparing for the next event. Here, they take a revealing look back at their first rough draft of history and the way they handled a story that would change the nation, themselves, and their profession forever.

Joe Urschel
Executive Director and Senior Vice President
Newseum

6 On Friday, November 22, 1963, a national radio audience tuned in to a popular music program on the ABC network was stunned when newscaster Don Gardiner broke in with the news that shots had been fired at President John F. Kennedy's motorcade in Dallas.

> *We interrupt this program to bring you a special bulletin from ABC Radio. Here is a special bulletin from Dallas, Texas. Three shots were fired at President Kennedy's motorcade today in downtown Dallas, Texas. This is ABC Radio.*

The sketchy first report filed by White House reporter Merriman Smith of United Press International—who was in the press-pool car five vehicles behind the president's limousine—had moved across UPI's teletypes just two minutes earlier, at 12:34 P.M. Central Standard Time.

6 In New York, CBS anchor Walter Cronkite broadcast the first television announcement of the shooting at 12:40 P.M. From that point on, the three television networks of the era—CBS, NBC, and ABC—stayed on the air nearly four days without commercials or regular programming. It was "the most massive and most concentrated broadcasting coverage in history," according to *Broadcasting* magazine. Only coverage of the September 11, 2001, terrorist attacks has since surpassed it in duration.

As the news broke, newspapers and magazines around the country tore up regular printing schedules and frantically began assembling "extra" and special editions to deal with the fast-breaking news. The printed word still had enormous impact. *Time* magazine reported that crowds waiting for first editions of newspapers in Munich broke into fights when supplies ran low, and news vendors in Rio de Janeiro had to call for police protection.

As the drama played out over four days in November, journalists faced the daunting task of reporting a fast-paced story with accuracy and dignity. At a time when security was far less rigorous and reporters got much closer to news events, many of them literally had front-row seats for what would be the most challenging news story of their careers.

Although reporters generally had greater access than they do today, their technology was far more primitive—TV cameras required time to warm up before operating and were tethered to hard-wired electrical systems. Television news mostly relied on film, not videotape or live broadcasts. That translated into time lost during processing and editing. Most people got breaking news from radio, not television. Print and broadcast newsrooms around the country largely were still dependent on the ringing bells of wire-service teletypes to alert them to breaking news.

Today, satellite and fiber-optic communications can instantaneously relay sound and images from anywhere on the globe. In the 1960s, the idea of a global cable news network was not even a dream. *Time* reported breathlessly in its November 29, 1963, edition that "words and pictures reached all the way to Japan, by television signals bounced off the U.S. satellite Relay 1."

33 Television also earned the dubious distinction of airing its first live murder when NBC broadcast the fatal attack on Lee Harvey Oswald as he was being moved from a Dallas jail on November 24. NBC correspondent Tom Pettit was just a few feet away when Oswald was shot by Dallas nightclub owner Jack Ruby. Pettit immediately shouted, "He's been shot! Oswald's been shot!" as cameras showed police officers swarming over Ruby's back. NBC was the only network to broadcast live from the jail. The *New York Times* called it "easily the most extraordinary moments of TV that a set-owner ever watched."

CBS, which had cameras at the scene but was taping the transfer for playback, broadcast its taped shooting less than a minute later. ABC lagged behind.

13 Working at full throttle, the news media helped inform and unify a traumatized nation. Reporters on the whole maintained professional composure throughout the weekend, grieving later in private. One memorable exception was the moment that veteran broadcaster Cronkite choked up and wiped his eyes when announcing the official confirmation of President Kennedy's death with the unforgettable words, "From Dallas, Texas, the flash, apparently official: President Kennedy died at 1:00 P.M. Central Standard Time, two o'clock Eastern Standard Time, some thirty-eight minutes ago."

Television came of age that weekend. It marked the moment that "we became a TV nation," *Entertainment Weekly* declared many years later. "Not only did television surpass print for primacy as a news source for the first time, it created a focal point for the public's grief." As many as 175 million viewers were estimated to be watching television at various times during the four-day period.

In covering the Kennedy assassination and its immediate aftermath, the networks logged two hundred hours of broadcasting at a cost of nearly $40 million in lost revenues and added costs, *Newsweek* calculated. Coverage had been relayed by satellite to twenty-three countries.

This book tells the story of the assassination of President Kennedy through the eyes of more than sixty print and broadcast journalists who were part of the coverage of various pieces of the tragedy and its aftermath in Dallas, Washington, D.C., on Air Force One, and in New York.

As with any work of this genre, it must be noted that time can alter memory. After forty years, no two individuals' memories of the same event are likely to be precisely the same. But taken as a whole, these sharply remembered and deeply personal recollections bring to life a story that is as vivid and searing today as it was when it happened.

Journalists were the historic recorders of the events that changed America forever. So many reporters and photographers were assigned to cover this story that several journalists witnessed almost every major event, including the announcement of the president's death and the interrogation and murder of Oswald. Some were privy to more intimate scenes:

• *Dallas Times Herald* photographer Bob Jackson and other journalists saw a rifle being pulled into a window on the sixth floor of the Texas School Book Depository shortly after shots were heard.
• NBC newsman Robert MacNeil and WFAA-TV news executive Pierce Allman are believed to have spoken to Oswald just minutes after the shooting, not realizing he was the shooter.
• *Dallas Morning News* reporters Hugh Aynesworth and Jim Ewell were at the Texas Theatre when Oswald was apprehended.
• *Fort Worth Star-Telegram* reporter Bob Schieffer (later a CBS correspondent) gave Oswald's mother a ride to the Dallas police station and listened as she complained that no one would feel sorry for her or help her out financially.
• *Newsweek* Washington bureau chief Ben Bradlee, a friend of the Kennedys, was at Bethesda Naval Hospital when a "shattered" Mrs. Kennedy arrived and asked, "Do you want to hear what happened?"

- *Life*'s Richard Stolley and Tommy Thompson hid Oswald's mother, wife, and children in a Dallas hotel room for a rare interview.
- Mike Cochran of the Associated Press, UPI's Preston McGraw, and several other reporters were pressed into service as pallbearers at Oswald's funeral.

Even more intimate moments were witnessed by the White House press officials whose recollections are gathered here. Press secretary Pierre Salinger was flying to Japan with Cabinet members. His radio communications with the White House vividly convey shock and uncertainty. Assistant press secretary Malcolm Kilduff accompanied Kennedy to Texas and provides an insider's view of the drama and chaos surrounding events there.

🔊 22 Radio relays to and from Air Force One also reveal some of newly sworn-in President Lyndon B. Johnson's first telephone conversations, including a call to Rose Kennedy, the slain president's mother, and anxious communications about the need to get the Johnsons' younger daughter, Luci, out of school and back to their residence under Secret Service protection.

It was a different era in journalism, both technologically and ethically. With few exceptions, reporters were dependent on manual typewriters and landline telephone communications to dictate breaking stories. No cell phones, electronic pagers, or laptop computers were available to speed and ease their work. Broadcast journalists lugged heavy tape recorders and cameras—which often were linked to trucks carrying electronic equipment. The old mobile unit that served NBC correspondents in Dallas that weekend broke down on Friday and had to be towed behind a wrecker for the rest of the weekend. Photographers used rolls of film, which during a breaking news story often would be tossed to "runners" to be relayed to labs or newsrooms for processing.

Reporters had more relaxed relationships with law enforcement. Before any official announcement, a Secret Service agent flatly told UPI's Smith that Kennedy was dead. The *Star-Telegram*'s Schieffer, who often wore a snap-brim hat to cover the police beat because it helped him blend in with detectives, got exclusive access to Oswald's mother for several hours in the Dallas police station through a sort of "don't ask, don't tell" approach: he wouldn't lie about his identity, but he didn't see the need to say he was a reporter unless someone asked.

This increased access sometimes led to cronyism and self-imposed censorship. Reporters did not always reveal private details, even when they constituted legitimate news. Several reporters could not bring themselves to describe the blood on Jacqueline Kennedy's suit that day. Schieffer did not write about a bizarre conversation he had with Oswald's mother because her comments were so appalling—only realizing later that "you have to be very careful about censoring what people tell you because oftentimes they're telling you what they want you to know."

Journalists could play hardball and did when it came to getting news fast and first. As the press-pool car rocketed toward the hospital just minutes after the shooting, UPI's Smith had a now-legendary scuffle with the AP's Jack Bell over access to the car's radio-telephone. "Smitty" won the wrestling match, filing the first wire-service bulletin about the shooting and refusing to give up the phone until the car had reached the hospital. "It was the ultimate rivalry for the story of the century," said Helen Thomas, longtime White House correspondent for UPI. "Smitty always knew how to look for the phone."

The assassination of President Kennedy on November 22, 1963, like the terrorist attacks on America on September 11, 2001, was a defining moment, shattering illusions and signaling that an era had ended and a new, more tumultuous one was under way. But the republic prevailed and the transfer of power was smooth. "It [seems like] a week since I got up," Johnson wearily told a Kennedy aide shortly after being informed that President Kennedy was dead. Less than an hour later, he was sworn in as the thirty-sixth president of the United States.

For those who were alive then—and for the millions who were not—this story deserves to be retold as an illumination of a gentler, less suspicious time, as a preface to harder times to come, and as a moment in history when journalists worked to their highest capabilities to provide the kind of public service essential to the successful survival of our nation.

Cathy Trost
Susan Bennett
Arlington, Virginia
September 2003

PRESIDENT
KENNEDY
HAS BEEN
SHOT

LEAVING FOR DALLAS

NOVEMBER 21   11:05 AM – NOVEMBER 22   11:30 AM

THE KENNEDY-JOHNSON TICKET needs Texas's twenty-five electoral votes in the 1964 presidential election. President John F. Kennedy and Vice President Lyndon B. Johnson are going to Texas to help mediate a rift in the Democratic Party there—a political feud that pits liberal Senator Ralph Yarborough against conservative Governor John B. Connally.

There are signs that the Kennedy administration might not get the warmest reception in Texas. Right-wing groups have been active there. Ambassador to the United Nations Adlai Stevenson was hit with a protester's sign less than a month earlier. Johnson and his wife, Lady Bird, were jeered in Dallas during the 1960 presidential campaign, even though they are native Texans.

President Kennedy, the nation's youngest elected president, seems eager to make the trip, especially because his wife, Jacqueline, is making a rare appearance with him. A reluctant campaigner, she is making her first official trip since the death of their infant son, Patrick, who died shortly after he was born in August.

Air Force One departs Andrews Air Force Base, near Washington, D.C., at 11:05 A.M. Eastern Standard Time on Thursday, November 21, bound for stops in San Antonio, Houston, and Fort Worth, before continuing to Dallas, Austin, and a visit to the vice president's ranch on Friday. A backup plane carrying the vice president and a press plane with forty-two reporters aboard follow Air Force One.

Despite concerns, Texans turn out enthusiastically at Thursday's stops, and excitement grows about the president's planned motorcade through downtown Dallas on Friday. The *Dallas Times Herald* even publishes a map of the motorcade route on Thursday so people can determine the best sites to view the president.

The presidential party spends the night in Fort Worth, and the next morning, President Kennedy greets a crowd that has gathered in the rain in a parking lot across from his hotel. He speaks at a local chamber of commerce breakfast, and prepares to make the short flight aboard Air Force One from Carswell Air Force Base in Fort Worth to Love Field in Dallas.

The morning is marred only by a vitriolic black-bordered, full-page ad in the *Dallas Morning News* accusing the president of pro-communist sympathies. The ad, backed partially by a local coordinator of the right-wing John Birch Society, troubles the president's aides, but Kennedy is undeterred.

THURSDAY, NOVEMBER 21
ABOARD THE WHITE HOUSE PRESS PLANE, EN ROUTE TO TEXAS

HUGH SIDEY
White House correspondent,
Time

The big story was that this was one of [Kennedy's] opening campaign trips for [the 1964 presidential election]. He was trying to sample the South and to heal the wounds there of

President and Mrs. Kennedy (backs to camera, lower left) greet well-wishers upon arriving in Fort Worth on November 21, 1963.

some of his aggressive civil rights acts. And then there was dissent in the Texas Democratic delegation. Ralph Yarborough, the liberal senator, was at odds with Lyndon Johnson and John Connally. So this wasn't just some kind of surveillance reporting, but an effort to get a look at Kennedy at this stage of the game, coming after the Cuban missile crisis, which elevated him in the eyes of the world, and the headway he seemed to be making—not in legislation but in leadership—and the feeling that [Republican Senator Barry] Goldwater was perhaps going to be [his opponent], and how he would stack up against him. There wasn't any feeling that this was dangerous. It was the furthest thing from anybody's mind, particularly with this president who was so popular.

DALLAS

HUGH AYNESWORTH
science/aviation/space editor,
Dallas Morning News

A month before, Adlai Stevenson had been struck with a sign, and Lyndon Johnson and his wife had been [jeered] at the Adolphus Hotel. People were anticipatory because they were afraid something embarrassing would happen. The city had passed a regulation that protesters could only be so close to the people they were picketing. That was a first for Dallas, and it was meant to be at the Trade Mart, where some people were going to dress up in Uncle Sam suits and picket the president. The ordinance also said you couldn't shout obscenities, that that was against the law too. They thought there would be some kind of a protest at the Trade Mart. But that was all.

KEITH SHELTON
political writer,
Dallas Times Herald

We had prepared extensively because it was a big story. We thought there would be demonstrations, but no one had any thought of any kind of assassination attempt. The political climate was such in Dallas that it was extremely conservative, very much pro-Goldwater. The John Birch Society was very strong. They opposed the United Nations. Some of them opposed public schools. So it was a little bit of a surprise that the crowds [the next day] were very big.

TERRANCE W. MCGARRY
reporter,
United Press International,
Dallas

As I was checking out with Jack Fallon, [UPI's] Southwest Division manager, I said something to him like, "Gee, Jack, wouldn't it be something if one of the local nuts took a shot at the president tomorrow?" We were thinking along those lines because there had been a shot fired at General [Edwin] Walker [in April]. Walker was the right-wing general who had led troops in desegregating Little Rock and then retired from the Army. Also, Adlai Stevenson had been clubbed by a picketer with a picket sign shortly before that. So we were thinking in those terms. I forget exactly what Fallon said. It was something on the order of, "Don't even think about that."

ABOARD THE WHITE HOUSE PRESS PLANE

ROBERT PIERPOINT
White House correspondent,
CBS News

We were a little worried when we left for Texas. The general atmosphere in Texas was very anti-Kennedy, so we were concerned even before we left that there might be some incidents.

MALCOLM KILDUFF
assistant White House
press secretary

Just before we landed, I remarked to Evelyn Lincoln, President Kennedy's personal secretary, that I'd be glad when this [trip to Texas] was over. It was the only one I had any concern about.

SAN ANTONIO

JOHN BENNETT
reporter,
San Antonio News

I was assigned to cover a speech that Kennedy was to make, so I went to the airport and finally ended up at Brooks Aerospace Medical Center, where Johnson and Kennedy both spoke. I had stepped out to smoke a cigarette in a little open space enclosed only by tape. To my surprise, Kennedy and his wife, Jacqueline, walked out. They walked over, and I walked over, and we started chatting. It was just that simple. I made a reference to the Latino citizens who were around the tape and talked about how Latinos were strongly in support of the Democratic Party and his candidacy. He knew an awful lot about people who were significant players on the local level. Three times Mrs. Kennedy broke in and said in a very sibilant

President and Mrs. Kennedy and their Secret Service escorts arrive in Fort Worth.

voice, "So nice to see you." She was absolutely the most beautiful woman I had ever seen.

KEITH SHELTON
Dallas Times Herald

Jackie was a great political asset. She went to a League of United Latin American Citizens meeting and talked to them in Spanish, which was a big hit.

DALLAS

MARY ELIZABETH WOODWARD
society section reporter,
Dallas Morning News

On the night of November 21, a group of friends and I went out to dinner after work. The dinner conversation was charged with excited talk of the big day coming up—the day when we would see our president and, best of all, his beautiful, charming first lady. At last, we were going to get a look at Jackie, the first lady who had caught all our imaginations with her beauty, charm, youth, intelligence, and interest in the fine arts. We were all young and felt a kinship with her that we had never felt with a first lady before. When the dinner party broke up, we drove back to town and scouted out the best place for us to view the motorcade and decided on Dealey Plaza across the street from the Texas School Book Depository. I was anxious to get home because I wanted to give myself a manicure. I knew the president wouldn't see my hands reaching out from the crowd, but somehow I couldn't bear the thought of going to cheer the president looking less than my best.

FORT WORTH

BOB SCHIEFFER
night police reporter,
Fort Worth Star-Telegram

When we heard that President Kennedy was coming to Fort Worth, this was a huge story. Presidents didn't travel nearly as much in those days as they do now. So it was a big story because on this tour of Texas cities, he was going to spend the night in Fort Worth before going on to Dallas the next day. The part that I didn't like was that my boss told me I wouldn't be needed to take part in the coverage. That would be handled by the political reporters, and I was told to report to my duty station at the police station. Like any reporter who is not part of a big story happening in his town, I was pretty upset. However, I did go down to the Fort Worth Press Club the night that Kennedy came to town. We kept it open so that all the reporters covering the White House could come by and have a drink, and we were all excited because these were the bylines that we all knew—these were kind of our heroes. Late in the evening, there was this beer joint, basically, only it didn't sell beer, called The Cellar, in Fort Worth. It was a coffeehouse, an after-hours place. The thing that set it apart was the waitresses wore underwear. That was their business attire, as it were, and people sat around on cushions on the floor. All the visiting reporters wanted to go down there, and Phil Record, who was the night city editor of the *Fort Worth Star-Telegram*, and I were appointed to be their guides. While there, we were joined by some Secret Service agents from Kennedy's detail. They were off-duty, but they wanted to go. They weren't drinking. But we managed to see the dawn come up and see the sun rise in Fort Worth before we left the place.

MIKE COCHRAN
correspondent,
Associated Press

One of our major concerns, of course, was being able to wine and dine the [Washington] press corps. In 1963, Texas didn't have liquor by the drink and we also had a midnight curfew to buy beer at the Press Club. So we not only invited everybody that came in that night to the Press Club, but we kept it open into the wee hours, at which time Bob Schieffer and some other local guys guided the Secret Service and everybody over to The Cellar. Ten months later, they were all testifying before a Senate panel—one of Ohio's senators was checking into just what the Secret Service guys were doing at The Cellar.

Several of us had gone by Doug Cornell's room to invite him to go to the Press Club. He was one of [the AP writers] traveling with Kennedy. He was sitting there and he had his typewriter out—and it was one of those things that will always stick with me forever and ever because of circumstances—and he says, "No, I think not. I've got a feeling tomorrow's going to be a hell of a day."

FRIDAY, NOVEMBER 22
DALLAS

JAMES CHAMBERS JR.
president,
Dallas Times Herald

I was in my office about 8:15 [A.M.] or so, the phone rang, and it was the president. He said, "Can you get me some Macanudo cigars?" He loved a good cigar occasionally. He said, "They don't have any over here in Fort Worth." I said, "Sure." He said, "Well, get me about a half a dozen." I said, "Fine." I went to the United Cigar store and got him six Macanudo cigars that I was going to give him at the luncheon [that day]. And of course that was the last time I heard from him.

FORT WORTH

MALCOLM KILDUFF
White House

I recall the hate ad that appeared in the *Dallas Morning News* that morning. The president didn't even know about that ad until he was on the plane [to Dallas]. Matter of fact, [presidential aides] Kenny O'Donnell and Larry O'Brien and I were eating breakfast in Kenny's room, and I had read the paper early in the morning, and I said, "Did you see this ad in the paper?" They said no. I showed it to them, and they showed it to the president before he arrived in Dallas. He sloughed it off.

ROBERT MACNEIL
White House correspondent,
NBC News

Most of the reporters and White House staffers were talking about the night they had spent, first at the Fort Worth Press Club, then at some grimy nightclub where things got pretty wild. I was glad that I had been too tired to go. We drank our coffee beside our typewriters and studied advance copies of the speech JFK was to deliver at the lunch in Dallas. It was a spirited attack on his conservative critics.

CHARLES ROBERTS
White House correspondent,
Newsweek

The whole thing was on a tremendously high note. We started out in Fort Worth at the Texas Hotel, having spent the night there. The president got up very early and went down to a Democratic rally. He came down with Lyndon Johnson, and he had on the platform with him both [Ralph] Yarborough and John Connally, who in a way were...at least part of what this trip was all about, getting them together, and they had succeeded in doing that. [Kennedy] made, for that early in the morning, a very funny speech, a clever speech, about Texas and the Democratic Party. There was a light rain, but the crowd was tremendously enthusiastic.

He went back to the hotel to this breakfast arranged by the Chamber of Commerce. Mrs. Kennedy hadn't gotten up as early as he did, so he went on without her. Not long before he spoke, she came down. Then in his speech he used the same gag that had gotten such a laugh in Paris, identifying himself as the man who came to Texas with Jackie Kennedy.

PRESIDENT KENNEDY:

*hear...

track 2

Two years ago I introduced myself in Paris by saying I was the man who accompanied Mrs. Kennedy to Paris. I'm getting somewhat that same sensation as I travel around Texas. Nobody wonders what Lyndon and I wear...[the crowd roars with laughter].

ROBERT MACNEIL
NBC News

I went over and saw Jackie wearing a broad mischievous smile waiting outside [the kitchen] with the Secret Service men. The preliminary speeches finally ended and Jackie was announced. The band struck up, the cameras whirred and followed her through the crowd until she emerged in the lights at the end of the head table, resplendent in a suit the color of strawberry ice cream, with a pillbox hat and a dark blouse. She caused a sensation. She was cheered all the way to her seat. And in the back of the room the reporters laughed and wondered how they could describe so blatant a bit of staging without going too far.

We were seven minutes behind schedule leaving for Dallas. Our press bus ran straight up to the press plane, a Pan Am Boeing 707. We raced aboard and immediately taxied out for the takeoff. As soon as the doors were closed, the stewardesses began dispensing the Bloody Marys that were traditional on press planes. The flight lasted eight minutes.

President Kennedy speaks to a rally in Fort Worth on the morning of November 22, 1963. Behind him, from left, are Senator Ralph Yarborough, Governor John Connally, and Vice President Lyndon Johnson.

Anti-Kennedy ad that appeared on page 2 of the Dallas Morning News *on November 22, 1963.*

THE ASSASSINATION

NOVEMBER 22   11:38 AM – 12:57 PM (CST)

AIR FORCE ONE touches down at Love Field in Dallas at 11:38 A.M. Central Standard Time on Friday, November 22. The official welcoming party presents Jacqueline Kennedy with a bouquet of red roses. The president stops to shake hands with people gathered at the airport, and his wife joins him. The weather begins to clear, and it grows warm and sunny—temperate enough to remove the clear bubble-top from the presidential limousine, which was flown in from Washington for the motorcade.

The ten-mile motorcade route is to snake through downtown Dallas, ending at the Dallas Trade Mart, where the president will speak. The lead car, a white Ford driven by Dallas Police Chief Jesse Curry, is trailed by three motorcycles. The presidential limousine carries six passengers, including two Secret Service men. The president and his wife, who is dressed in a brilliant pink suit and pillbox hat, ride in the back of the limousine. In front of the Kennedys sit Texas Governor John Connally and his wife, Nellie. Four motorcycles follow the limousine. The follow-up convertible, code-named Halfback, carries more Secret Service agents, including four standing on the running boards. Behind it is the vice president's convertible carrying Lyndon Johnson, his wife, and Senator Ralph Yarborough. That is followed by another Secret

Service car, code-named Varsity. Behind it is the pool car, which carries the four reporters who make up the White House pool, responsible for filing a press report for the news media that are not present. After that come photographers' convertibles, two press buses, and an array of vehicles carrying other members of the party, including the president's physician.

At 11:55 A.M., two motorcycle policemen clear the way for the motorcade to begin. Despite fears about anti-Kennedy sentiments and sketchy crowds at the beginning of the route, there are throngs of people in downtown Dallas waiting to see the president and his wife.

After traveling through downtown Dallas on Main Street, the motorcade turns onto Houston Street, then makes a final turn onto Elm Street in front of the Texas School Book Depository—a seven-story warehouse for textbooks—before heading through a triple underpass to a freeway. As the motorcade passes the depository, Nellie Connally turns to the president and says, "Mr. President, you can't say Dallas doesn't love you."

FRIDAY, NOVEMBER 22
DALLAS

BERT SHIPP
assistant news director,
WFAA-TV

The sky was gray, it looked like somebody had poured cement over a fried egg, kind of an ugly day. My mind went back to that newspaper ad that somebody had put in the paper [that morning] with a big old black border telling Mr. Kennedy this wasn't his kind of territory and they didn't appreciate him coming.

President Kennedy shakes hands with supporters at Love Field in Dallas on November 22, 1963.

Cameramen Tom Craven of CBS (left) and Dave Wiegman of NBC record the arrival of President and Mrs. Kennedy at Love Field.

JACK BEERS
photographer,
Dallas Morning News

I arrived at Love Field about an hour before the scheduled arrival time for the presidential party. It was raining and still very overcast and threatening to rain even harder. There were many signs displayed such as, "Let's Bury King John"..."Forward With Vigah"..."Onward J.F.K."..."Help J.F.K. Stamp Out Democracy." I discussed the famed bubble-top for the car with a Secret Service man. He explained that it was stowed in the trunk and the car had to be stopped and the bubble assembled by hand in case it was needed. Little did anyone know just how ironic it was that the rain had moved on and the beautiful sunshine would make it unnecessary to use the bubble.

11:38 A.M. (CST)
LOVE FIELD

Reporters are at Love Field when Air Force One lands with President and Mrs. Kennedy aboard. The Kennedys shake hands with the crowd that has gathered to see them, and then enter the presidential limousine for the motorcade through downtown Dallas en route to the Trade Mart.

Largest Daily Circulation In Texas
235,621 WEEKDAYS
258,447 SUNDAYS
ABC Publisher's Statement March 31, 1963

The Dallas Morning News

Nixon Says JFK May Drop Johnson in '64
Story, Sec. 4, Page 1.

VOL. 115—NO. 53 | TELEPHONE: Riverside 1-3811 | DALLAS, TEXAS, FRIDAY, NOVEMBER 22, 1963—54 PAGES IN 4 SECTIONS | ★★★★ | PRICE 5 CENTS

Storm of Political Controversy Swirls Around Kennedy on Visit

By PAUL CRUME

ON A RECENT trip to Austin I visited the new undergraduate academic center at the University of Texas and have to report that things have changed. Study has become a luxury.

This new building is as close an approximation to the Palace of Versailles as an undergraduate is entitled to. Its great halls faced in shining marbles and other polished stones open on large courtyards where tackle-sized statues lie around on pedestals, presumably to remind the student that he had better not lie down on the job. At the front are a couple of enormous figures in stone that look like the sprint relay team making a world's record with the torch of learning.

There are richly furnished sitting rooms in this building and a great many comfortable nooks for chatting, and some of the halls are lined with oils of famous old university men. There was one of Dean Parlin looking like a particularly merry monk in his academic robes. Dr. Mather in his spade beard looked like Mephistopheles.

This undergraduate study hall is so richly done and so elegant that you wonder what the university has in mind for its graduate students.

THE IDEA of the center is to give the student direct access to the materials for learning, especially books, even rare books. The student helps himself. When he leaves, he shows his belongings to a policeman at the door so that none of the university's more precious possessions will be carried out for home work.

We were informed that this policeman has been nicknamed Charlie because he is The Checkpoint.

Dewitt Reddick said the new building often saves a student as much as 45 minutes in getting a book. In my day, we weren't in that much of a hurry to get to a book.

On the day we visited the center, though, it was pretty crowded with kids that looked like your high school daughter or son, all poring over books. They say that this is true even on Saturday afternoon when the nation's Number 1 football team is at its labors in the stadium a few blocks away. The college youngsters seem more serious now than they were in our day—and handsomer and prettier and altogether appealing.

An old grad is somewhat stunned by displays in the undergraduate center. You suddenly realize that the university isn't a new, raw school any more, that it is getting old, and that its past is rich in men, ideas and history.

YOU CAN run into almost anything in this building. Clitus Jones was up there on the day we visited it when he should have been out recruiting. Up on the fourth floor we met Arno Nowotny, the dean of student life, for the first time in years, the kind of wonderful man who stays around our schools, thank the Lord.

Henderson Shuffler was up there in his Texas collection. He had on display some thousands of volumes from the university's rare books on the West including a large section from Frank Dobie's collection of books and western art. He said he hoped with this to interest students in collecting and in some of the great collectors.

After a couple of hours in this building, I thought Henderson's project a little dubious. Probably there aren't any more books to collect.

The university seems to have them all.

Sellout Expected For Andre Previn

Advance ticket sales indicate that Andre Previn's return to Dallas in the season's first One Dollar Concert, Thursday, Dec. 5, will be a repeat of last year's sellout.

To avoid disappointment, order your tickets by mail today or pick them up at one of the several convenient Dallas locations.

For complete details and a handy mail order blank, see ad, Sec. 1, Page 17.

Love Field Braces for Thousands

By CARL FREUND

Dallas police said Thursday night they anticipate that "thousands of welcomers" will jam Love Field to greet President Kennedy when his jet airliner lands there Friday morning.

Police Capt. Glen King said officers anticipate parking lots at the airport will be filled long before the scheduled arrival of the President at 11:35 a.m.

Capt. King said police will divert additional cars into an auxiliary lot which motorists may reach by turning right off Cedar Springs Road after passing the Ramada Inn.

Meanwhile, the U.S. Weather Bureau forecast cloudy skies and occasional showers.

A motorcade will carry President Kennedy, Vice-President Lyndon Johnson, Sen. Ralph Yarborough, Gov. John Connally and most Texas congressmen from the airport through flag-bedecked Downtown Dallas to the Trade Mart on Stemmons Freeway.

Ed Reynolds, president of the Dallas Retail Merchants Association, urged owners and tenants of Main Street buildings to fly the U.S. flag. He said the association also arranged for overhead decorations.

Former Vice-President Richard Nixon, who ran against President Kennedy in 1960, joined police in urging Dallas residents to give President and Mrs. Kennedy "a courteous reception."

Nixon, who was in Dallas for a meeting of soft drink bottlers, said discourteous groups "harm their own cause and help their opponents."

One anti-Kennedy faction scattered leaflets which condemned the President for his stand on integration. The leaflets also criticized U.S. foreign policy.

U.S. Atty. Barefoot Sanders said he was investigating to determine whether the leaflets violated federal laws. Police Chief Jesse Curry said anyone found scattering leaflets would face prosecution for violating "litterbug" ordinances.

Most downtown firms will give employes time off to see the motorcade.

President Kennedy will ride in a blue convertible. If rain is falling, a plexiglass bubble will protect him.

The specially built car was flown here for use in the motorcade.

Police said the motorcade will move slowly so that crowds can "get a good view" of President Kennedy and his wife.

Democratic leaders said they were still hoping President Kennedy will make an impromptu speech when he leaves his plane at gate 28 on the east concourse of Love Field. This is the area where Mexicana Airlines flights normally load and unload.

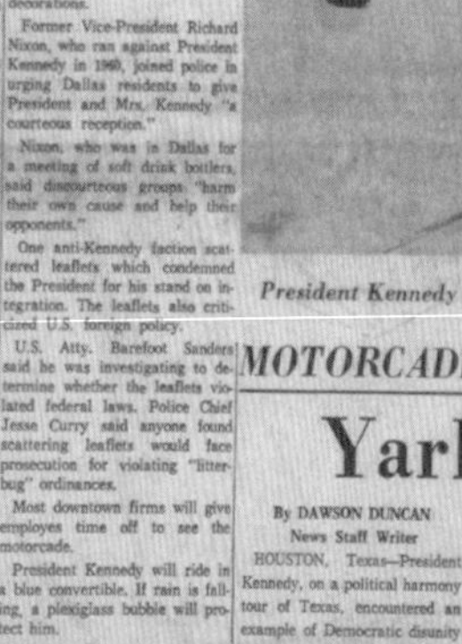

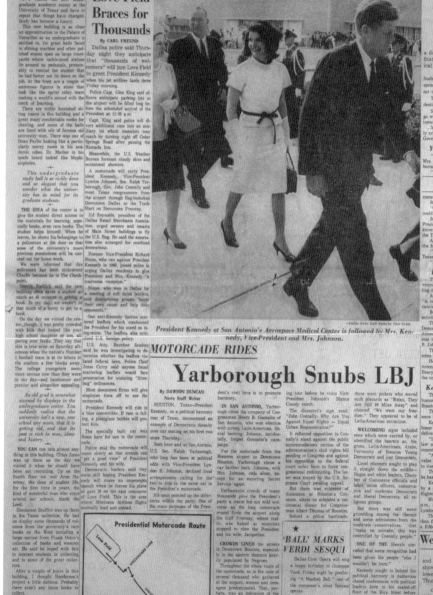

—Dallas News Staff Photo by Clint Grant.

President Kennedy at San Antonio's Aerospace Medical Center is followed by Mrs. Kennedy, Vice-President and Mrs. Johnson.

Split State Party Continues Feuds

By ROBERT E. BASKIN
News Staff Writer

HOUSTON, Texas—President Kennedy wound up a day of "nonpolitical" campaigning in the Lone Star State Thursday night with almost a hurricane of political controversy swirling about him.

The divided Texas Democratic party continued its feuds as the President visited San Antonio and Houston in balmy springlike weather with large and mostly curious crowds turning out to see him and the First Lady.

The day got off to a bad start, politically, even before the presidential Jet 707 reached San Antonio in early afternoon.

Sen. Ralph Yarborough, in the same plane as the President, let go with a blast at Gov. John B. Connally as the big plane speeded toward Texas.

Yarborough, in effect, issued a statement in which he was sharply critical of Connally for failing to invite him to a reception at the Governor's Mansion Friday evening.

Yarborough Statement Criticizes Connally

"I've had many telephone calls and letters from friends because Mrs. Yarborough and I were not invited to the mansion," Yarborough said.

"I want everyone to join hands in harmony for the greatest wel-

Other articles about visit on Pages 11, 12 and 16 of Sec. 1 and Page 1 of Sec. 4.

come to the President and Mrs. Kennedy in the history of Texas."

But then Yarborough added:

"Gov. Connally is so terribly uneducated governmentally, how could you expect anything else?"

Subsequently, Connally and Yarborough both rode with the President on the flight from San Antonio to Houston, but it was not known whether any effort was made by the President to patch up the Texas Democratic internecine battle.

Asked for comment on Yarborough's remarks, Connally issued the following statement Thursday night:

"The purpose of all our efforts has been to warmly welcome to Texas the President and vice-president and their ladies.

"I am glad they have been so received in a true Texan manner."

President Pays Tribute to Rep. Thomas

The President came here Thursday to pay tribute to Houston's veteran congressman, Albert Thomas, who was instrumental in getting the Manned Spacecraft Center for his city.

At a testimonial dinner he hailed Thomas as a congressman who "is consistently loyal to his party—but stays above petty partisan rancor."

But the political situation overshadowed all of the President's activities.

The Yarborough feud with the dominant machinery of the state Democratic party carried over into the motorcades in both San Antonio and Houston, with Yarborough refusing to take his assigned seat in both cities in cars bearing Vice-President and Mrs. Lyndon B. Johnson.

There was widespread speculation that Kennedy might take some action to try to heal the rift in the Texas party.

He talked to Yarborough and Connally together on the San Antonio-Houston flight, in the presence of Congressman Thomas and Henry B. Gonzalez of San Antonio and others. But the substance of the conversation was not learned.

Kennedys Appear in Radiant Good Humor

The President and Mrs. Kennedy appeared in radiant good humor as they drove in motorcades through San Antonio and Houston.

There were no demonstrations, but a few "Goldwater-64" signs were flourished along the route in San Antonio.

Kennedy's praise of Congressman Thomas at the dinner in his honor was almost unprecedented in the enthusiasm with which he delivered it.

"In Texas and the nation," Kennedy said, "change has been the law of life. Growth has meant new opportunities. Progress has meant new achievements.

"And men such as Albert Thomas—men who recognized the value of growth and progress—have enabled this city and this state to rise with the tides of change instead of being swept aside."

The 65-year-old Thomas has been considering retirement, but he has said that his doctors will be the final arbiters on his decision.

Kennedy flew to Fort Worth late Thursday night and was greeted by a crowd estimated at 5,500 by Fort Worth Police Chief Cato Hightower.

His plane touched down at Carswell Air Force Base at 11:07 p.m., about four minutes after another jet carrying Vice-President Lyndon Johnson and his party landed.

The President will speak at a Fort Worth breakfast Friday, then fly to Dallas for a luncheon before proceeding to Austin for a $100-a-plate fund-raising dinner Friday night.

MOTORCADE RIDES

Yarborough Snubs LBJ

By DAWSON DUNCAN
News Staff Writer

HOUSTON, Texas—President Kennedy, on a political harmony tour of Texas, encountered an example of Democratic disunity over car seating on his first two stops Thursday.

Both here and at San Antonio, U.S. Sen. Ralph Yarborough, who long has been at political odds with Vice-President Lyndon B. Johnson, declined local arrangements calling for the two to ride in the same car in the President's motorcade.

His snub pointed up the differences within the party. One of the main purposes of the President's visit here is to promote harmony.

IN SAN ANTONIO, Yarborough chose the company of Congressman Henry B. Gonzalez of San Antonio, who won election with strong Latin-American, liberal backing. Johnson, incidentally, helped Gonzalez's campaign.

For the motorcade from the Houston airport to Downtown Houston, Yarborough chose a car farther back. Johnson, with Mrs. Johnson, rode alone, except for an escorting Secret Service agent.

Enthusiastic crowds of many thousands gave the President's party a warm but not wild welcome as the long motorcade wound from the airport along the Gulf Freeway, where traffic was halted as motorists stopped to view the President and his wife, Jacqueline.

CROWDS LINED the streets in Downtown Houston, especially in the eastern districts heavily populated by Negroes.

Throughout the whole route of the motorcade, as in the case of several thousand who gathered at the airport, women and teenagers predominated. That, perhaps, was an indication of the drawing power of Mrs. Kennedy on her first trip to Texas.

For the President, however, a Texas visit was nothing new. This is his fifth since he became President, plus others when he was a candidate or as President-elect.

No protest demonstrators appeared. Also lacking were derogatory placards. A few signs of praise and in welcome of the President were in evidence.

ONE LONE sign carrier in the airport crowd, however, was not an admirer of Gov. John Connally, the President's official host on his 2-day speaking tour before he visits Vice-President Johnson's Blanco County ranch.

The dissenter's sign read: "John Connally, Why Are You Against Equal Rights — Equal Urban Representation?"

It reflected opposition to Connally's stand against the public accommodations section of the administration's civil rights bill pending in Congress and against his opposition to the federal court order here to force congressional redistricting. The latter was stayed by the U.S. Supreme Court pending appeal.

But there was evidence of dissension at Houston's Coliseum, where he attended a testimonial dinner for Congressman Albert Thomas of Houston.

Behind a police barricade, there were pickets who waved such placards as "Relax, They Are Still 90 Miles Away" and chanted "We want our freedom." They appeared to be of Latin-American extraction.

WELCOMING signs included ones which were carried by, or identified the bearers as, Negroes, Latin-Americans, Arabs, University of Houston Young Democrats and just Democrats.

Local planners sought to play it straight down the middle—Negro and white leaders, Chamber of Commerce officials and labor union officers, conservative and moderate Democrats and liberal Democrats, all religious groups.

But there was still some grumbling among the liberals and some admissions from the moderate-conservatives that "make no mistake, this was controlled by Connally people."

ONE OF THE liberals conceded that some recognition had been given his people "else I wouldn't be here."

Kennedy sought to bolster his political harmony in numerous closed conferences with political leaders here in his sealed-off floor of the Rice Hotel before the affair he came officially to attend—a testimonial dinner for veteran Congressman Albert Thomas of Houston. How successful those private confabs were will be determined by the lineups in next year's Democratic primary contests.

He also sought to cement his support, which contributed heavily to his election in 1960, among the Latin-Americans. He departed from schedule before the Thomas dinner to speak briefly to the League of United Latin American Citizens holding a convention here. Jacqueline added her bit by addressing them in Spanish.

★

'BALL' MARKS VERDI SESQUI

Dallas Civic Opera will sing a happy birthday to Giuseppe Verdi Friday night by producing "A Masked Ball," one of the composer's most famous operas.

The production, opening at 8 p.m. in the Music Hall and to be repeated at 2 p.m. Sunday, is being staged especially in honor of the 150th anniversary of Verdi's birth year.

Heading the DCO cast will be Antonietta Stella, Giuseppe di Stefano, Mario Sereni, Margherita Guglielmi, Bianca Berini, Norman Triegle and Nicola Zaccaria. Nicola Rescigno will conduct, and Carlo Maestrini has staged the production.

Savings in Mercantile Bank on deposit a year or more at interest paying date, earn 4% interest. Member F.D.I.C.—(Adv.)

Weather . . . Today's Index

Dallas and Vicinity. — Considerable cloudiness and turning cooler Friday with scattered thundershowers ending in the afternoon. High Friday in the lower 70's. Low Saturday morning in the upper 40's. Thursday's high: 74.

Gov. Rockefeller promises he won't raid **Pennsylvania delegation** before 1964 GOP convention. Sec. 1, Page 4.

U.S. Chamber of Commerce president blasts **washed-out** ARA project in East Texas. By John Mashek, Sec. 1, Page 5.

Despite news of AT&T stock split, the **stock market** suffers its second worst selloff of 1963. Sec. 2, Page 6.

Accused bookmaker is told that lie detector fails to prove charges of police brutality. By James Ewell, Sec. 4, Page 1.

On your next trip to New York, treat yourself to the elegance of a Braniff Silver Service Flight. Adv.

News in depth at 7 a.m. including News around the World on Radio Station WBAP-570. (Adv.)

MIKE QUINN
reporter,
Dallas Morning News

I saw Kennedy step past the back door of the plane, then saw his arm reach back for something or someone. It happened to be Mrs. Kennedy. That first impression of her stepping to the door will linger forever. She had on a rose suit, or pink, I guess, but it was beautiful, and the color seemed to reflect the sun. As she stepped out ahead of the president the crowd seemed awestruck, then started applauding and—if you will pardon— squealing. I understood then why Kennedy liked to have Mrs. Kennedy along.

KEITH SHELTON
political writer,
Dallas Times Herald

I asked her press secretary to describe her outfit for me because I knew nothing about fashion. I was told very forcefully that her suit was raspberry; it was not pink.

CHARLES ROBERTS
White House correspondent,
Newsweek

I remember the president going the whole length of a chain-link fence at the airport with Jackie at his side. When they got to the end of that fence, when they had literally run out of spectators and people to shake hands with and were turning to go back in the limousine, I asked Jackie how she liked campaigning. She said, "It's wonderful, it's wonderful."

A WFAA-TV mobile unit was on hand to provide pool coverage of the Kennedys' arrival at Love Field.

The first lady greets well-wisher Annie S. Dunbar at Love Field in Dallas.

ROBERT PIERPOINT
White House correspondent,
CBS News

It was one of the few times I ever saw her actively engaged in any kind of crowd-pleasing politics. She seemed more supportive of him than she had been in the past, at least in the political sense.

VAL IMM
society editor,
Dallas Times Herald

I was assigned to cover the Kennedy arrival at Love Field along with Jim Lehrer. We were right there at the fence line. It's one thing to read it and it's another thing to experience it—[Kennedy] was equipped with just a tremendous charisma. It was actually like waves that went out in the crowd, including myself.

ROBERT DONOVAN
Washington bureau chief,
Los Angeles Times

I said when I came back on the press bus that if Hollywood had tried to cast for their purpose a president and his wife, they could never have dreamed up John F. Kennedy and Jacqueline Kennedy. They were just two beautiful people that day, glamorous, and they had a screaming reception. There was never a point in the public life of the Kennedys, in a way, that was as high as that moment in Dallas.

CHARLES ROBERTS
Newsweek

We ran toward the press buses and the president got in his open car. He had inquired about the weather that morning and decided that they would not have the top on [the limousine]. They had a choice of three tops: a fabric top, which would have obscured him from the public; the plastic top, which the Secret Service had told me would deflect a bullet, but would not stop it; and a metal top. He did not want any of those that morning, and so we started into downtown Dallas with him in an open car. There were, I think, twelve cars in the motorcade, and I was in the first press bus.

BERT SHIPP
WFAA-TV

We only had eight people [covering the story]. Each reporter/ photographer was inclusive. They wrote their own stories, shot their own film. With everybody in place it was a routine visit—just get him in, get him out, [because] he was here just to shore up fences that [the vice president] had let lie down on the ground.

Jacqueline Kennedy at Love Field. Behind her is Time *magazine White House correspondent Hugh Sidey.*

JACK BELL
political writer,
Associated Press

Kennedy had overruled the Secret Service, which wanted to take him directly from the airport to the Dallas Trade Mart where he was supposed to make a speech. Johnson had not wanted that. He wanted Kennedy to go through Dallas and demonstrate to these people—and to the world—that Dallas loved Kennedy.

EDDIE BARKER
news director,
KRLD-TV and Radio

Originally, there was not going to be a parade here because Democratic loyalists felt that the big-money crowd was taking this thing over. He was going to go from the airport to the Trade Mart, make his speech, get back on the plane, and go down to Austin for the weekend. There was a Methodist preacher here named Baxton Bryant. Baxton was more political than he was religious. He was always around wanting something or another. He started really making a big thing about "we common Democrats are not even going to get to see our president." So that went on for a few days and then they decided we would have a parade.

The Kennedys arrive at Love Field.

Merriman Smith, White House correspondent for United Press International, is riding in the front seat of the White House press-pool car, a black sedan provided by AT&T. The pool comprises reporters chosen on a rotating basis to have the closest access to the president. They, in turn, must provide reports to other White House reporters on all that they see and hear. The pool always includes representatives of the wire services, at least one newspaper, and one broadcast outlet. The pool car has a radiotelephone in the front seat. Smith takes the front seat next to the phone, between the driver and Malcolm Kilduff, acting White House press secretary. Jack Bell of the Associated Press, Bob Clark of ABC News, and Robert Baskin, Washington bureau chief of the *Dallas Morning News*, are in the back seat.

BOB CLARK
Washington correspondent,
ABC News

When we got in the motorcade, Merriman Smith took the front seat. Smitty was great at using his elbows and taking advantage of anything possible.

CHARLES ROBERTS
Newsweek

Dallas, which had been a stronghold of not just conservatives, but reactionaries, had voted against Kennedy and Johnson quite overwhelmingly in 1960, but had turned out big this day, and the motorcade just had to inch its way through the crowd. They had a fairly heavy escort of police motorcycles, but the crowd would surge in behind the motorcycles and bring the car to a stop [to try to] shake his hand.

I think somebody figured there were two hundred thousand windows along the parade route he took. Well, you'd need a couple of divisions to cover, say, every tenth window, and then they'd have to be airborne divisions because on a trip like this they'd have to leapfrog ahead of him to establish the kind of security that some people think you can have.

HUGH SIDEY
White House correspondent,
Time

I was [in one of the press buses] behind the driver, and to be honest I was bored. It was just another motorcade. At one point we stopped. The sidewalks were filled and they were obviously secretaries and clerks and young people from the buildings, basically workers. I'll always remember John Kennedy commenting one time, long before that, about how he would go along in these high-rise areas during the [presidential] campaign and down below, people were cheering and wonderful—these were the young people in the streets—but he would look up and behind the glass in the corporate precincts, people were giving him the finger! I thought about that that day. These were the people that liked him, the young people, the workers. We went over to a little clutch of women and [Peter Lisagor of the *Chicago Daily News*] said, "What do you see in this guy?" One of the women looked at Pete and said, "He looks like he would play." He had sex appeal.

11:55 A.M. (CST)
NEAR THE TRIPLE UNDERPASS IN DALLAS

MARY ELIZABETH WOODWARD
society section reporter,
Dallas Morning News

Friday is a busy day in women's news since we put out both the Saturday paper and the two Sunday sections, so everyone was concentrating on keeping busy. I gathered up a lunch of apples and crackers, and with three friends from the department, started down Houston Street to take my place in the crowd. The crowd was so heavy we decided to cross Elm Street

The Kennedy motorcade turns onto Main Street in Dallas about ten minutes before the assassination.

and wait for the parade on the grassy slopes between the Texas School Book Depository and the triple underpass. I looked around at the railroad trestle going over the triple underpass and remarked that it seemed like an ideal place for a sniper, but reassured myself that it was well guarded. At last the presidential limousine was in our range of view. We started our own cheering section and President and Mrs. Kennedy turned around, looked directly at us, flashed their well-known smiles, gave us a wave of recognition, then looked forward again.

PEGGY SIMPSON
reporter,
AP, Dallas

I was out there as one of the AP "on-the-street" people, just watching the motorcade go by. John Connally was giving a reception that night in Austin for President Kennedy once they got through Dallas, and they had barred the media. So [Dallas AP bureau chief] Bob Johnson said, "Well, that's not going to stop us. You find one of these state legislators who's single and get a date with him, and you be inside that dinner." So that's what I had done. But I had a lot of time; it wasn't going to be until eight o'clock that night, so he had said, "Why don't you just go out and take notes on the motorcade?"

HUGH AYNESWORTH
science/aviation/space editor,
Dallas Morning News

I was really a little pissed because I didn't have any assignment connected with the Kennedy thing at all. So I decided to walk over and see what was going on. I was in the middle of Elm Street; it was blocked off. Everybody was excited. I remember there was this black woman who was so excited when she saw Jackie. She said, "She's got my dress on! She's got my dress on!"

PIERCE ALLMAN
manager of programming
and production,
WFAA-TV and Radio

Kennedy had this marvelous—it wasn't a wave, it was an acknowledgment with his hand up. He was sitting up straight. Of course, he was wearing a back brace. I thought to myself, "They look so good. They look so vibrant." Kennedy had a lot of color, looked tan. I guess part of that was the medication. But the guy looked great, and I hollered out something when they went by [like] "Welcome to Dallas," or "Glad you're here."

Photographer Bob Jackson (right) of the Dallas Times Herald, *in one of the motorcade's press cars about five minutes before the president was shot.*

12:30 P.M. (CST)
WITH THE PRESIDENTIAL MOTORCADE

CHARLES ROBERTS
Newsweek

We turned left off Main Street and got over to Elm Street. The last thing I remember was looking up at the sign on this building as we came to a park and sort of turned to the right to go down this incline under the triple underpass. I saw the words "Texas School Book Depository" and thought it was a weird name for a building and wondered what it was. Just seconds after that I heard what I thought was a [motorcycle] backfire.

JACK BELL
AP

I thought somebody had set off a cherry bomb. I thought to myself, "My God, these Texans don't ever know when to quit. They've given the man everything they could. Here they are shooting off firecrackers and cherry bombs."

TOM DILLARD
chief photographer,
Dallas Morning News

My car had just turned north on Houston Street and was at the county jail entrance when the first shot was fired. I said, "They've thrown a torpedo." At the second shot, "No, it's heavy rifle fire," and at the third shot I said, "They've killed him." Bob Jackson, a photographer in my car, said, "There's the rifle in that open window." In the three or four seconds it took me to locate that particular open window and make a picture, the rifle had been withdrawn.

BOB JACKSON
photographer,
Dallas Times Herald

We had prearranged for me to drop off film that I shot along the route to a reporter. I had unloaded the camera, put the film in an envelope, and as we turned the corner onto Houston, I tossed the envelope out to the reporter. And that's when we heard the first shot, and then two more shots closer together. I remember Tom Dillard, the photographer sitting next to me, we looked at each other. We knew it was a gunshot, no doubt about it. On the fifth floor I saw two men

The president and first lady respond to Dallas residents along the route of the presidential motorcade just minutes before the president was shot.

leaning out and looking up. And my eyes went up to the next window and I could see the rifle on the ledge and I could see it being drawn in. I could not see who was holding it. And I said, "There's a rifle." I pointed it out to Tom and, of course, he photographed the empty window. Of course, I'm sitting there with an empty camera, with a long lens.

MALCOLM COUCH
cameraman,
WFAA-TV

We were right in front of the Texas School Book Depository and right about that time I looked up and saw about a foot of the rifle going back in the window.

MERRIMAN SMITH
White House correspondent,
United Press International

Suddenly, we heard three loud, almost painfully loud cracks. The first sounded as if it might have been a large firecracker. But the second and third blasts were unmistakable. Gunfire.

BOB CLARK
ABC News

[Merriman Smith] said, "Those were gunshots." I certainly knew Smitty was a gun fancier and occasionally did target practice. When he said those were gunshots, I think we all in the car just accepted they were gunshots. They were loud and clear and more significant—for the historical record—they were equally loud and equally clear and were clearly fired from almost over our head where [someone] was firing from almost directly above us at that point.

MALCOLM KILDUFF
assistant White House
press secretary

We saw a flash of pink—which of course was Mrs. Kennedy. We realized she was doing something. I saw the Secret Service agent in the follow-up car raise the rifle. At that point we realized these were shots.

CHARLES ROBERTS
Newsweek

I saw a policeman running across the park, pulling his pistol out of a holster, reaching back to his hip and pulling it out. Of course, I realized—this confirmed—that something terrible had happened. You never bare a weapon in front of the president unless there's an emergency, so I knew there was an emergency.

ROBERT MACNEIL
White House correspondent,
NBC News

I said, "Was that a shot?" Several people said, "No, no." Others said, "I don't know." Then there were two more explosions, very distinct to me. I jumped up and said, "They were shots! Stop the bus! Stop the bus!" The driver opened the door and I jumped out. I couldn't see the president's car but I really started to believe there was a shooting because on the grass on both sides of the roadway people were throwing themselves down and covering their children with their bodies. The air was filled with screaming, a high unison soprano wail. The sun was intensely bright. I saw several people running up the grassy hill beside the road. I thought they were chasing whoever had done the shooting and I ran after them.

HUGH SIDEY
Time

It looked like a giant hand or wind had swept the place, everybody was lying down on the grassy knoll. At the curb there was this young man with a little boy. He was hammering the ground with his fist, with his other arm over the boy protecting him, just in anguish.

MERRIMAN SMITH
UPI

The president's car, about 150 or 200 yards ahead, seemed to falter briefly. We saw a flurry of activity in the Secret Service follow-up car behind the chief executive's limousine. Next in line was the car bearing Vice President Lyndon B. Johnson. Behind that, another follow-up car bearing agents assigned to the vice president's protection. We were behind that car. Our car stood still for probably only a few seconds, but it seemed like a lifetime.

CHARLES ROBERTS
Newsweek

Our bus came to a halt. Everybody started screaming different advice to the bus driver. A few of us jumped out onto the pavement but didn't get far from the bus because from long experience with motorcades you know that they start up suddenly. If sixty people get out of a bus and the motorcade starts up, they simply can't get back in. I think that I saw the back of the "Queen Mary," the big security car that was immediately behind the president. And I think I saw a man standing in the back of that car with an automatic rifle or a submachine gun. This was in a flash. This thing was like an explosion in a shingle factory—it happened so fast you didn't know where to look.

MALCOLM COUCH
WFAA-TV

We tried to get our driver to stop but he was panicky. We were screaming for him to stop, slow down, so we could peel off. Finally, we just grabbed his coat and started shaking at him, yelling at him, "Stop the car! Stop the car!" He slowed down enough for us to peel off. We all just leaped off. I'll never forget running back hollering at the top of my lungs, looking up at the sky, probably talking to God, "They can't do that, they can't shoot the president." I had the camera in my hand and just kept running as fast as I could.

MALCOLM KILDUFF
White House

We went around Vice President Johnson's car because it had slowed up and we wanted to get up and catch up with the president's car. We sped off down the highway. The normal emergency procedure with shots is to just speed out, to get out of there as quickly as possible. At this point it was still perfectly normal—until we passed the Trade Mart. I asked the driver of our car, "What is that large building up there ahead?" He said, "Parkland Hospital." Naturally you realized that somebody had been hurt, at least. It didn't occur to a single person in that car that the president of the United States really had been shot, or certainly that he was in the condition he was in.

TOM WICKER
reporter,
New York Times

At first no one knew what happened, or how, or where, much less why. Gradually, bits and pieces began to fall together.... Even now, however, I know no reporter who was there who has a clear and orderly picture of that surrealistic afternoon;

THE ABRAHAM ZAPRUDER FILM:

This home-movie footage shows the presidential limousine on Elm Street seconds before the first of three shots rang out.

President Kennedy and Governor Connally react as they are struck by the same bullet.

This frame shows President Kennedy and Governor Connally immediately after they were shot.

it is still a matter of bits and pieces thrown hastily into something like a whole.

MARY ELIZABETH WOODWARD
Dallas Morning News

I saw the bystanders fall to the ground, saw the president slump, heard Mrs. Kennedy's anguished cry, and saw her crawl out of the car and drag the Secret Service man in before the car sped away from view. Now there was no doubt in my mind. The eagerly awaited noontime break had turned into a nightmare of horror as I eyewitnessed the assassination of the president.

PIERCE ALLMAN
WFAA-TV and Radio

There were three shots. They were very distinct. Later on, in asking to recreate the time sequence, my timing on it was six and a half seconds. It was a very, very vivid memory. Mr. Kennedy really didn't slump. He sort of jerked up and his arms went up and his hands went up towards his chin. As the shots continued, Jackie screamed something and tried to get up. Kennedy began slumping to the left and Jackie got out of

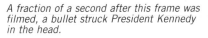
A fraction of a second after this frame was filmed, a bullet struck President Kennedy in the head.

Jacqueline Kennedy crawls from the back seat of the limousine as Secret Service agent Clint Hill leaps onto the vehicle.

The second of three press buses in the motorcade passes the grassy knoll above Elm Street about a minute after the shooting.

her seat and was going over toward her husband as he was coming toward her. About that time, the Secret Service man sprinted in from the trailing car and vaulted over the left rear fender and put himself on top of both of them and shoved them down. That's when they were both down in the back seat and Kennedy's foot was dangling over the side.

HUGH AYNESWORTH
Dallas Morning News

It was just complete chaos, because people didn't know where to run. Nobody knew where the shots were coming from. Nobody knew who had been hit, if anybody. Nobody knew where to run to protect themselves. Some threw their kids down and covered them. The lady [wearing the same pink dress as Jackie] threw up, she was sick. Other people were bumping into each other and shouting and trying to find a place of refuge. I started interviewing people, but I didn't have a pencil or paper. I reached in my back pocket. I had two utility bills that I hadn't mailed. I used the backs of those envelopes. I saw a little kid that had one of these big jumbo pens, had a big American flag on it. And I grabbed that because I had to start writing and interviewing. I gave him a quarter or two.

DALLAS POLICE DEPARTMENT RADIO TRANSMISSION (CHANNEL 2):

POLICE CHIEF JESSE E. CURRY:
Approaching triple underpass.
DISPATCHER:
12:30 P.M. KKB 364.
CURRY:
Go to the hospital—Parkland Hospital. Have them stand by.
CURRY:
Get a man on top of that triple underpass and see what happened up there.

Law enforcement officers and bystanders rush to the site of the shooting on Elm Street.

BOB CLARK
ABC News

There was one pool telephone in the car. [Merriman Smith] was sitting next to it and that was because of his experience and his years as a White House reporter. Part of the press mythology is that Smitty immediately grabbed the phone and began talking, dictating a bulletin. He did not. It was sort of a difficult wire service bulletin to compose. Before he picked up the phone he just sat for a minute or two—a minute or two where [the AP's Jack] Bell could have reached forward from the back and gotten the phone. But he did not.

Eventually Smitty started dictating. He was having trouble at the other end. His lines had to be repeated for him. But Bell slowly realized that Smitty was driving an axe through his skull on a very big story. He started shouting, "Smitty, you have had your turn, give it to me now." Just before we went swinging into the driveway of the hospital, Bell reached forward and was grappling with Smitty, trying to get the phone out of his hands. I guess Smitty was hit a couple of times during that scuffle for the telephone. Jack did not succeed in getting the telephone. Then the car screeched to a halt and we all jumped out.

ROBERT BASKIN
Washington bureau chief,
Dallas Morning News

Smith grabbed the radiotelephone, which hung just in front of him on the dashboard and got through to UPI quickly. "Where did that happen? Where did that happen?" he shouted at me. For the life of me, I could not get the words out, and the driver told him it was at the triple underpass. Jack Bell began to demand the telephone as we raced along, but Smith would not relinquish it. A wrestling match for the phone ensued between the two of them.

MALCOLM KILDUFF
White House

Jack Bell got tired of waiting to dictate. He reached over, grabbed the phone, and swiped at Smith with it—and hit me instead.

HELEN THOMAS
White House correspondent,
UPI

It was the ultimate rivalry for the story of the century. [Smith] always knew how to look for the phone.

Ike Altgen of the Associated Press photographed Secret Service agent Clint Hill leaping aboard the presidential limousine to aid the first lady.

*hear...
track 4*

DALLAS POLICE DEPARTMENT RADIO TRANSMISSION (CHANNEL 2):

POLICE CHIEF CURRY:
Looks like the president has been hit. Have Parkland stand by.

12:34 P.M. (CST)
DALLAS BUREAU, UNITED PRESS INTERNATIONAL

Smith calls UPI's Dallas bureau and begins dictating to Wilborn Hampton, a young reporter who has been on the job only two months.

WILBORN HAMPTON
reporter,
UPI, Dallas

I was standing next to the news desk. One of the telephones rang and I picked it up, and this voice was shouting, "Three shots were fired at the motorcade! Make it a bulletin precede" [an alert that new developments had occurred in an earlier story]. I literally nearly dropped the phone. I cradled it next to my ear, and rolled into the typewriter what were called books—

these were three or four pieces of paper that were separated by very flimsy carbons, so as you typed you could make three copies. I wanted to confirm what I'd heard. What I said to him was not the most brilliant thing. I said, "I can't hear you." He screamed, "Three shots were fired at the motorcade! Make it a bulletin precede." So I typed the words he said to me: "Bulletin precede. Three shots were fired today at President Kennedy's motorcade in downtown Dallas." I said, "I'm having trouble hearing you." He shouted a third time. This time I was stepping over to [UPI division news manager] Jack Fallon and I was almost afraid to interrupt him. I almost whispered, "Jack, it's Smitty." He said, "What does he want?" "He said there were three shots fired at the motorcade." Jack said, "What?" and grabbed the phone from my hand.

JACK FALLON
Southwest Division
news manager, UPI

When Smith called, Hampton picked up the phone. He was a kid fresh out of the University of Texas. He was a bright boy and we were going to break him in. He got broken in, all right.

WILBORN HAMPTON
UPI

The teletype operator, Jim Tolbert, had overheard me telling Jack this, and he tore off the tape. In those days you punched stories into tape and they were fed into a machine and it activated teletype machines all around the country. He tore off the tape and just sat there waiting. Jack gave a copy of

A photographer runs to catch up to the second of three press cars heading into the triple underpass in pursuit of the presidential limousine moments after the shooting.

the bulletin to Jim Tolbert and he sent it. In those days, you could stop a story in progress by pushing a little lever if you had a bulletin. A story about a murder trial in Minneapolis was moving on the [main national news wire]. Jim pressed the little lever that would stop the story in progress, cut it off in mid-sentence. Jim hit the send button, then rang five bells on the machine to signify it was a bulletin.

UPI WIRE:

```
MOREDA 1234 PCS
UPI A 7N DA
BULLETIN PRECEDE KENNEDY
DALLAS, NOV. 22 (UPI) — THREE SHOTS WERE FIRED TODAY
AT PRESIDENT KENNEDY'S MOTORCADE IN DOWNTOWN DALLAS
JT1234PCS
```

12:34 P.M. (CST)
NEW YORK CITY

WALTER CRONKITE
anchor,
CBS Evening News

I was at my desk. Ed Bliss, who was our editor, was standing at the teleprinters in one corner of the newsroom when the bulletin came on the United Press wire. Ed shouted across the newsroom. This was very unusual for him. He was very calm most of the time and very cool. But he did raise his voice to say, "There's been a shooting in Dallas, at Kennedy apparently."

12:34 P.M. (CST)
DALLAS

DALLAS POLICE DEPARTMENT RADIO TRANSMISSION (CHANNEL 1):

DISPATCHER:
Report to Inwood and Stemmons. Cut all traffic for the ambulance going to Parkland. Code 3. [An emergency—use red lights and sirens.]

ABC NEWS:

We interrupt this program to bring you a special bulletin from ABC Radio. Here is a special bulletin from Dallas, Texas. Three shots were fired at President Kennedy's motorcade today in downtown Dallas, Texas. This is ABC Radio.

DALLAS POLICE DEPARTMENT RADIO TRANSMISSION (CHANNEL 2):

OFFICER 260:
I have a witness that says that [the gunfire] came from the fifth floor of the Texas Book Depository Store.

The presidential limousine speeds toward Parkland Memorial Hospital after the shooting.

NBC's Robert MacNeil races inside the Texas School Book Depository, looking for a phone to file the news, as do several local newsmen. Both MacNeil and WFAA's Pierce Allman are later told they may have talked to Lee Harvey Oswald, the alleged sniper, on his way out of the building.

ROBERT MACNEIL
NBC News

I ran into the first building I came to that looked as though it might have a phone. It was the Texas Book Depository. As I ran up the steps and through the door, a young man in shirt-sleeves was coming out. In great agitation I asked him where there was a phone. He pointed inside.

PIERCE ALLMAN
WFAA-TV and Radio

I ran up to the door of the Depository building and I asked a guy who was just leaving, "Where's the phone?" and he jerked his thumb and said, "In there."

TOM ALYEA
newsman,
WFAA-TV

After covering the panic on the grassy knoll, I noticed a man at the corner of Elm and Houston looking at the upper floors of the Texas School Book Depository. I assumed that the police were in the building because I could see no activity outside. I raced for the door and found myself jammed in a cluster of plainclothes and uniformed police officers who were responding to a police dispatch that the shooting suspect was in the building. When we were inside, one officer ordered two uniformed officers to seal it and let nobody in or out unless they had a badge.

KENT BIFFLE
reporter,
Dallas Morning News

Getting in was no problem. I just hid my press badge and went in with the first wave of cops. Plainclothesmen and uniform policemen alike had their guns drawn. Several had riot guns. They moved fast, these policemen. One group took the first floor, another group took the second, and another group headed for the third. I decided to go with the men searching the second floor. I was surprised to find wailing women in several offices. It had not occurred to me that there would be anyone but the sniper in the building.

TOM ALYEA
WFAA-TV

On the fifth floor, I was following one of the detectives as we came upon a paper sack. He touched it with the toe of his shoe and a couple of dried chicken bones spilled out. They looked to be about two or three days old. A Dr Pepper bottle was sitting upright next to the sack. It was dusty and dry inside and out. The officer walked on. I filmed this debris thinking it might later be important.

KENT BIFFLE
Dallas Morning News

I needed to phone the city desk. There was a phone in the office with a button switch for two lines. I grabbed it and put it to my ear. A man was telling his broker to "sell everything except telephone." I turned the button and on the other line another man was giving his broker similar instructions.

The policemen had moved to other offices while I interviewed the women. When I opened the door into the corridor to follow them, I nearly got it. Patrolmen at either end of the hall drew down on me with riot guns.

Police officers and newsmen inspect the "sniper's nest" in the Texas School Book Depository.

TERRANCE W. MCGARRY
reporter,
UPI

I ran into a police roadblock, a couple of cars parked across the intersection, not letting people into the downtown area. I figured, "This is the story of my life. I am absolutely not going to stop and talk to these guys." So I slowed down as if I was going to turn, then went around the roadblock and onto the sidewalk. I [drove] right down the sidewalk. Today, of course, I would probably get shot.

12:36 P.M. (CST)
DALLAS BUREAU, UNITED PRESS INTERNATIONAL

WILBORN HAMPTON
UPI

Suddenly it occurred to me who would know what was going on—a police dispatcher. Everybody else in the office had sprung into action on the phones. I picked up the phone and called the Dallas police main number, and tried to muster all the authority I didn't feel and said, "This is Bill Hampton, UPI. Give me dispatch." To my utter amazement, somebody picked up the phone and said, "Dispatch." I said, "What can you tell me about the shots that were fired at the president's motorcade?" He said, "The president has been hit. I just got off the phone with the motorcycle policeman right next to the car and they're going to Parkland Hospital." I said, "How bad?" He said, "I don't know, there's blood in the back of the car and the president has fallen over and they're going to Parkland right now."

12:36 P.M. (CST)
PARKLAND MEMORIAL HOSPITAL

The first contingent of journalists to reach the hospital comprises the four reporters in the pool car. They arrive so quickly that the mortally wounded president is still in the limousine, lying face down, cradled by Mrs. Kennedy. Governor Connally is lying on his back in the arms of his wife. Remarkably, the reporters are able to walk directly up to the car and witness the wrenching scene.

Dallas Morning News *reporter Jim Ewell (left) was among the journalists and law enforcement officers who converged on the Texas School Book Depository after the shooting.*

MERRIMAN SMITH
UPI

We skidded around a sharp turn and spilled out of the pool car as it entered the hospital driveway. I ran to the side of the [presidential limousine]. The president was face down on the back seat. Mrs. Kennedy made a cradle of her arms around the president's head and bent over him as if she were whispering to him. Governor Connally was on his back on the floor of the car. His head and shoulders resting in the arms of his wife, Nellie, who kept shaking her head and shaking with dry sobs. Blood oozed from the front of the governor's suit. I could not see the president's wound. But I could see blood splattered around the interior of the rear seat and a dark stain spreading down the right side of the president's dark gray suit.

BOB CLARK
ABC News

Relations were much better with the Secret Service in those days. Today, they'd keep the press a quarter of a mile away if they could in a situation like that. In those days, nobody tried to stop us at all. They knew all the reporters. They simply let us go up and stand as close as we could. We were standing literally a couple of feet from the car, staring down at Kennedy. He was stretched out in the back seat. He was lying with the side of his head exposed and his head in Jackie's lap. I was not conscious of any wound in the head, so that part of his head had to be hidden, probably deliberately by Jackie. It was just a frozen scene. Jackie was sitting there, saying nothing. We had to wait a minute or so for the stretchers to come out.

I asked them where there were phones. I had been trained under Smitty in high pressure reporting. Smitty always, the first thing he did, anywhere he moved, was to spot a telephone. If you had a story, it didn't do any good if you didn't have the means to file it. They steered me into an adjoining room where there was a vacant telephone. Senator Ralph Yarborough was in that room, sitting, weeping quietly. Yarborough had been the liberal along on the trip and the fella who was not getting along with the Connally faction in Texas. I didn't speak to him. I grabbed a telephone and called New York and got through immediately.

We have our reporter in Dallas, Bob Clark. He was immediately behind the president's automobile. We have Bob Clark on the telephone. We will switch immediately to Bob Clark, ABC in Dallas.

BOB CLARK

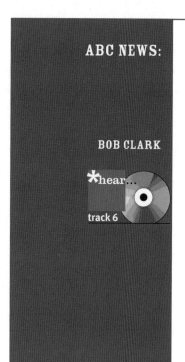

*hear...

track 6

Three shots were fired at the president's motorcade as it passed out of the downtown area of Dallas. The Secret Service immediately gave orders for the procession to speed out of the crowds and took the president directly to Parkland Memorial Hospital. I am at the hospital now. The president was taken in a few minutes ago. Lifted from the car, placed on a stretcher, he was motionless. The first lady leaned over him, crying. Lyndon Johnson also appears to have been struck by one of the bullets, though he was able to walk into the hospital. Governor Connally of Texas was also wounded; it's uncertain at this moment how seriously. There is no word yet from the surgical room of the hospital as to Mr. Kennedy's condition.

JACK BELL
AP

He just looked like a man who had been killed. He lay on the back seat on his face. It was a horror of all horrors to imagine that some stupid murderer had snuffed out the life of a man who held such promise for his country, who had got it up off its hind end, who was moving it in a direction toward the future—that this could have happened; that our civilization could breed people like that—to kill a man just to be killing him.

MERRIMAN SMITH
UPI

Clint Hill, the Secret Service agent in charge of the detail assigned to Mrs. Kennedy, was leaning over into the rear of the car. "How badly was he hit, Clint?" I asked. "He's dead," Hill replied curtly.

MALCOLM KILDUFF
White House

I ran in the hospital and tried to find some phones for the AP and UPI reporters who were in the car. I went back outside and they had just taken Governor Connally out of the car—they had to get him out first to get President Kennedy out. Then they took President Kennedy out and his condition was pretty apparent. There was talk among some of the agents that in fact he was dead. He was loaded on the stretcher and

At Parkland Memorial Hospital, police officers and Secret Service agents attempt to clean the bloodied interior of the presidential limousine.

one thing was the sight of Jacqueline Kennedy helping to push the stretcher through the halls, with her hair flying and dripping with blood. To me it was the most pathetic sight in the world. Then they went into the emergency room, and we all followed in. It was one of those helpless situations, you know, what can I do? [Presidential aides] Dave Powers, Kenny O'Donnell, Larry O'Brien were there—what can we do? I got hold of [White House transportation official] Wayne Hawks and told him to get hold of the telephone company and start moving phones in. At this point, I was pretty much a basket case, but I still felt this was history and we had to get information out—we had to do it and do it fast.

UPI's Merriman Smith grabs a telephone in a hospital cubicle and dictates a flash that sets off ten bells and interrupts the addition to his first bulletin in midword. The flash is worded awkwardly, reflecting the concern Smith must have had about reporting that the president was dead without more confirmation.

UPI WIRE:

```
UPI A8N DA

URGENT

1ST ADD SHOTS, DALLAS (A7N) XXX DOWNTOWN DALLAS.

NO CASUALTIES WERE REPORTED.

   THE INCIDENT OCCURRED NEAR THE COUNTY SHERIFF'S

OFFICE ON MAIN STREET, JUST EAST OF AN UNDERPASS

LEADING TOWARD THE TRADE MART WHERE THE PRESIDENT

WAS TO MA


FLASH          FLASH

KENNEDY SERIOUSLY WOUNDED

PERHAPS SERIOUSLY

PERHAPS FATALLY BY ASSASSINS BULLET

JT 1239 PCS
```

WALTER CRONKITE
CBS News

I dashed out of my little glass-enclosed office, which was on the corner of the newsroom. I dashed over toward the United Press machines. Just at that point, they came in with the second bulletin, that possibly Kennedy had been shot and that his car had broken away from the motorcade and appeared to be going to the hospital. With that, we were beginning to shout, "Let's get on the air, let's get on the air!" Unfortunately at that time, we did not have a camera in the newsroom. Our nearest camera was down in the studio in the Grand Central

Mike Wallace (center) examines a teletype news report in the CBS newsroom in New York.

Building and they had to get the camera up to the newsroom. In those days, it took twenty minutes for the camera to warm up to be ready to go on the air. So besides lugging the camera up to the newsroom, then you had to turn it on, and then you had to wait twenty minutes for this thing to be ready to go. As a result of that experience, a camera was installed in the newsroom, always on, twenty-four hours a day, seven days a week, because of being caught short that way.

So instead, we went into the radio booth, a small booth that had radio capability, to get on the radio network. We interrupted the program in progress on the television network, which was *As the World Turns*, for a bulletin, which I ad-libbed.

CBS News breaks into the live soap opera *As the World Turns* just as actress Helen Wagner is telling the actor playing her grandfather about the marital problems of her son. A black "bulletin" slide fills the television screen and anchorman Walter Cronkite's voice is heard over it.

CBS NEWS:
WALTER CRONKITE
*hear...
track 6

Here is a bulletin from CBS News. In Dallas, Texas, three shots were fired at President Kennedy's motorcade in downtown Dallas. The first reports say that President Kennedy has been seriously wounded by this shooting.

WALTER CRONKITE
CBS News

[After they got the camera upstairs and warmed up] I went from the radio booth directly to the news desk and we began broadcasting live from New York with an increasingly detailed story about the fact that the president seemed to be wounded and the president's car had veered off and went to Parkland Hospital.

12:40 P.M. (CST)
ABOARD THE STATE DEPARTMENT BOEING 707
SOMEWHERE OVER THE PACIFIC

Six members of the president's Cabinet, including Secretary of State Dean Rusk, are en route to Tokyo from Hawaii for trade talks. Aircraft 86972 is about 900 miles west of Honolulu when the news of the shooting begins coming over the plane's teletype news "ticker." White House press secretary Pierre Salinger is summoned to Rusk's cabin, where he finds Rusk holding a piece of teletype paper with the garbled UPI flash saying that shots had been fired at President Kennedy, who was "perhaps seriously wounded," "perhaps fatally" by an assassin's bullet. Salinger, whose code name is Wayside, begins communicating with the White House, code-named Crown, trying to reach the White House Situation Room.

PIERRE SALINGER:

White House Situation Room, this is Wayside, do you read me? Over.

WHITE HOUSE:

This is White House. This is White House. I read you loud and clear, Wayside.

SALINGER:

Can you give me the latest information on president? Over.

WHITE HOUSE:

This is Crown, this is Crown. Do you want Situation Room?

SALINGER:

I want Situation Room. That's affirmative.

WHITE HOUSE:

Roger, roger. Getting them now. Stand by please. Wayside, Wayside, this is Crown. Situation Room is on, go ahead.

SALINGER:

Situation Room, this is Wayside, do you read me? Over.

SITUATION ROOM:

This is Situation Room, I read you. Go ahead.

SALINGER:

Give me all available information on president. Over.

SITUATION ROOM:

All available information on president follows. He and Governor Connally of Texas have been hit in the car in which they were riding. We do not know how serious the situation is. We have no information. [National Security Council executive secretary] Mr. Bromley Smith is back here in the Situation Room now. We are getting our information over the tickers. Over.

SALINGER:

Please keep us advised out here. This plane, on which secretary of state and other Cabinet ministers headed for Japan, turning around returning to Honolulu, will arrive there in approximately two hours. Over.

SITUATION ROOM:

Understand those departing Honolulu are turning around, will be back there in about two hours. Is that correct? Over.

SALINGER:

That is affirmative, affirmative. We will need all information to decide whether some members of this party should go directly to Dallas. Over.

12:44 P.M. (CST)
DALLAS

DALLAS POLICE DEPARTMENT RADIO TRANSMISSION (CHANNEL 1):

DISPATCHER:
Attention all squads, report to downtown area, Code 3 to Elm and Houston, with caution.

12:44 P.M. (CST)
WASHINGTON, D.C.

RICHARD REIDEL
press liaison aide,
U.S. Senate

(From an interview on CBS News) I immediately went into the Senate chamber over in front of the desk of Majority Leader Senator Mike Mansfield, raised my voice so that he and the senators at the surrounding desks could hear and said, "Senators, the president has been shot." It, of course, was like a shock wave, a jolt. I crossed the aisle to the Republican side where Senator [Everett] Dirksen was seated and in the same manner told Senator Dirksen and the Republican senators.... I then happened to recall that a few moments before, the president's brother, Senator Edward Kennedy of Massachusetts, was presiding over the Senate. I turned and he was still occupying the chair. I knew that someone would have to inform him. I thought I might as well.... I rushed up to the chair and said, "Senator, Senator Kennedy, your brother, the president, has been shot." He gave a jerk of his body, his body tensed, but he was absolutely calm and, as I recall, said, "No!" and that was all.

The CBS newsroom in New York bustled with activity following the shooting of President Kennedy.

12:45 P.M. (CST)

NBC NEWS: President Kennedy was shot at in Dallas, Texas, today. Blood was seen on the president's head as they rushed him to the hospital. Mrs. Kennedy was heard to exclaim, "Oh, no."

DAVID BRINKLEY
co-anchor,
Huntley-Brinkley Report,
NBC News

[Chet] Huntley and I were told to get into our New York and Washington studios and keep the news going.... At that hour in the afternoon, the network normally is not busy and the affiliate stations are running local programs. But in less than two minutes, it was all pulled together and stayed together for seventy hours and twenty-seven minutes, all day and all night, giving the American people the horrible news and showing them everything as fast as we could bring it in. From that Friday afternoon we went, as all the networks did, without a halt until 1:16 A.M. the following Tuesday morning with no entertainment programs and no commercials.

BEN BRADLEE
Washington bureau chief,
Newsweek

I was in Brentano's [bookstore] in the bottom of the National Press Building. I used to spend some lunches there going through books that I would never read. You could see people start to whisper in a very unusual way and then you could hear words like "Kennedy" and "shot." I went up to my office on the twelfth floor and as I walked in, there was a ticker machine with a soundproof box, and the bell was going like hell. Everybody was gathered around it and they were all telling me that Kennedy was shot, that he wasn't going to make it.

ABC NEWS:

Here is some more information that is just coming in. This is from the Associated Press. It says President Kennedy was shot today just as his motorcade left downtown Dallas. Mrs. Kennedy jumped up and grabbed Mr. Kennedy. She cried, "Oh, no!" and the motorcade then sped on. And from the United Press, President Kennedy and Governor John Connally of Texas were cut down by an assassin's bullet.

NICK GEORGE

Just as an advisory, we are staying on the air as long as we need to.

12:45 P.M. (CST)
ABOARD THE STATE DEPARTMENT BOEING 707
SOMEWHERE OVER THE PACIFIC

The White House Situation Room relays more information about the shooting to Salinger on the Cabinet plane. After hearing the news, Secretary Rusk orders a fully fueled Boeing 707 to stand by on the runway at Honolulu to take Assistant Secretary of State Robert Manning, himself, and Salinger to Dallas.

hear... track 8

SITUATION ROOM:

The Associated Press is coming out now with a bulletin to the effect that they believe the president was hit in the head. That just came in. Over.

PIERRE SALINGER:

The president was hit in the head. Over.

SITUATION ROOM:

Roger. We will pass on any additional information we get from here to you...Hold on the line there, Wayside, we have some more information coming up...Wayside, Wayside, this is Situation Room. I read from the AP bulletin. Kennedy apparently shot in head, he fell face down in back seat of his car, blood was on his head. Mrs. Kennedy cried, "Oh, no" and tried to hold up his head. Connally remained half seated and slumped to the left. There was blood on his face and forehead. The president and governor were rushed to Parkland Hospital near the Dallas Trade Mart where Kennedy was to have made a speech. Over.

SALINGER:

I read that, over.

SITUATION ROOM:

This is Situation Room, I have nothing further for you now—I will contact you if we get more.

SALINGER:

From Wayside, roger and out.

12:45 P.M. (CST)
NEW YORK CITY

OSBORN ELLIOTT
editor,
Newsweek

[Washington Post Company president] Katharine Graham had invited Arthur Schlesinger [Jr.] to come up from Washington and [John Kenneth] Galbraith to come down from Cambridge for lunch in her executive dining room, which was right down the hall from the editorial offices and my own office. Her purpose was to get these two distinguished guys to talk to the top editors of *Newsweek* about how to make the magazine better. Frankly, I did not look forward much to this lunch. I quite outrageously said to myself, "What do these guys know about making magazines that I don't know?"

We were still sitting in Kay Graham's office, having a drink before lunch, when the door opened and a fellow from our copy desk called Al McCollough poked his head in, caught my eye, and said, "I'm sorry to interrupt, Oz, but the president has just been shot."

IKE PAPPAS
reporter,
WNEW Radio

It was my day off. It was a brilliant beautiful cool day in New York. I had plans to go to my dentist, "Painless Pete" Coutros, and have lunch in [Greenwich] Village and cocktails later with friends. I was getting out of the subway at West Fourth Street. Immediately a woman came running up. She was screaming, crying, "The president has been shot! The president has been shot!" I looked at it rather cynically, you know, "another nut in Greenwich Village." I put a nickel in the phone box—it cost a nickel in those days—and called my office.

12:45 P.M. (CST)
DALLAS TRADE MART

WES WISE
sports director,
KRLD-TV

My wife and I were sitting at a table with some other people at the Trade Mart and they had just served the meal. I had taken the motion pictures of UN Ambassador Adlai Stevenson about a month earlier when he was leaving what was called the UN Day Celebration at the Memorial Theater in downtown Dallas. A woman came out of the crowd and hit him on the ear with a placard. The Secret Service people I had come to know and the FBI people that I had come to know from this area asked me if I would go to the Trade Mart the day President Kennedy was to have spoken there, and if I saw any of the people that I had seen at the Adlai Stevenson event, either looking suspicious or in the background or anything, that I would notify them. I was doubling, trying to help them and to broadcast the fact that he was arriving.

Back in those days, there was such a warm relationship between journalists and law enforcement in general that [a conflict] never even occurred to me. I think the local Dallas police would have thought that if they were negligent in their duty I would have reported it that way. So, no, I had no problem with that, especially when it was concerning the security of the president of the United States.

I saw one of the Secret Service walking fast down the hall. I got up and stopped one of them and said, "What's going on?" He said, "The worst has happened."

EDDIE BARKER
KRLD-TV and Radio

We were the CBS affiliates. I was news director of both properties and the anchor on the news too. I had assigned myself to be at the Trade Mart because that was going to be the capstone of the visit. The people who were out to view him at that luncheon, I would doubt that 10 percent had voted for him. He was not popular here at all. So all of these people out to see him were people with deep pockets and really the upper crust of Dallas—the mayor and you name it. I was up on the balcony of the Trade Mart with a view down to the head table. Shortly, we got word that shots had been fired, so I went on air, just ad-libbing what I had heard about the entourage leaving, and the shooting.

Adlai Stevenson (back to camera) moments before he was struck in the head with a placard after a speech in Dallas one month before President Kennedy's visit.

CHARLES ROBERTS
Newsweek

There's no precedent. When somebody shoots at the president, there is simply no precedent for what you do with the press— who goes where. Within a few minutes, they released the press bus and we went on to the hall where the president was to speak—the Dallas Trade Mart. By this time, all of us were convinced the president had been shot at, but we had no earthly way of knowing aboard that press bus that he'd been hit. We lumbered up to the back of the Trade Mart, burst into this hall, literally pushed these double doors open and swarmed into the place. And this was kind of an otherworldly scene. They were sitting there with no knowledge of what had happened, and the water fountains playing softly. I think there was music piped into the place. And here were perhaps a thousand lunch guests sitting there waiting for the president, and they looked up at us like we were men from Mars or nuts of some kind.

MARIANNE MEANS
White House correspondent, Hearst Newspapers

We rushed for the phones and I happened to get through to our New York office before anybody else, and our man in New York, Eddie Killian, said, "Kennedy's been shot, he's at Parkland Hospital." [Merriman Smith] had broadcast the UPI bulletin and Eddie was looking at the wire. So I screamed, "Kennedy's shot! He's at Parkland!" and everybody dropped what they were doing and we rushed to the exits. We hijacked some bus, as I recall, and scrambled to get to Parkland.

TOM WICKER
New York Times

At the Trade Mart, rumor was sweeping the hundreds of Texans already eating their lunch. It was the only rumor that I had ever seen; it was moving across that crowd like a wind over a wheat field. With the other reporters—I suppose thirty-five of them—I went on through the huge hall to the upstairs press room. We were hardly there when Marianne Means of Hearst Headline Service hung up a telephone, ran to a group of us and said, "The president's been shot. He's at Parkland Hospital."

One thing I learned that day; I suppose I already knew it, but that day made it plain. A reporter must trust his instincts. When Miss Means said those eight words—I never learned who told her—I knew absolutely they were true. Everyone did. We ran for the press buses. A man seized my arm—an official-looking man. "No running in here," he said sternly. I pulled free and ran on. Doug Kiker of the [New York] *Herald Tribune* barreled head-on into a waiter carrying a plate of potatoes. Waiter and potatoes flew about the room. Kiker ran on. He was in his first week with the *Trib*, and his first presidential trip.

12:45 P.M. (CST)
KRLD-TV AND RADIO

Dan Rather, a thirty-two-year-old CBS newsman who is chief of the new CBS bureau in New Orleans, has been asked to set up the network's coverage for Kennedy's trip to Texas. Because CBS is one man short to staff film-drops along the motorcade route, Rather fills in, waiting near the triple underpass for the last drop. Suddenly, a speeding police car passes him, followed by a blur that he believes to be the presidential limousine. He races back to the newsroom of the CBS Dallas affiliate, KRLD-TV and Radio, and immediately calls Parkland Memorial Hospital. A switchboard operator tells him the president has been shot, and then puts a doctor on the phone. The doctor says he believes that the president is dead, but hangs up without identifying himself.

DAN RATHER
New Orleans bureau chief,
CBS News

I got back to the station and started desperately making telephone calls trying to find out what was going on. It was clearly a fact that the president had been shot at, and while it may not have been an absolute, totally confirmed fact, I operated on the basis that he had been shot at, and indeed, hit, and there was a high probability he had been seriously hit and that he might be dead. The key there was making the [telephone] call quickly. If I had made the call, I think certainly minutes later, and possibly seconds later, I probably couldn't have gotten through at all.

12:45 P.M. (CST)
DALLAS TRADE MART

CHARLES ROBERTS
Newsweek

I ran out into the parking lot and ran into another police-man with a three-wheel motorcycle. He was listening to this tremendous radio traffic that had been touched off by the [shooting]. I asked him where the president had gone. And he said, "The president has been shot. They're taking him to

Frank McGee (left), Chet Huntley, and Bill Ryan on the set of NBC News reporting on the shooting.

Parkland Hospital." I ran up to the front of the building and the first person I ran into was George Burkley, Admiral Burkley, the president's personal physician. He had been back in the motorcade probably just a car or two ahead of the press bus, somewhere after the security car and the vice president's car. He had been cut off and had gone to the Trade Mart, not knowing. But he had gotten the word somehow from the policeman there over his police radio.

He had a physical therapist with him, the man that used to give, I guess, massages or back rubs to President Kennedy and accompanied him on all trips. They were piling into this car. I asked him to give me a ride. He wouldn't do it…for which I've since forgiven him. I ran to a police sergeant a few feet away and said, "I've got to get to Parkland Hospital, fast." He walked out into that freeway, flagged the first car that came along. It was a car driven by a Mexican-American woman. She had a teenage daughter with her. The sergeant said, "You take this man to Parkland Hospital. And take him there fast." And she did. She drove me to Parkland and right through the first gate. I think by then they had about one cop at the main gate of the place, but he didn't challenge us. She drove me right up to the emergency entrance of the hospital.

BERT SHIPP
WFAA-TV

We got to Parkland right behind the presidential motorcade and the people that were in the motorcade. In those days, we had access to everything. We could walk into banks, check out the vault, go into police stations. I used to sit in on interrogations. Everything was open to us.

ROBERT DONOVAN
Los Angeles Times

[*Chicago Daily News* Washington bureau chief] Peter Lisagor and I and some other reporters got into the station wagon. It was a horrifying ride. As we approached the hospital on a double-lane highway, [the driver] saw traffic piling up ahead. He turned in and went against the approaching traffic, horn blowing. Well, the police seeing this station wagon coming up the wrong side of the street with its horn blowing assumed it was filled with officials and stopped all traffic and waved us in to the hospital grounds.

DORIS JACOBY
photographer,
Dallas Morning News

I convinced one of the policemen I luckily knew that it was imperative that I get [to Parkland] immediately on his motorcycle. He had the three-wheel kind, with a seat on the back. He told me to get on, and I did, with one hand clutching my camera and power pack, as he blasted off. He was trying to break some speed record. I wildly thought, "This is a most inopportune time to arrive at Parkland Hospital as an emergency."

12:45 P.M. (CST)
DALLAS TIMES HERALD

CHARLIE DAMERON
assistant managing editor,
Dallas Times Herald

I immediately ran back to the composing room and told them to start ripping up the page. I had them go over and find what we used to call the old blockbuster type. This was used for these big, wild advertising pieces and things like that. I said, "Send me two headlines, one that the president was shot, and one the president dead." Then I went back, and of course, the story started rolling.

12:45 P.M. (CST)
DEALEY PLAZA, DALLAS

DARWIN PAYNE
reporter,
Dallas Times Herald

I ran across two or three women who said their boss had taken film of it. Of course, I immediately was interested in that. They said it was Abraham Zapruder. I asked them to take me to him and they did. I talked to him briefly and told him what I wanted. He did not want to give the film to the *Times Herald*. I told him that if he would come with me, with his camera, with the film—the camera was on top of a filing cabinet right there in the outer office—we would see about having the film developed, see what was on it. It seemed to me it might be awfully good because he had described to me what he had seen through the viewfinder.

He was saying [President Kennedy's] head exploded like a firecracker. He said he knew he was dead. He was in tears much of the time. He was very upset about it. They were watching the [television] accounts saying President Kennedy has been shot, was wounded, perhaps seriously wounded. Zapruder was saying, "No, he's dead. I know it because I saw it through my viewfinder."

Before long, a number of men came into the office wearing hats, looking like Secret Service or FBI men. With them was a reporter for the *Dallas Morning News* named Harry McCormick, a legendary police reporter who then must have been in his early seventies. He went in with them, so I started following in with them as well. They said the press can't come in. I said, "Well, there's Harry McCormick. If he's in there, I have to be in there." So they told McCormick to leave. That was my instant, ethical decision to make—whether or not to blow the whistle on the other reporter, which I did. Soon they left with Zapruder. They developed the film that night at the Kodak plant here in Dallas. The next morning he took bids for it.

12:45 P.M. (CST)

DALLAS POLICE DEPARTMENT RADIO TRANSMISSION (CHANNEL 1):

DISPATCHER:
Attention all squads, the suspect is reported to be a white male, approximately thirty, slender build, 5 feet 10 inches, weighs 165 pounds, reported to be armed with what is thought to be a thirty-caliber rifle. No further description at this time or information.

12:45 P.M. (CST)
Parkland Memorial Hospital

WILBORN HAMPTON
UPI

I got to Parkland, and by this time, there was already bumper-to-bumper traffic on Harry Hines Boulevard, the road that runs in front of the hospital, just creeping along. I got up on the median strip and drove as close as I could to the hospital, and just left the car and started running across the lawn. [UPI manager Jack Fallon] had told me to find [Merriman Smith] and help him. On the way to the hospital I had been telling myself, "You have one job—one job—to find out whether the president of the United States is alive or dead." I went around the back and there were maybe fifty, sixty newsmen there. I started to go up toward the emergency entrance and there were two men with automatic weapons—submachine guns—standing at the front door.

MARIANNE MEANS
Hearst Newspapers

We fought for phones at the hospital. I remember wrestling with the nurse for a phone on her desk. She was cursing me and I was saying, "I have to have this phone!" We were both frantic. I got it.

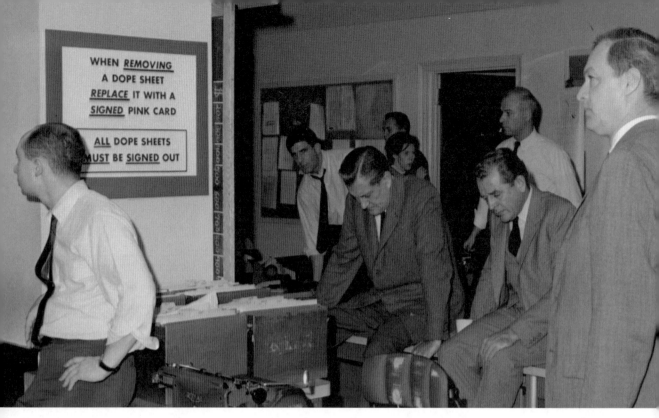

CBS journalists in New York listen somberly to coverage of the shooting in Dallas. Seated on a desk are Eric Sevareid (left) and Charles Collingwood.

MALCOLM COUCH
WFAA-TV

I'll never forget Mrs. Cabell, the mayor's wife, was sitting in the convertible limousine under the tree there at the hospital, totally shocked. She had flowers in her hand and they were draped over her lap, just a bundle of flowers. She was just sitting there, totally shocked, unable to speak.

CHARLES ROBERTS
Newsweek

I started to walk into the emergency entrance and was turned back, then stood in the driveway and talked to Senator [Ralph] Yarborough for a minute. The Secret Service men were then starting to mop up the back seat of the big Lincoln the president was in. A few minutes later, they started putting the fabric top on it. Having been in the vice president's car, very close behind, [Yarborough] knew better than any of us did in the driveway at that moment that the president couldn't possibly survive. I asked him, "Where was the president hit?" And he said, "I can't tell you that." And at the same time, he put his hand up to the right rear corner of his head, which is exactly, of course, where the president had been hit.

TOM WICKER
New York Times

Senator Yarborough is an East Texan, which is to say a Southerner, a man of quick emotion, old-fashioned rhetoric. "Gentlemen," he said, pale, shaken, near tears. "It is a deed of horror." I had chosen that day to be without a notebook. I took notes on the back of my mimeographed schedule of the two-day tour of Texas we had been so near to concluding.

HUGH SIDEY
Time

It was just an eerie scene. A young man, I assume he was a Secret Service man, with a sponge and a bucket of red water, and he was trying to wipe up the blood and what looked like flakes of flesh and brains in the back seat. The red roses were on the front seat. It comes at moments like that how our existence, our civilization, so much hinges on people who are so fragile, and how it comes apart just in an inkling like that.

A television image of Walter Cronkite on the air on November 22, 1963, used in a TV Guide report on assassination coverage in January 1964.

The White House Situation Room continues to brief the Cabinet plane.

SITUATION ROOM:

Wayside, this is Situation Room. I read you latest bulletin. President Kennedy has been given blood transfusions today at Parkland Hospital in an effort to save his life after he and Governor John Connally of Texas were shot in an assassination attempt. Over the TV we have the information that the governor has been moved to the operating room and the president is still in the emergency room. Do you read me so far, over?

PIERRE SALINGER:

Wayside. I read you loud and clear.

SITUATION ROOM:

Wayside, this is Situation Room. Are you getting the press coverage or do you want us to continue to relay it to you? Over.

SALINGER:

[Inaudible]

SITUATION ROOM:

This is Situation Room. Roger. New subject—we will have information for you on whether to proceed to Dallas by the time you land at Honolulu, over.

SALINGER:

Affirmative, affirmative. [Inaudible]

SITUATION ROOM:

This is Situation Room. Will do. Get determination whether secretary of state should also go to Dallas.

SALINGER:

Wayside. Out, over.

A plane carrying Secretary Rusk and five other Cabinet officers to Japan has turned back and will return to Honolulu prior to flying back to the U.S. immediately. The plane on which Mr. Rusk was flying also carried Treasury Secretary Dillon, Commerce Secretary Hodges, Interior Secretary Udall, Agriculture Secretary Freeman, and Labor Secretary Wirtz. This is John Scali, ABC, Honolulu.

Employees of CBS News check teletype reports in the network's New York headquarters after the shooting.

12:51 P.M. (CST)
DALLAS

DALLAS POLICE DEPARTMENT RADIO TRANSMISSION (CHANNEL 2):

DISPATCHER:
125, can you obtain from 1 if the president is going to appear at the Trade Mart?

POLICE CHIEF CURRY:
It's very doubtful.

12:54 P.M. (CST)

DALLAS POLICE DEPARTMENT RADIO TRANSMISSION (CHANNEL 1):

DISPATCHER:
78. [Patrolman J.D. Tippit]
TIPPIT:
78.
DISPATCHER:
You are in the Oak Cliff area, are you not?
TIPPIT:
Lancaster and Eighth.
DISPATCHER:
You will be at large for any emergency that comes in.
TIPPIT:
10-4.

CHARLES ROBERTS
Newsweek

I think it was at 12:57 that we saw the priest arrive, the priest who turned out to be Father [Oscar] Huber, in whose parish Parkland Hospital was. A cop there observed that "it must be the last rites." And, of course, he was right. Some of us reconnoitered the hospital, and the word was seeping out that the president was dead.

MERRIMAN SMITH
UPI

As I stood in the drab buff hallway leading into the emergency ward trying to reconstruct the shooting for the UPI man on the other end of the telephone...I watched a swift and confused panorama sweep before me. [Malcolm] Kilduff of the White House press staff raced up and down the hall. Police captains barked at each other, "Clear this area." Two priests hurried in behind a Secret Service agent, their narrow purple stoles rolled up tightly in their hands. A police lieutenant ran down the hall with a large carton of blood for transfusions. A doctor came in and said he was responding to a call for "all neurosurgeons."

Journalists and police await the latest news in the triage area of Parkland Memorial Hospital.

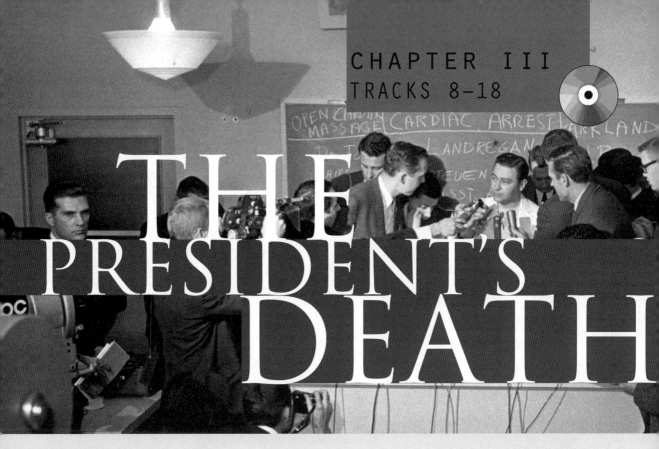

THE PRESIDENT'S DEATH

NOVEMBER 22   1:00 PM – 2:13 PM (CST)

THE PRESIDENT IS shot in the back of the neck with a bullet that exits at his throat and then strikes Governor Connally, sitting in front of him. Another shot hits the back of the president's head and he slumps toward his wife.

Secret Service agents in the follow-up car jump out with automatic weapons drawn, and Agent Clint Hill leaps toward the back of the limousine as Mrs. Kennedy appears to be crawling across the back of the car. In the vice president's car, Lady Bird Johnson hears someone shout over the radio system, "Let's get out of here!" Rufus Youngblood, the Secret Service man assigned to the vice president, vaults over the front seat on top of the vice president, throws him to the floor, and says, "Get down!" The cars speed toward Parkland Memorial Hospital, arriving less than ten minutes after the shooting.

The president and Governor Connally are carried into the hospital. Doctors insert a breathing tube in the president's mouth and another through a hole in his throat, and he is given blood transfusions. A doctor tries to stimulate his heart with chest massage, but an electrocardiograph shows no heartbeat. The president is pronounced dead at 1:00 P.M. Central Standard Time, but the news is not officially released for another half hour, while confused aides try to decide where the new president—Lyndon B. Johnson—should take the oath of office. Lady Bird Johnson finds Mrs. Kennedy in a small hall, looking "quite alone."

Police surround the Texas School Book Depository within minutes of the shooting because witnesses say the shots came from there. Several people report seeing a rifle being quickly withdrawn from an upper-floor window. Police searching the building find a rifle and a barricade of book cartons on the sixth floor that is believed to be the sniper's nest.

Less than an hour later, just a few miles from Dealey Plaza, a Dallas police officer is shot to death. A suspect is seen fleeing into a local theater, where police corner him and take him into custody. He is identified as Lee Harvey Oswald.

A decision is made to escort Lyndon Johnson and his wife in an unmarked car to Love Field, where he will take the oath of office aboard Air Force One before flying back to Washington. Mrs. Kennedy is taken to board the plane along with her husband's coffin, which she will not leave.

1:00 P.M. (CST)
ABOARD THE STATE DEPARTMENT BOEING 707
SOMEWHERE OVER THE PACIFIC

Aircraft 86972 carrying the Cabinet officials receives conflicting reports from the White House Situation Room, alarming Pierre Salinger and others on the plane, who wonder if the shooting might be part of a conspiracy or war, and worry that their own plane might be a target.

*hear...

track 8

MURRAY JACKSON:
This is [Special Assistant to Secretary of State Rusk] Murray Jackson at the State Department. I talked to 7-2 a little while ago. Could you get me 7-2 on single sideband again?

COMMUNICATIONS OPERATOR:
Mr. Jackson, be advised that 7-2 is in a patch with the Situation Room at the present time, sir. If you wish to stand by...

JACKSON:
Oh, that's all right. They're talking to them now?

OPERATOR:
Yes sir, they're in a patch at the present time.

JACKSON:
Very good, can you listen in on this? What we want to tell the plane is Undersecretary Ball requests that [Rusk] and all the passengers return directly to Washington instead of going to Dallas.

PIERRE SALINGER
White House press secretary

It was instructions for Rusk from acting Secretary of State George Ball to tell the plane to return to Washington with everyone aboard. We were not to go to Dallas. That frightened me even more.

1:04 P.M. (CST)
PARKLAND MEMORIAL HOSPITAL

MALCOLM KILDUFF
assistant White House press secretary

At 1:04 [CST] they were still trying to work on him—I think that was Dr. [Malcolm] Perry's statement later. It was only a few minutes later that in talking to Kenny O'Donnell that we knew the president was, in fact, dead.

1:11 P.M. (CST)
TEXAS SCHOOL BOOK DEPOSITORY

DALLAS POLICE DEPARTMENT RADIO TRANSMISSION (CHANNEL 2):

OFFICER 9:
On the [sixth] floor of this book company down here, we found empty rifle hulls and it looked like the man had been here for some time. We are checking it out now.

TOM ALYEA
newsman,
WFAA-TV

We had almost completed the search on the fifth floor when Dallas Police Captain Will Fritz arrived. He was now in charge of the search. Captain Fritz ordered us to the elevator to continue our search on the sixth floor. As we filed out of the elevator, we passed within three feet of the hidden rifle and didn't see it. After searching the sixth floor for about five minutes, a uniformed officer called to Captain Fritz. The officer had discovered the sniper's nest behind a row of book cartons. It was a solid row of book cartons about four and a half feet tall.

Captain Fritz and I couldn't see what the officers had found until we looked over the top. We saw the half-open window with the two shooting support boxes on the brick window ledge. The shell casings were clustered in front of the adjacent window. It took me about three minutes to film this evidence and the crime scene. This included Captain Fritz entering the open east end of the enclosure and holding the three casings over the top of the barricade for me to shoot a close-up of this evidence. I had the only camera in the building.

Captain Fritz put the casings in his pocket and ordered a detective to notify the crime lab at City Hall to come to the Texas School Book Depository but to stay on the first floor until the possibility of a firefight was neutralized. After inspecting the scene for a few minutes, Captain Fritz ordered us to the elevator for our trip to the seventh floor to continue our search for the suspect. The seventh was clear. A small stairway led to the roof, where we went next.

1:11 P.M. (CST)

ABC NEWS: The New York stock exchanges—the New York Stock Exchange and the American Exchange—closed early today a few minutes after two o'clock because of the shooting of President Kennedy.

From Hyannis Port, Massachusetts, ABC correspondent Larry Newman says the president's mother, Mrs. Rose Kennedy, has been given the news that the president has been shot and his condition is serious. State and local police seal off the area of Hyannis Port where the Kennedys live. No one is permitted to approach the area.

Working their sources, two newsmen—CBS network correspondent Dan Rather and CBS affiliate KRLD news director Eddie Barker—are separately hearing that the president is dead. Barker, a well-connected local newsman who is at the Trade Mart, hears it there from a doctor who is on staff at Parkland Memorial Hospital. After hearing earlier from an unidentified doctor at Parkland that the president was believed to be dead, Rather gets through to the hospital switchboard a second time and speaks to a priest, who tells him the president is dead.

1:11 P.M. (CST)
DALLAS TRADE MART

EDDIE BARKER
news director,
KRLD-TV and Radio

A doctor that I knew came up to me and tapped me on the shoulder and whispered in my ear, "Eddie, he is dead." I said, "How do you know?" He said, "I called the emergency room and he was DOA."

1:11 P.M. (CST)
KRLD-TV AND RADIO

DAN RATHER
New Orleans bureau chief,
CBS News

The hospital was, I don't want to say panicked, but you could hear in the background tense voices, and the woman on the switchboard was, she was courteous, she was Texas courteous. I was urging her to—was there somebody I could talk to, somebody who knew what was going on? She said something along the lines of, "All the doctors are busy." She said it in a way, like, "Don't you understand what's going on here?" Then she told me there were two Catholic fathers there, and I asked her if I could speak to one. He said, "What can I help you with?" I told him, "I'm Dan Rather with CBS News" and told him what I was trying to do, that I was trying to confirm the president had been shot. I wasn't prepared for his answer, which was, "Yes, he's been shot and he is dead."

Rather recalls speaking on an open telephone line from the KRLD newsroom to Barker at the Trade Mart and comparing notes; Barker doesn't recall speaking to Rather until later in the day, when he returned to the KRLD newsroom. Both men acknowledge they have different recollections of some of the details of that chaotic day.

DAN RATHER
CBS News

We discussed [Barker's source saying the president was dead] in the context of what I had. My recollection of it is that I said, "Eddie, you put that together with what I've gotten out of the hospital"—and I remembered thinking and I believe I said to Eddie—"if we were still working the police beat, we would know what we have here is a dead man." But because it was the president of the United States...

1:11 P.M. (CST)

In a local television report aired by CBS, Barker says he has an unconfirmed report that the president is dead.

CBS NEWS:
EDDIE BARKER

As you can imagine, there are many stories that are coming in now as to the actual condition of the president. One is that he is dead. This cannot be confirmed.

1:16 P.M. (CST)

Barker now reports that he has learned from a doctor at Parkland Hospital that the president is dead, but again stresses this is unconfirmed.

CBS NEWS:
WALTER CRONKITE

EDDIE BARKER

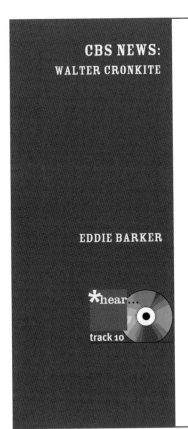

*hear...
track 10

KRLD is reporting they've been told by somebody at the hospital the president is dead. Only a rumor, but they've been told that. KRLD is saying...

Well, that's a repeat of something that you heard reported to you directly a moment ago from KRLD Television in Dallas, and that is the rumor that has reached them...that the president is dead, totally unconfirmed apparently as yet. However, let's go back to KRLD in Dallas.

We do not know what his condition is, but the report is that the president is dead.... This is something that the word just came to us a minute ago. The word we have is that President Kennedy is dead. This we do not know for a fact. Word we have is that he is dead, that he was shot by an assassin at the intersection of Elm and Houston Streets just as he was going into the underpass. The word we have is from a doctor on the staff of Parkland Hospital who says that it is true. He was in tears when he told me just a moment ago. This is still not officially confirmed, but, as I say, the source would normally be a good one.

EDDIE BARKER
KRLD-TV and Radio

I just went on the air with it. I said an unimpeachable source has told me that he is dead on arrival at the hospital. In those days, we were so close to the police or the FBI or the medical people. I knew my source. What you're always trying to teach young reporters is sources, sources, sources.

After I said that he was dead, CBS was carrying this, which I did not know. They figured that we had a pretty good reputation as a news operation. They figured we would be on top of it so they picked it up and were carrying it. Well in New York, they panicked. My dear friend Walter Cronkite kept giving me great credit—I'm saying it, not him. That was how the word got out that he was dead.

WALTER CRONKITE
anchor,
CBS Evening News

Eddie Barker was the news director at KRLD. Barker was relaying reports minute by minute. He had inside information because he was a Dallas news director. He had people inside the hospital that were feeding information to him.

Dallas police officer J.D. Tippit is shot in the Oak Cliff area of Dallas about forty-five minutes after the attack on the president. Witnesses say Tippit pulled his car over to question a man walking on Tenth Street. The man pulled a gun, shot him, then ran away. A passerby, Domingo Benavides, uses the patrolman's radio to alert dispatchers to the shooting.

track 11

DALLAS POLICE DEPARTMENT RADIO TRANSMISSION (CHANNEL 1):

CITIZEN:
Hello, police operator?

DISPATCHER:
Go ahead. Go ahead, citizen using the police [radio].

CITIZEN:
We've had a shooting out here.

DISPATCHER:
Where's it at?

DISPATCHER:
The citizen using police radio…

CITIZEN:
On Tenth Street.

DISPATCHER:
What location on Tenth Street?

CITIZEN:
Between Marsalis and Beckley. It's a police officer. Somebody shot him. What's this?…404 Tenth Street.

DISPATCHER:
78 [Patrolman J.D. Tippit].

CITIZEN:
You got that? It's in a police car, number ten. You got that?

DISPATCHER:
78.

CITIZEN:
Hello, police operator, did you get that? A police officer—510 East Jefferson.

DISPATCHER:
Signal 19 [a shooting], involving a police officer, 510 East Jefferson.

HUGH AYNESWORTH
science/aviation/space editor,
Dallas Morning News

I've always learned that in a crisis, stay close to the police radio. So there was a three-wheeler parked right down here in front. [*Dallas Morning News* police reporter Jim Ewell] and I got close to the radio, and that's when we heard the report coming in from Oak Cliff that an officer had been shot. I remember saying to Jim, "Hey Jim, this has got to be connected, that's only three or four miles away." I jumped in a Channel 8 car and said, "Let's get over to West Tenth Street." We ran every red light. We were screaming, "Hey, look out!" We got over there pretty damn fast.

The first person we saw was Helen Markham, who was a woman waiting at the bus stop when she saw Oswald shoot Tippit. She was in tears, she was spasmodic. She gave us a description, told us which way he ran.

1:19 P.M. (CST)
DALLAS

track 11

DALLAS POLICE DEPARTMENT RADIO TRANSMISSION (CHANNEL 1):

DISPATCHER:
The subject's running west on Jefferson from the location.
OFFICER 85:
10-4.
DISPATCHER:
No physical description.
CITIZEN:
Hello, hello, hello.
602 [AMBULANCE]:
602.

CITIZEN:
From out here on Tenth Street, 500 block. This police officer's just shot. I think he's dead.
DISPATCHER:
10-4. We have the information. The citizen using the radio, remain off the radio now.

1:19 P.M. (CST)
KRLD-TV AND RADIO

Dan Rather discusses the unconfirmed reports of the president's death with CBS officials in New York.

DAN RATHER
CBS News

Putting those two things together [what he and Barker had both learned], I was on the phone with [CBS Radio officials in] New York and I told them what the situation was, and a man named—I believe it was Mort Dank Sr.—said, "The president is dead?" And I said, "Yes, I think he's dead."

Now, frankly, there wasn't any doubt in my mind he was dead, but I thought we were going to discuss what we were going to do with this information. And then the next thing I heard was CBS Radio playing "The Star-Spangled Banner" and [announcer] Alan Jackson saying the president was dead. It dawned on me that if for any reason this was not true, that I had probably committed a blunder—but I didn't believe at the time it was a blunder. I was just sort of taken aback by the enormity of their playing "The Star-Spangled Banner"and saying the president is dead, and they're doing it on the basis of what I've said here. At my age and stage—I would argue at any age and stage—that was pretty heavy.

ROBERT SKEDGELL
radio newsroom supervisor,
CBS News

Mort Dank was on the phone with Rather and I heard him ask, "You say he's dead?" Then I took the phone from Mort. I asked, "Are you sure? Are you absolutely certain?" He said he was, so I took a piece of yellow copy paper and wrote "JFK DEAD" and handed it to Alan, who then went on the air.

1:22 P.M. (CST)

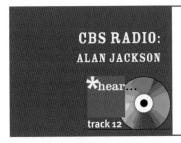

CBS RADIO:
ALAN JACKSON

hear...

track 12

Ladies and gentlemen, the president of the United States is dead. John F. Kennedy has died of the wounds received in the assassination in Dallas less than an hour ago. We repeat—it has just been announced that President Kennedy is dead.

1:26 P.M. (CST)
PARKLAND MEMORIAL HOSPITAL

Lyndon Johnson leaves the hospital bound for Love Field.

MALCOLM KILDUFF
White House

I got hold of Kenny [O'Donnell] and I said, "Kenny, this is a terrible time to have to approach you on this but the world has got to know that President Kennedy is dead." He said, "Well, don't they know it already?" I said, "No, I haven't told them." He said, "Well, you're going to have to make the announcement, but you better check with Mr. Johnson."

I walked through the hall through the emergency room into the small cubicle where [Lyndon Johnson] was sitting with Mrs. Johnson and with Rufus Youngblood, the Secret Service agent who'd been with him. I walked up to him and for the first time when I looked at him, very frankly I didn't know what to call him—I just blurted out "Mr. President." He turned around—I'll never forget the look on his face—I'm fairly sure this was the first time he'd been called "Mr. President." I said, "I have to announce the death of President Kennedy, is it all right with you?" He reacted immediately. He said, "No, Mac, I think we better wait for a few minutes. I think I'd better get out of here and get back to the plane before you announce it. We don't know whether this is a worldwide conspiracy, whether they're after me as well as they were after President Kennedy, or whether they're after [House] Speaker McCormack or Senator Hayden [president pro tempore of the Senate]. We just don't know." He also mentioned at that time the attempt on the life of Secretary of State Seward at the time of Lincoln's assassination.

He said, "Are they prepared to get me out of here?" I went back and talked to one of the agents, Roy Kellerman, who was the agent in charge of this trip and who was riding in the right front seat of President Kennedy's car when [Kennedy] was shot. He gathered a few agents together. I talked to President Johnson and I said, "I'm going to make the announcement as soon as you leave." They sent an agent outside to get the car lined up to take him back. They got the motorcycle escort lined up to get him back to the airport, then the two of us, President Johnson and myself, walked out of the emergency room entrance together. Everyone was screaming at me, "What can you tell us, what can you tell us?" It was a scene of absolute confusion. In that confusion, President Johnson had gotten into a car and left.

1:27 P.M. (CST)

CBS reports that Rather has confirmed that the president is dead.

CBS NEWS:
WALTER CRONKITE

✳hear...
◉
track 12

We just have a report from our correspondent, Dan Rather, in Dallas, that he has confirmed that President Kennedy is dead. There is still no official confirmation of this, however.

WALTER CRONKITE
CBS News

The next major bulletin we had on our own was when Dan Rather said that he had heard at the hospital that Kennedy was dead. Well, we debated this one at the news desk. He heard it, but he couldn't confirm it. And we couldn't confirm it any other way. So we labored with whether we should

In Washington, D.C., passers-by throng in front of the ABC-TV studio for news of events in Dallas. ABC affixed the latest wire-service reports to the window.

report it. A very short time after that, the word became official that the president was dead.

DAN RATHER
CBS News

My recollection, which is vivid, is that Ernie Leiser, who was in charge of things, and whoever else was with him [at CBS Television News in New York] knew that we had broadcast it on radio, had heard my information, and at least Leiser took it as, "OK, he's dead, but what can we do about that?" My impression at the time was—and I think I'm right about this— was that they accepted the information was true, but made a decision: "Listen, we're just not going to say it on television until there's an official announcement." We were already on the record with radio.

BERT SHIPP
assistant news director,
WFAA-TV

The sheriff came out and I said, "Mr. Decker, how's it look?" He said, "Bert, you ever seen deer hit in the back of the head? Gone." I said, "A man can't live with the back of his head gone." I got on the phone and told the station for all practical purposes the president's dead. [Radio reporter] John Allen says, "You tell 'em. I ain't gonna do it." So I became, along with twenty-two hundred other people, the first one to ever announce that Kennedy was dead. I went on live. I said I was just in contact with Sheriff Decker who said there was a wound in the back of Kennedy's head so severe that it was impossible for life to be maintained. I still left it open about the fact that he was gone.

Two priests who were with Kennedy leave the hospital.

TOM WICKER
reporter,
New York Times

As I was passing the open convertible in which Vice President and Mrs. Johnson and Senator [Ralph] Yarborough had been riding in the motorcade, a voice boomed from its radio: "The president of the United States is dead. I repeat— it has just been announced that the president of the United States is dead." There was no authority, no word of who had announced it. But—instinct again—I believed it instantly. It sounded true. I knew it was true. I stood still a moment, then began running.

Ordinarily, I couldn't jump a tennis net if I'd just beaten [Pancho] Gonzales. That day, carrying a briefcase and a typewriter, I jumped a chain fence looping around the drive, not even breaking stride. Hugh Sidey of *Time*, a close friend of the president, was walking slowly ahead of me. "Hugh," I said, "the president's dead."…Sidey, I learned a few minutes later, stood where he was a minute. Then he saw two Catholic priests. He spoke to them. Yes, they told him, the president was dead.

HUGH SIDEY
White House correspondent,
Time

We saw the priests come out, [Hearst correspondent] Marianne Means and myself. Marianne said, "What can you tell us?" One of them said, "We can't tell you anything." One of them got in a car and Marianne said to the other one, "Can't you tell us whether he is dead or alive?" The priest said, "He's dead all right." There is no mistake about it. I heard it standing four feet from him.

SID DAVIS
White House correspondent,
Westinghouse Broadcasting
Company

I saw a couple of priests down the hallway and they were talking to some other reporters. I ran down and I heard the priest say, "He's dead all right." The priest's name was Father Oscar Huber. He was the local parish priest. I ran back to the phone and, I don't know why I did this, but I did not put that on the air. I just felt because it was the president—I know a priest probably knew what a dead person looked like, he'd said he'd given the last rites of the church—but I just felt I wasn't going to go with that until I had the official announcement.

White House press pass issued for the Texas trip to Sid Davis of Westinghouse Broadcasting.

DALLAS POLICE DEPARTMENT RADIO TRANSMISSION (CHANNEL 2):

DISPATCHER:
Stand by. Notify 1 [Police Chief Curry] that officer involved in this shooting, officer J.D. Tippit, we believe, was pronounced DOA at Methodist 1:28 P.M.

OFFICER 4:
Is there any indication that it has any connection with this other shooting?

DISPATCHER:
Well, the descriptions on the suspect are similar and it is possible.

ABC NEWS:
Here is a flash from the Associated Press. Two priests who were with Mr. Kennedy say he is dead of bullet wounds. There are conflicting reports—one moment is one way and another moment is another way. Until we can get official word we will stay on the air.

Cronkite reports that two priests say the president is dead.

CBS NEWS:
WALTER CRONKITE

This is the bulletin that just cleared from Dallas, that the two priests who were in the emergency room, where President Kennedy lay after being taken from the Dallas street corner where he was shot, say that he is dead. Our man, Dan Rather, in Dallas reported that about ten minutes ago, too.

MERRIMAN SMITH
White House correspondent,
United Press International

[Assistant press secretary Malcolm] Kilduff and Wayne Hawks of the White House staff ran by me, shouting that Kilduff would make a statement shortly in the so-called Nurses Room above and at the far end of the hospital. I threw down the phone and sped after them.

CHARLES ROBERTS
White House correspondent,
Newsweek

Mac Kilduff came in at 1:33.... He had a cigarette in one hand and a very short piece of paper in the other with a simple, perhaps thirty-word statement. He read it with his hands trembling.

ROBERT MACNEIL
White House correspondent,
NBC News

Kilduff stood behind a wooden desk on a small platform. The cameras were switched on. His face was very white and he kept twisting it to avoid crying, but his cheeks were shining with tears. His hands were shaking and he tried to steady them by pressing down firmly with his fingers on the desk. With great difficulty in controlling his voice, [he] said..."President John F. Kennedy died at approximately one o'clock Central Standard Time of a gunshot wound in the brain."

SID DAVIS
Westinghouse

I remember the familiar cigarette was in [Kilduff's] hand. He had been very emotional; I guess I'd say he'd been crying. He could barely get the words out of his mouth. He later said he opened his mouth and nothing came out. He could not bring himself to say that John Kennedy was dead. It was bedlam—we just charged for the phones.

MALCOLM KILDUFF
White House

I'd been assistant press secretary for the White House for a year and a half. This was the first trip I'd ever taken with President Kennedy alone. I got up there and I thought, "This is really the first press conference on a road trip I've had to hold." I started to say it, and all I could say was, "Excuse me, let me catch my breath." I thought in my mind, "What am I going to say and how am I going to say it?" The simplest thing was: "President John F. Kennedy died at approximately one o'clock here in Dallas of a gunshot wound in the brain."

MIKE COCHRAN
correspondent,
Associated Press

When we walked through the entrance of Parkland Hospital, we had only gone a few steps and a wave of nurses came down the hall. They were just hysterical and crying. Malcolm Kilduff had just announced that Kennedy had died.

WILBORN HAMPTON
reporter,
UPI

I shouted into the receiver. "He's dead, Don, my God, he's dead. It's official. He died at 1:00 P.M." "Who said it?" "The White House guy. Kilduff." I could hear Don Smith shout, "Jack, it's official. He died at 1:00 P.M." Then I could hear Jack [Fallon] shout to Jim Tolbert: "Flash! President Kennedy dead." In addition to the ten bells that rang, the flash was what we called keyboarded. Jim stopped the wire wherever it was and typed in the word "Flash" and the news. This is the [wire] that everybody dreaded.

UPI WIRE:

```
FLASH
PRESIDENT KENNEDY DEAD
JT135PCS
```

1:35 P.M. (CST)
ABOARD THE STATE DEPARTMENT BOEING 707
SOMEWHERE OVER THE PACIFIC

Aircraft 86972, carrying the Cabinet officials, receives a transmission from the White House relaying confirmation of the president's death.

hear...

track 14

SITUATION ROOM:
This is Situation Room, relay following to Wayside. We have report quoting Mr. Kilduff in Dallas that the president is dead, that he died about thirty-five minutes ago. Do you have that? Over.

PIERRE SALINGER:
The president is dead. Is that correct?

SITUATION ROOM:
That is correct. That is correct. New subject. Front office desires plane return Washington with no stop Dallas. Over.

SALINGER:
Wayside copied all OK and we return direct to Washington without stopping in Dallas. Roger.

Assistant White House press secretary Malcolm Kilduff makes the official announcement at Parkland Memorial Hospital that President Kennedy is dead.

(above) Journalists gather in a classroom area of Parkland Memorial Hospital, where most press announcements about the president's condition were made.

Bert Shipp (left) and Jay Watson of WFAA-TV, in a broadcast from the station's newsroom, discuss the shooting of President Kennedy just minutes before the official announcement of his death.

PIERRE SALINGER
White House

I walked slowly back to [Secretary of State Dean] Rusk's cabin. Tears were already streaking down my face. "The president is dead," I told the Cabinet officers. Without another word being said, everyone bent his head and said his private prayer. Secretary Rusk then walked to the microphone in the front of the plane and announced the president's death to the twenty-eight passengers. There was a cumulative cry of anguish from the passengers. I was standing at the front of the aisle, sobbing. My wife, Nancy, came up and held me, tears rushing down her face. Other wives reached for their husbands and the aisle was clogged.

1:35 P.M. (CST)
DALLAS

DALLAS POLICE DEPARTMENT RADIO TRANSMISSION (CHANNEL 1):

DISPATCHER:
Go ahead, 223.

OFFICER 223:
He is in the library, Jefferson, East 500 block, Marsalis and Jefferson. [Some garble.]

DISPATCHER:
What location, 223?

OFFICER 223:
Library, Jefferson and Marsalis. I'm going around the back. Get them here fast.

DISPATCHER:
Any unit near Marsalis and Jefferson.

OFFICER 85:
En route.

HUGH AYNESWORTH
Dallas Morning News

Once again, I got close to a police radio. The police radio said, "Go to the public library. Suspect in the public library." We ran like hell there and we found out that this was nothing at all—a man who ran in and said, "The president's been shot." Everybody jumped on him and beat the hell out of him.

CBS News anchor Walter Cronkite announces President Kennedy's death.

1:38 P.M. (CST)
New York City

WALTER CRONKITE
CBS News

I had to report that the president was dead. At the moment it happened, I choked up.

CBS NEWS:
WALTER CRONKITE

*hear...

track 13

From Dallas, Texas, the flash, apparently official: President Kennedy died at 1:00 P.M., Central Standard Time, two o'clock, Eastern Standard Time—some thirty-eight minutes ago.

WALTER CRONKITE
CBS News

I don't recall crying at all but I did wipe my eyes, so I guess I must have felt a tear or two. That was a very momentary thing. I did show emotion quite clearly, but I think I managed to swallow that problem pretty quickly and got on with the broadcast. I'm proud of that and I'm not ashamed of choking up for the moment at all.

OSBORN ELLIOTT
editor,
Newsweek

Kay [Graham] and Arthur [Schlesinger Jr.] and [John Kenneth] Galbraith and I all dashed down the hall to my office, which was where the nearest television set was, flicked it on, put on CBS, and like the rest of America, watched Walter Cronkite as he delivered the awful news. And needless to say, everybody was stunned, shocked, and saddened. Gradually, our little group dissipated, and I went about my job of trying to tear apart a magazine [that] was already pretty much at the press.

1:38 P.M. (CST)
PARKLAND MEMORIAL HOSPITAL

BOB HUFFAKER
reporter,
KRLD-TV

I finally got hold of Congressman Jim Wright and was talking with him at the very moment we discovered the president was dead. I had some difficulty continuing to speak. I handed the mike to the congressman and said, "No one wants to speak at a time like this but do you have anything to say?" Bless his old heart, he took the mike and said a prayer.

There was not much more to be said except reporting on the condition of the governor. People were crowded around and weeping. It was quite a scene. I just continued to talk even though I hated to go on. I did not feel like talking.

TOM WICKER
New York Times

I wandered down the hall, found a doctor's office, walked in, and told him I had to use his phone. He got up without a word and left.

HUGH SIDEY
Time

After the announcement, I went around back because I didn't have to do any instant stuff, and there [Malcolm Kilduff] was alone, sobbing, weeping.

I had covered the president as long and as intently as any single reporter. Many [news organizations] didn't have the money to send them around the world with Kennedy, but I had been with him really all of six years because *Time* had the dough and wanted me to do it. He was a friend, but it went beyond that—a friend had been killed, an administration, the New Frontier, was over with, finished. I knew probably better than others because I had been around Johnson, I knew how different the two were, and how the nature of the presidency flowed from the man in the Oval Office, and now, here he is dead, and this is the heartbeat of the most powerful nation on earth. In those moments, you suddenly realize that we are on this Earth by the grace of God.

CBS NEWS:
WALTER CRONKITE

✱hear...

track 13

Vice President Lyndon Johnson has left the hospital in Dallas but we do not know to where he has proceeded; presumably he will be taking the oath of office shortly and become the thirty-sixth president of the United States.

WALTER CRONKITE
CBS News

We began to be concerned about where Lyndon Johnson was, and when he might be taking the oath of office. We were speculating on that. We finally determined he was in one of the other cars, and had proceeded to the airport, where the presidential airplane had been awaiting the president's party.

1:38 P.M. (CST)
DALLAS

KEITH SHELTON
political writer,
Dallas Times Herald

We were very careful to try to double-check things. There was a lot of bad information. People said they saw Johnson shot. People said they saw the Secret Service exchanging gunfire with people. So the problem was sorting out the false information from the real information. Today, with immediate cable television, we probably would have used some of it as speculation. But in those days we just didn't put it in until we checked it out.

TOM WICKER
New York Times

That day, a reporter had none of the ordinary means or time to check and double-check matters given as fact. He had to go on what he knew of people he talked to, what he knew of human reaction, what two isolated "facts" added to in sum—above all on what he felt in his bones…. In a crisis, if a reporter can't trust his instinct for truth, he can't trust anything…. Throughout the day, every reporter on the scene seemed to me to do his best to help everyone else…. Nobody thought about an exclusive; it didn't seem important.

1:38 P.M. (CST)
DALLAS SHERIFF'S DEPARTMENT

TERRANCE W. MCGARRY
reporter,
UPI

The sheriff had a guy in custody. I asked one of the sheriff's deputies, "Is that him? Did he do it?" He said, "We don't know." This poor guy, as it came out later, was the manager of an office machine or equipment company who'd come downtown with a group of friends to see Kennedy. He needed to take a whiz, walked into an office building to look for a bathroom, and while he was in there, Kennedy was shot outside. He walked out, having no notion of what had happened. Some workers up above yelled down to the people in the street, "There he is. There he goes." He comes out of this building and this lynch mob jumps him. [The sheriff's deputy] said, "People were fixin' to start beatin' on him. I grabbed him, pulled him over here."…While [the deputy] was pulling him over, some people were swinging at him. A woman took a picture of him with a camera and then took the hot flashbulb and threw it in his face.

I hung around [the sheriff's office] a little bit more and then [the deputy] said, "OK, boys, we're letting this gentleman go. We're convinced he had nothing to do with the incident." He said, "I think I should tell you before you ask him any questions we have not told him why he is here. That's part of the interrogation technique. We don't tell people why they are being questioned, apparently to see if they reveal any knowledge of it. So if you want to talk to him you will have to explain what he's doing here." This guy is just standing there with sort of a shell-shocked expression. He looked over at us. He said, "Is somebody going to tell me what this is all about?" I said, "You really don't know why you are here?" "No," he said. "Why?" I said, "You were arrested on suspicion of assassinating the president of the United States." He just went white. He said, "What?" As it turned out, this guy attended the same church that I did in Dallas. Whenever I would go to church and he would recognize me, he would get this horrible expression on his face. He clearly connected my face with one of the low points in his life.

1:38 P.M. (CST)
DALLAS TRADE MART

KEITH SHELTON
Dallas Times Herald

There was an announcement that the president had been delayed. Then there was an announcement that the president had been hit. And then finally an announcement that he was dead. The head of the ministers' association said a prayer. The mayor said a few words, and then everybody left. There were yellow roses on all the tables, the "Yellow Rose of Texas" theme. I noticed the presidential seal was on the podium and it disappeared almost immediately.

1:38 P.M. (CST)
LOS ANGELES

RICHARD STOLLEY
Los Angeles regional editor,
Life

I grabbed [*Life* correspondent Tommy Thompson] and two photographers who happened to be in the office and we just jumped in a car. [Staff writer] Shana Alexander drove us to the L.A. airport with no bags, nothing, except that the photographers brought their camera bags. We were entering Los Angeles International Airport when we heard the news on the radio that Kennedy was dead. We got on a

National Airlines plane, an airline that no longer exists. It was the strangest flight I ever took, because a lot of newspeople from L.A. were on that plane. All safety regulations were abandoned. They put these huge TV cameras in the aisles. They didn't check them, they weren't strapped down, they weren't anything. People were sitting on other people's laps. It was bizarre. And the captain kept keeping us up-to-date from the radio.

1:38 P.M. (CST)
DALLAS

A cashier at the Texas Theatre, a few blocks from the place where Dallas police officer J.D. Tippit has been shot, phones police to say a man acting suspiciously has entered the movie house.

1:46 P.M. (CST)

hear…
track 15

DALLAS POLICE DEPARTMENT RADIO TRANSMISSION (CHANNEL 1):

DISPATCHER:
Have information a suspect just went in the Texas Theatre on West Jefferson.
OFFICER 79:
10-4.
DISPATCHER:
10-4. Supposed to be hiding in the balcony.

HUGH AYNESWORTH
Dallas Morning News

We converged on the Texas Theatre. The first person I saw there was Julie Postal, the woman who sold tickets in front of the theater. She said, "He's in there, he's in there!" I said, "Did he buy a ticket?" I don't know why I asked her that. She said, "I don't remember."

So about that time, [reporter] Jim Ewell comes over and we went into the building. I peeked through and I saw they dimmed the lights about half, and the show was still on. Then I saw a couple of people on each side walking up [the aisle], talking to people. All of a sudden two people came to [the suspect's] row. I was not more than fifteen to eighteen feet from him, right to my left, third row. Coming up on my right side were a couple of others. Officer Nick McDonald grabbed [the suspect]. It wasn't ten seconds until a couple other people jumped in, too, which saved McDonald's life. [The suspect had a pistol and McDonald had gotten his hand between the pistol's firing pin and hammer, preventing the suspect from shooting him.] It was so fast. They dragged [the suspect] like a piece of meat. I mean, they were angry. I remember what he said, he said it twice: "I protest this police brutality! I protest this police brutality!"

1:46 P.M. (CST)
PARKLAND MEMORIAL HOSPITAL

BERT SHIPP
WFAA-TV

I go out to the intersection there in front of Parkland Hospital and thought, "Well, the next car that comes along I'll just hop in and have 'em take me downtown to the station." This old car stopped there, one of those old DeSotos with the tail fins all over. I pulled the door open and there was a senior citizen sitting there. I startled him. I said, "I'm Bert Shipp, Channel 8 News, the president's been shot, I've got to get to the station, and you're about the only chance I got." He says, "I'm not going that way." I just reached over and put my foot on top of his on the accelerator and said, "You got a green light, we're both going that way." He says, "You're gonna get us killed." I said, "You just drive and I'll do the gas." We went through stoplights and I was trying to get the news on the radio, and he says, "You're liable to ruin that radio." I said, "Drive!" I looked over and the blood was drained out of his face. It was a harrowing experience for him, I know. [I can imagine] that evening: he walks in and puts his coat up on the rack, sits down, his wife's got him some liver and onions or something, and she says,

"How was your day?" I would have given anything to have been there.

1:51 P.M. (CST)
DALLAS

DALLAS POLICE DEPARTMENT RADIO TRANSMISSION (CHANNEL 1):

550/2:
Suspect on shooting of police officer is apprehended and en route to the station.
DISPATCHER:
10-4. At the Texas Theatre?
550/2:
Caught him in the lower floor of the Texas Theatre after a fight.

Shooting suspect Lee Harvey Oswald is hustled into custody by Dallas police officers.

1:51 P.M. (CST)
WASHINGTON, D.C.

BEN BRADLEE
Washington bureau chief,
Newsweek

It was a Friday, and Friday is a pivot day for *Newsweek*. That's the day that the book is supposed to freeze. You go from there to the printer in as fast and as orderly manner as you can. I think we threw the whole goddamn thing out. So we had various conferences about who would do what.

We had this other thing in addition to the professional part. [The Kennedys] were friends of ours, my wife and me. I've always felt it was kind of a blessing [to work], because if you have a personal sort of explosion in your life, if you are left with nothing to do, you just get depressed about it. I had so much to do then, not only getting the bureau's coverage going but editing it. I was talking to [*Newsweek* editor Osborn] Elliott all the time and talking to all the reporters, squeezing in a few tears when it sort of hits you. Then they decided they wanted me to write a piece that later turned out to be "That Special Grace." I think I tried to get out of it several times. It was going to be so difficult to stay out of the piece and not be maudlin. Oz Elliott, who was really a great editor, said, "You just keep going. You're doing fine. You're doing fine." They kind of pulled it out of me. But it was twenty-minute bursts.

OSBORN ELLIOTT
Newsweek

Ben [Bradlee] of course was a very good friend of Kennedy's and was absolutely devastated by this news. I know at least one time when I spoke to him, he was in tears. I had thought, who better to write a personal appreciation of the president than his good friend Ben? Obviously, Ben was so devastated that he said, of course, "I just can't do it." And we talked back and forth over the next few hours, and I would be trying to be the professional, saying, "Look, Ben, you've just got to figure out some way to separate the personal feelings from your professional life here, and I know how tough it is, but can't you *possibly* do a personal appreciation for one page?" Well, he finally set about doing it and ended up turning out an incredibly good piece.

From left, Benjamin Bradlee, Jacqueline Kennedy, Tony Bradlee, and President John Kennedy in the White House on the president's birthday in May 1963.

2:08 P.M. (CST)
PARKLAND MEMORIAL HOSPITAL

Mrs. Kennedy refuses to leave the hospital without her husband's body. The Dallas County medical examiner insists that local regulations require that an autopsy be performed in Dallas, and that the president's body cannot be taken back to Washington before then. After a fight with the medical examiner, the president's staff prevails. Plans are made for Kennedy's body, accompanied by his wife, to be taken to the airfield with a police escort and to then be transported to Washington on Air Force One, where Lyndon Johnson soon will be sworn in as president.

DALLAS POLICE DEPARTMENT RADIO TRANSMISSION (CHANNEL 1):

DISPATCHER:
Report to Parkland, entrance to Parkland, Code 2. [Urgent—use red lights and siren as needed.]
OFFICER 29:
To Parkland, Code 2.

CHARLES ROBERTS
Newsweek

At the [hospital] door was a hearse from the Oneal Funeral Home. Hugh Sidey of *Time* and I talked to Vernon Oneal, and I guess he was the first one from whom we learned that they were planning to fly the president's body back to Washington. Oneal was sitting in the front seat of this hearse and said, "They expect me to take this body out to the airport and put it aboard a plane. I can't take the body out to the airport because I don't have a certificate or permit." Apparently, he was quite convinced he had to follow the letter of the law.

I stepped into the corridor [leading to the emergency operating room] just minutes before they brought the president's body out in the bronze casket that Oneal had brought in that hearse. The casket was on one of these little rubber-tired dollies and Mrs. Kennedy was walking on the right side of it. A policeman pinned me up against the wall as they passed by. She was walking with her left hand on the casket and a completely glazed look on her face, obviously in shock. It was deathly still in that corridor as this casket was wheeled out. I had a feeling that if somebody had literally fired a pistol in front of her face that she would just have blinked. It seemed that she was absolutely out of this world.

They put the bronze casket in the back door of the hearse. The curtains of it were drawn, and Mrs. Kennedy insisted on riding in the back of the hearse rather than in the front seat.

HUGH SIDEY
Time

We stood there as the casket came out and it went down a sloping ramp, Jackie beside it with her hand resting on the casket. I remember [Kennedy aide] Larry O'Brien with tears running down his cheeks. These were my friends. It just tore your heart out. Do you be a journalist and stand there and make notes, or do you say something? We stood there.

BOB CLARK
Washington correspondent, ABC News

I was just making a call to New York when here comes the casket with Jackie. So I gave a live description to New York on Jackie coming down the hallway with the casket. Just a very somber scene. Nobody was speaking to her.

ROBERT PIERPOINT
White House correspondent, CBS News

I had phoned New York and for the next half-hour I was on the phone. I didn't know how much of my words were going to [Walter] Cronkite on television; all I know is I kept talking about everything I had seen. All of a sudden I saw Lyndon Johnson and Lady Bird hurrying out the door. I described that and, a few minutes later, I saw a casket rolling out with Mrs. Kennedy's hand on the casket. I described that. I did not report, and I regret it to this day, I just couldn't talk about the fact that Mrs. Kennedy in that beautiful watermelon-colored dress, her legs were covered almost to the waist in blood. I just broke down as a reporter and couldn't describe it. The function of a reporter in a situation like that is to avoid the state of shock and do your job, but I was just kind of in a state of shock.

MERRIMAN SMITH
UPI

Jiggs Fauver of the White House transportation staff grabbed me and said [Malcolm] Kilduff wanted a pool of three men immediately to fly back to Washington on Air Force One, the presidential aircraft.... Down the stairs I ran and into the driveway, only to discover that Kilduff had just pulled out in our telephone car. Charles Roberts of *Newsweek* magazine, Sid Davis of Westinghouse Broadcasting, and I implored a police officer to take us to the airport in his squad car.

SID DAVIS
Westinghouse

Jiggs Fauver, the White House transportation officer, grabbed me by the shoulder and said, "You've got to come with me." I said, "I'm on the air live and I can't come with you." He said, "No, you must come with me at this very moment. We don't have a minute to lose. We need a pool. We need a broadcaster."

I remember writing in my notepad my office telephone number and [my manager] Jim Snyder's number. I wrote, "Call Jim Snyder" and I handed it to the cop who was driving the car and asked him to radio his office and ask them to send it.

CHARLES ROBERTS
Newsweek

So three of us jumped into an unmarked police car, no siren. We had to go like hell to get there. For all we knew they were going to put that casket aboard a plane and fly out immediately. We went through mid-afternoon traffic at about... sometimes I think we got up to eighty miles an hour without a siren. We went through red lights and crossed median strips. The driver kept telling us that they couldn't use sirens. The idea was they were not to attract attention to the airport.

2:10 P.M. (CST)

DALLAS

DALLAS POLICE DEPARTMENT RADIO TRANSMISSION (CHANNEL 2):

OFFICER 251:
Could you contact someone out there at the airport and have them advise Mr. Kilduff, he's in the White House staff, and tell him the pool men he's concerned about are en route; that I'm bringing them to the plane?

DISPATCHER:
4 [Deputy Police Chief N.T. Fisher], did you receive?

N.T. FISHER:
The pool men he's concerned with are what?

DISPATCHER:
Are en route to that location.

OFFICER 251:
[These] gentlemen also wish to know if it would be possible for your office to make a collect call to Washington to deliver a message for them.

DISPATCHER:
I'm sorry my phones are all tied up.

ABC RADIO: Vice President Johnson has now started making his plans to be sworn into office. He has left the hospital. The vice president, though he seemed to have been wounded, was not hurt in the assassination of President Kennedy today.

2:10 P.M. (CST)

NEW YORK CITY

HENRY GRUNWALD
foreign editor, Time

A German-born researcher burst into my office, in tears. She was weeping not only for the president, but crying in rage about a conversation between two writers she had just over-heard. "Can you imagine," she said between sobs, "those bastards were talking about the stock market, how the stock market would react. How can they, at a time like this!"

The *Time* cover for that week, already on press, was to have been the jazz pianist Thelonius Monk.... Surely this was one of those rare occasions when the *Time* tradition of not putting dead people on the cover might be broken. But, unhes-itatingly, [*Time* managing editor] Otto Fuerbringer ruled that the week's cover would be the next president, Lyndon John-son, as a symbol of the nation's continuity. To colleagues who pleaded for Kennedy, he said firmly, "The king is dead, long live the king."

OSBORN ELLIOTT
Newsweek

In effect, we had to redo the entire issue of *Newsweek*, begin-ning at 2:30 on Friday afternoon, and try to get it to press on Saturday evening within some reasonable target of our normal closing time.

The running story, the appreciation of Kennedy, the John-son story, everything was, in my view, superior to others in the field. But in particular, it was a matter of taste that I will always remember. It had to do with the space normally occupied by our letter to the readers, you know, letter from the editor, publisher's letter, up front in the magazine, which normally is used to promote stories in the magazine, boasting about our wonderful reporting. And I was absolutely flum-moxed as to what to do with that particular space that par-ticular week. We didn't want to boast, obviously, so I didn't know what to do.

Finally, my number two, Kermit Lansner—he was one of two number twos—who was a wonderfully intellectual editor, he said, "Well, why don't we quote from Walt Whit-man, his poem about 'When Lilacs Last in the Door-yard Bloom'd'?"—which of course was written about the Lincoln assassination. And this is obviously a brilliant idea, so that's what we did. Well, that week *Time*, in its publisher's letter, did exactly what we wanted to avoid. They said, "Last week, *Time* lost one of its favorite subscribers," or words to that effect. And they put LBJ on the cover. *Time* had a lifelong tradition of never putting a dead man on the cover. We didn't have that tradition, so we obviously automatically went to Kennedy on the cover.

HUGH SIDEY
Time

I was disappointed in *Time* because we put Lyndon Johnson on the cover. [*Time* co-founder Henry R.] Luce had once said, "We don't put dead people on the cover," so they put LBJ on, and I just thought it didn't work in that moment. But I don't know that either of the newsmagazines did all that good. The news was too big and newsmagazines don't do all that well when the news gets that big. I don't think *Newsweek* beat us that much, though I do think they did a wonderful job, but *Time*, in its own way, aside from that cover portrait, did a very good job.

CBS NEWS:
WALTER CRONKITE

*hear...
track 16

The messages are beginning to come in from around the world and from the cities of the United States where a nation is—in almost—I say it advisedly—almost uncontrollable shock, it seems. They're weeping on the streets. Schools have to be dismissed. My own school is dismissed because the children were weeping so much they couldn't stay in class. Quite a tragic day—as we all obviously know.

Commuters absorb the news of the assassination.

2:10 P.M. (CST)
DALLAS

TOM WICKER
New York Times

In those hours after the president's death, and I'm trying to write a story at the time, I had paid some kid to keep the telephone open for me [in a] telephone booth downstairs. I'd write a few hundred words and go down and dictate and go back and write a few hundred words, on a portable typewriter.

track 17

OPERATOR:
Will you accept the charge on a call from Mr. Wicker?
NEW YORK TIMES:
Yes, put him on.
TOM WICKER:
Hello, I've got some dictation for you on the Kennedy story.
NEW YORK TIMES:
Where are you, Tom?
WICKER:
I'm in Dallas.
NEW YORK TIMES:
Now, take it easy.
WICKER:
OK, this is Dallas, November 22nd. I don't have too much... Dallas November 22nd...President [Wicker's voice breaks]— President John F. Kennedy was shot and killed here today, period. The president suffered a massive gunshot wound in the brain and was pronounced dead at 1:00 P.M. Central Standard Time, period, paragraph.

His assassin or assassins, plural, had not been apprehended late today, period, paragraph.

Lyndon B. Johnson, comma, who was riding in the third car behind the president in a motorcade when the shooting took place, comma, was sworn in at 2:39 P.M. Central Standard Time as the thirty-sixth president of the United States [Wicker's voice breaks again], period, paragraph.

...I'm sorry for being emotional about this. I hope you can make all that out.

TOM WICKER
New York Times

That tape may suggest that I was personally moved and of course I was. I would have been moved whoever the president had been to have a thing like that happen. Every so often, just as on that dictation, the emotion would come over you, but most of the time you just had to keep working as a professional. It was a day you had to follow your instincts.

2:10 P.M. (CST)
NEW YORK CITY

IKE PAPPAS
reporter,
WNEW Radio

When I got to the studio, they gave me a tape recorder, about $500 in cash, and all the copy I could carry off the wire. I ran outside and gave the cabbie $20 and said, "I've got to get to Idlewild Airport."

I knew I had only one shot to do this right and I had to get to the right airport. New York City was absolutely choked with traffic; you couldn't get across the bridges. The city was in chaos. We didn't know what was going to happen—it was a very insecure time. We didn't know if there was going to be an attack by the Soviet Union.

The cabbie drove all kinds of crazy routes. I believe he cut through several lines of clothing in back yards and he cut across lawns. I gave the guy another five dollars to stay there and I went to [an airline counter] and I said, "Are you going to Dallas?" He said, "The whole airport is closed. There is nothing moving, but we hear there's a special flight being organized." [That flight] was supposed to go to California but the story was that it had been commandeered by the FBI and Secret Service. I think that's true. I got on. We first flew to pick up some FBI and Secret Service in Washington, then to Dallas.

WFAA-TV:

*hear...

track 18

PROGRAM DIRECTOR JAY WATSON:

A gentleman just walked in our studio that I am meeting for the first time as well as you. This is WFAA-TV in Dallas, Texas. May I have your name please, sir?

ABRAHAM ZAPRUDER:

My name is Abraham Zapruder.

WATSON:

Mr. Zapruda?

ZAPRUDER:

Zapruder, yes sir.

WATSON:

Zapruda. And would you tell us your story please, sir?

ZAPRUDER:

I got out in, uh, about a half-hour earlier to get a good spot to shoot some pictures. And I found a spot, one of these concrete blocks they have down near that park, near the underpass. And I got on top there, there was another girl from my office, she was right behind me. And as I was shooting, as the president was coming down from Houston Street making his turn, it was about halfway down there, I heard a shot, and he slumped to the side, like this. Then I heard another shot or two, I couldn't say it was one or two, and I saw his head practically open up, all blood and everything, and I kept on shooting. That's about all, I'm just sick, I can't...

WATSON:

I think that pretty well expresses the entire feelings of the whole world.

2:10 P.M. (CST)
DALLAS MORNING NEWS

BILL RIVES
managing editor,
Dallas Morning News

I shall never forget the anguish that swept the city room when word came that the president had died. There were no outcries at the moment—just a frozen look of futility on every face, and then, back to work, as silently as possible, grimly, swiftly, effectively. Many elements complicated the coverage, including the fact that the emotional impact of the assassination was almost overwhelming. Where other businesses virtually ground to a halt, our personnel had to put in a peak performance, submerging the distressing factors of the story. The impact of all this was too much for even a seasoned reporter like [Washington bureau chief Robert] Baskin. When he came into the office at my request, he was white-faced and trembling. Someone gave him a drink of whiskey, hoping it would quiet his racing nerves. We got him a cup of coffee, too, and his hand shook so much that he splashed coffee into the saucer as he raised the cup to his mouth.

2:10 P.M. (CST)
DALLAS TIMES HERALD

KEITH SHELTON
Dallas Times Herald

We were putting out new issues just as soon as we could. We would replate three or four pages every time we had enough new information. Normally, we had basically four editions. The fourth edition was a financial edition that only changed the stock market. But the three star, which had about an 11:30 A.M. deadline normally, was our main edition of the day. After that, I guess we put out three or four other replates. The [Dallas] Times Herald printing plant was in the same building downtown with the newspaper. People lined up in the street to get papers coming off the press. A lot of people were watching television, but they were still looking to the newspaper as the first source.

Afternoon newspaper sales were brisk in Dallas and elsewhere after President Kennedy was assassinated.

2:10 P.M. (CST)
KRLD-TV AND RADIO

EDDIE BARKER
KRLD-TV and Radio

In those days, we didn't have minicams. The only thing we had were film cameras. We had a lot of film from down at the site, from Parkland Hospital. You can't do like you do now with a piece of videotape. You have to develop film. Of course, CBS was going crazy wanting our film so just as soon as we would [process] it, they were taking it right up the line.

2:10 P.M. (CST)
FORT WORTH POLICE DEPARTMENT

BOB SCHIEFFER
night police reporter,
Fort Worth Star-Telegram

I went to the police station, and shortly thereafter a person was brought into the police station who had been stopped at an Arlington [Texas] gas station. The gas station attendant had called the police and said he believed this person might have been the assassin. Well, it turned out this poor man, who was a demolition contractor, had simply stopped to get some gas—he had heard on the radio that the president had been shot and mentioned it to the gas station attendant. [The attendant] hadn't heard it and figured that anybody who knew about this must have been the person who did it. So he called the police. The police arrested this poor man and brought him into the Fort Worth jail and for a few moments he was thought to be the assassin. As they brought him down the steps at the police station, I remembered a trick that the police had always taught me that sometimes you can shock people, so I just stepped to the front of the line and said, "You son of a bitch! Why did you do this?" He said, "I didn't," and they took him back into the jail. Well, as it turned out, the police quickly realized they had arrested an innocent person.

2:10 P.M. (CST)
TEXAS SCHOOL BOOK DEPOSITORY

TOM ALYEA
WFAA-TV

Captain Fritz held a conference with search team members on how to conduct the search [from the roof] back down [to the first floor]. It was agreed that flashlights would be a great help. A deputy mentioned that he could get flashlights from the sheriff's office only a block away. Captain Fritz said, "OK," and added that he and the search team would wait for the lights. The building had been sealed by armed guards and we all assumed that the suspect was still armed and trapped somewhere inside the building.

My immediate objective was to get my film of the sniper's nest to the newsroom. I decided to utilize this lull in activity to give it a try. I left the roof with two deputies, hoping we would not be the next targets. I followed the deputies out of the building as far as the front steps. A mob of newsmen had gathered on the sidewalk. A [co-worker] whom I had seen earlier from the fifth-floor window was in the front row. I tossed my film cans to him and he turned to race it back to the station. I was surprised that the guards let me out, but I assumed that they thought I was one of the officers leaving the building. I didn't want to risk it, so I reentered the building. I was not challenged.

Minutes later, Captain Fritz became impatient and ordered us to start our search back down. We were about two or three minutes into our second search of the sixth floor when the flashlights arrived. We were still looking for the shooting suspect, but a few minutes later, the rifle was located with the aid of a flashlight. It was inside a small, dark, barricaded enclosure. It was concealed by three overhanging cartons of advertising folders. Only four inches of the rifle butt could be seen. Captain Fritz made his way into the enclosure. I took about three or four seconds of the hidden rifle before the federal officer in our group

Tom Alyea of WFAA-TV photographed police officers examining a rifle found on the sixth floor of the Texas School Book Depository.

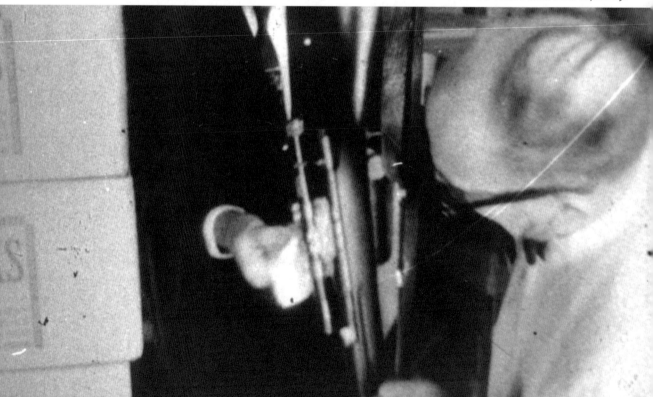

ordered me to stop taking pictures and leave the floor. I turned to a local officer and asked if he would take the picture of the hidden rifle for me. I told him how to steady the camera by holding it next to a box. He said, "OK, let the Fed try to stop me." After filming another four or five seconds, I told the officer to stop. The Fed glared at us both.

It was apparent that the suspect no longer had his weapon. Captain Fritz ordered a detective to go down to the first floor and bring up the two crime lab men. During our wait, we learned that the president was dead. This stunned us all. One officer hit a nearby book carton with his fist. We were no longer looking at the butt end of a shooting suspect's rifle; we were looking at the weapon that killed our president. Several minutes later, I tried to leave the building with my film. This time the guards would not let me out. I spotted our news editor, A.J. L'Hoste, on the steps outside. The next time the door was opened for an officer, I tossed my exposed film to A.J. It was on the air by the time I was permitted to leave and go back to the station.

2:13 P.M. (CST)

NBC NEWS:
TOM WHELAN

The weapon which was used to kill the president, and which wounded Governor Connally, has been found in the Texas School Book Depository on the sixth floor.... Three empty cartridge cases were found beside the weapon.

2:13 P.M. (CST)
DALLAS

JACK FALLON
Southwest Division
news manager, UPI

We were ahead. I was keeping two wires going at one time. I wrote another lead and another lead and I never typed so much in my goddamn life. Suddenly we got this report that the police had arrested a gunman in a movie theater as he was trying to shoot another cop, a man named McDonald. He managed to save himself because [the gunman had] a Smith & Wesson with a hammer. The cop grabbed it and the firing hammer hit the flesh between his finger and thumb. He brought this guy in, and I got [the gunman's] name and sent it up on the message wire to New York to circulate. Well, this got around the world and hit the Paris bureau and a woman named Aline Mosby, it rang a bell with her. She had been in Moscow and interviewed a Marine who deserted. It was Lee Harvey Oswald.

2:13 P.M. (CST)
PARKLAND MEMORIAL HOSPITAL

WILBORN HAMPTON
UPI

As I was leaving, walking across the lawn, under a huge tree, suddenly it hit me. You get involved in covering stories like this and because you're in a great rush you don't sometimes take in the full story because you're concentrating on the specifics. I just stopped under the tree and began to cry. Whether you voted for him or not, he was a great symbol of a new America. He was bright and he was witty and he was handsome, and he carried so much hope for all of us who were young at that time. And he was gone just in a flash.

2:13 P.M. (CST)
DALLAS POLICE DEPARTMENT

DARWIN PAYNE
reporter,
Dallas Times Herald

There was a definite decision made by the city manager and the police chief to let the press in. They wanted the world to see that they had the accused assassin. They felt certain it was the right person. They wanted the press to see him, and I think they acted honorably in that way.

WILBORN HAMPTON
UPI

By the middle of the evening, people were coming from all over the world. Dallas police had never seen anything quite like this and they didn't quite know how to handle it.

LEE OSWALD HAS DENIED IT TO THE WORLD.....HE TOLD US, ALL THIS MORNING THAT
HE DIDN'T KILL THE PRESIDENT.....THAT HE WASN'T EVEN TOLD THAT THE PRESIDENT
WAS DEAD OSWALD IS A COOL CUSTOMER......HE SPOKE CLEARLY.....HE HAD BEEN
TOLD THAT HE WAS CHARGED WITH BEING THE ASSASSIN OF THE
PRESIDENT OF THE UNITED STATES...YET, IT APPEARED TO ME AS IF THE MESSAGE
NEVER GOT THROUGH.

        AS HE WAS LED INTO THE LINE UP ROOM HERE AT THE DALLAS POLICE
HEADQUARTERS...A ROOM JAMMED WITH REPORTERS, CAMERAMEN, MICROPHONES....
OSWALD KEPT HIS HEAD DOWN.....HE'S A THIN MAN, ABOUT 5 FEET
SIX INCHES TALL......YOU COULD DETECT A SLIGHT POUT ON HIS FACE AS HE TURNED
TO THE CAMERAS....SOMEONE YELLED: DID YOU KILL THE PRESIDENT AND HE REPLIED....
. I WAS QUESTIONED BY A JUDGE, HOWEVER AT THAT TIME I PROTESTED
THAT I WAS NOT ALLOWED LEGAL REPRESENTATION.....AT THAT VERY SHORT AND SWEET
HEARING.   I REALLY DONT KNOW WHAT THE SITUATION IS.....I'VE BEEN TOLD NOTHING
BUT THAT I AM ACCUSED OF KILLING A POLICEMAN...I KNOW NOTHING MORE THAN THAT.
I'M WAITING FOR SOMEONE TO COME FORWARD TO GIVE ME A LEGAL ASSISTANCE.
        DID YOU KILL THE PRESIDENT?   I HAVE NOT BEEN CHARGED WITH
THAT.   THE FIRST THING I HEARD ABOUT IT WAS WHEN THE NEWSPAPER REPORTERS IN
THE HALL, ASKED ME THAT QUESTION.
        WHAT DID YOU DO IN RUSSIA....THEN HE WAS LED OUT.

        THROUGH THE MAZE OF REPORTERS...BACK UP TO HIS CELL, TO AWAIT
ARRAIGNMENT AS THE ASSASSINATOR OF A PRESIDENT.

The typed notes of radio reporter Ike Pappas regarding suspect Lee Harvey Oswald.

BERT SHIPP
WFAA-TV

It was like third-grade soccer. Have you ever seen little kids play soccer? Just all over the place, running here and there. There was no organization to it at all—just a wolf pack snarling at each other. They were everywhere they shouldn't be.

EDDIE BARKER
KRLD-TV and Radio

About that time was when this first wave of the Eastern press came in. Most of them unfortunately had written their stories on the plane. It was just "Sin City," all of these bigots, and they had killed the president. It took a long time to get that straightened out.

TRAVIS MAYO
amusements writer,
Dallas Morning News

I was amazed that persons on the trolley who never speak to their neighbors on ordinary days talked freely with everyone else. Some frankly admitted they did not admire the president. Some thought he was a modern Messiah. "He was selling the country down the river," some said. "He was the last of the truly heroic men," others insisted. A heavyset Negro woman did not sit beside a white person on the trolley as she seemed delighted to do in the past. She came to rest well toward the back of the bus, sitting with another woman of her race. Their conversation was that of mourners. They expressed fear for the future of the civil rights movement. They were anxious of their own future under the Johnson administration.

2:13 P.M. (CST)
DALLAS TRADE MART

DORIS JACOBY
photographer,
Dallas Morning News

I entered in the rear, through the kitchens, where innumerable uneaten steaks were piled up. In the main hall, the tables had been cleared, except the head table, which was still intact, as if waiting for a party to arrive momentarily. There were several policemen guarding it. They told me that nothing was allowed to be touched, and the food already on it was to be taken away to be analyzed for poison. At the center of the table, a large black, very modern rocking chair had been placed. It looked eerie, and I quickly made my photographs. I was shown some large packages, very prettily gift-wrapped in a Western motif, containing gifts—now abandoned—for the Kennedy children. They were in a small side room, outfitted with a direct telephone line to Washington, and an early American rocking chair, intended for the president.

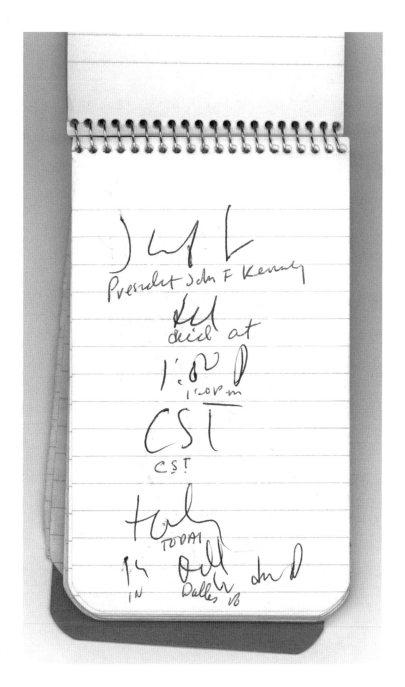

Details of the president's death are scrawled on Westinghouse correspondent Sid Davis' notebook.

THE DALLAS TIMES HERALD

FINAL EDITION

CONTINUOUSLY PUBLISHED FOR 87 YEARS   THE TIMES 1876   THE HERALD 1886   CONSOLIDATED 1888

87th Year—No. 292   ★ ★ ★   DALLAS, TEXAS, FRIDAY EVENING, NOVEMBER 22, 1963   Telephones—CENTRAL, RANDALL   3 Parts   Price Five Cents

PRESIDENT DEAD

Connally Also Hit By Sniper

By GEORGE CARTER

President Kennedy died of assassin's bullets in Dallas Friday afternoon.

The President and Gov. John Connally were ambushed as they drove in the President's open convertible in a downtown motorcade.

Two priests announced shortly before 1:30 that the President was dead.

Bullets apparently came from a high-powered rifle in a building at Houston and Elm.

A man was arrested and taken to the sheriff's office.

The President immediately clutched his chest and slumped into the arms of his wife. Gov. Connally, apparently shot in the chest, fell to the floor under his wife's feet.

Secret service agents immediately dispatched the motorcade at high speed to Parkland Hospital.

Gov. Connally was reported in critical condition.

Witnesses standing on a balcony at the courthouse gave this account of what they saw:

The motorcade had just turned into Houston Street from Main Street when a shot rang out. Pigeons flew up from the street. Then, two more shots rang out and Mr. Kennedy fell to the floor of the car.

The shots seemed to come from the extension of Elm Street from just beyond the Texas Textbook Depository building at the corner of Elm and Houston streets.

Police swarmed into the area toward the railroad tracks and the witnesses could not tell whether he was captured.

The cavalcade stopped there and there was bedlam.

Deputy Police Chief Ray Lunday, leading the procession through Dallas, said he thought the shots were fired as the President's car neared the Triple Underpass.

Police issued a pickup order for an unknown white male, about 30, slender, 5-10, 165 pounds, armed with a .30 caliber rifle.

Six or seven persons were believed hit by sniper's volley.

Police swarmed the building as the stunned crowd of persons watching the downtown parade watched.

The President was rushed to Parkland Hospital.

Sgt. G. D. Hensley, police dispatcher, directed all available police units to the downtown area near the western edge of downtown Dallas.

The Presidential convoy cut off its route and sped at high speed immediately toward Parkland Hospital where doctors were ordered to stand by.

The motorcade, originally set to turn off Industrial by the Trade Mart, sped straight down Industrial toward Harry Hines.

The police radio blared that the President had been hit.

Sheriff Decker came on the air around 12:25 p.m.

"I don't know what's happened. Take every available man from the jail and the office and go to the railroad yards off Elm near the triple underpass.

The crowds waiting inside the Trade Mart were not immediately told of the shooting.

A sobbing carpet salesman told police minutes after the shooting the President appeared to be hit twice.

"The first time he slumped and the second one really blasted him." These were the words of Charles Drehm, 28, of 2419 Kings Highway.

"After the first shot the President's wife rose slightly to hold the President and they both went down in the second shot. He was definitely hit badly," Mr. Drehm said.

Mr. Drehm said the President was half standing, waving give the crowd, when he heard the first of two shots. He said after the President was knocked down, apparently by the second shot, the President's car roared underneath the triple underpass.

President Kennedy and Gov. Connally were critically wounded by sniper's bullets near the downtown triple underpass shortly afternoon Friday.

Bullets apparently came from a building at Houston and Elm.

But reporters following the President in a motorcade said a man and woman were seen scrambling on a walk over the underpass.

The President and Connally were rushed to Parkland Hospital.

Minutes later they were reported still alive by Rep. Albert Thomas of Houston, who stood outside the emergency surgery door.

Police reports indicated President Kennedy was shot in the head. Connally was apparently shot in the chest.

Mrs. Kennedy apparently was safe. Mrs. Connally also was safe, it appeared. Both women were stunned.

Witnesses said six or seven shots were fired. The bursts were clearly heard.

Police swarmed the area immediately. Reporters about five car lengths behind the chief executive heard what sounded like three bursts of gunfire.

Secret Service agents in a follow-up car quickly unlimbered their automatic rifles.

The bubble top of the President's car was down.

They drew their pistols, but the damage was done.

The President was slumped over in the back seat of the car, face down. Connally lay on the floor of the rear seat.

It was impossible to tell at once where Kennedy was hit, but bullet wounds in Connally's chest were plainly visible, indicating the gunfire might possibly have come from an automatic weapon.

Dallas motorcycle officers escorting the President quickly leaped from their bikes and raced up a grassy hill.

The President, his limp body cradled in the arms of his wife, was rushed to Parkland Hospital. The Governor also was taken to Parkland.

Clint Hill, a Secret Service agent assigned to Mrs. Kennedy, said "he's dead," as the President was lifted from the rear of a White House touring car, the famous "Bubbletop" from Washington. He was rushed to an emergency room in the hospital.

Other White House officials were in doubt as the corridors of the hospital erupted in pandemonium.

The Secret Service said the President remained in the emergency room at Parkland and the Governor was moved to the general operating room.

One Secret Service man was overheard telling another that there was no need to move the President because emergency facilities were entirely adequate in the emergency room.

Two Roman Catholic priests were summoned to the emergency room where the President lay. One was identified as a Father Huber.

Malcolm Kilduff, acting White House press secretary, said that the two priests had been "asked for."

Pandemonium broke loose around the scene. The Secret Service waved the motorcade on at top speed to the hospital.

Even at high speed it took nearly five minutes to get the car to the ambulance entrance of the hospital.

Reporters saw Kennedy lying flat on his face on the seat of his car.

A reporter said a man and a woman were scrambling on the upper level of a walkway overlooking the underpass.

Lawrence O'Brien, presidential aide, said he had no information on owhether the President still was alive.

Mrs. Kennedy was weeping and trying to hold up her husband's head when reporters reached the car.

Fire equipment was rushed to the building from which the shots were believed to have been fired. Firemen roped off the area as Secret Service men and city police swarmed through the building.

Police Chief Jesse Curry advised Sgt. Hensley that no condition would be released immediately on the President's condition.

At the Triple Underpass, large numbers of the crowd were milling around half sobbing, half hysterically shouting, "The President's shot!"

Women and children and men stopped one another and police to ask plaintively, "Is the President alive? God, how horrible." Although most of the law officers present felt the bullets came from

See ASSASSINATION on Page 19

This picture was taken at Love Field on the President's arrival.

—1963 Photo by William Allen

Secret Service Checks in Vain

By JIM LEHRER
Staff Writer

Despite the extensive and painstaking steps taken by the vaunted Secret Service, tragedy struck in downtown Dallas.

The President's protectors had checked minutely everything, everything, so the fatal ride Kennedy went to eat, the flowers they would send out soldiers, the brands who would cheer, the opponents who would jeer, the roads they would travel and the newsmen who would report the story.

TRAGICALLY, ONE link was missing.

The quiet-spoken, reserved security team of the Secret Service had been the calmest this week of local law enforcement officers and other observers for their thoroughness.

First, there were several area proposals initially for Friday's luncheon. Secret Service men checked them all.

THE BALCONIES at the Trade Mart, the favorite of the local sponsors, made the security experts reluctant. But they studied and investigated once more and, finally approved the Trade Mart site.

A lot—by scores—of known agitators in Dallas who might possibly be inclined to stir up trouble was obtained. Agents became familiar with them, their pictures.

A dozen-odd posts was checked out next. Trouble spots were spotted both in traffic and possible crowd situations.

The decision on the Love Field arrangement was made. Agents gave the airport one of its most thorough checks, including what balconies, windows and vantage points were to look down on the President.

DETAILED SECURITY measures at the Trade Mart with its 14 different entrances to the main courtyard were set up. Uniformed guards with restriction ropes were arranged for each of the passageways and the entrances to the balconies.

A press list was assigned. Secret Service agents planned to check the tickets of everyone who entered the Trade Mart.

Thursday, roaming agents probed through 1,200 yellow roses as they were being installed at the Trade Mart to ensure that no bombs or other damaging weapons were included with the fragrant ride.

THE ORDER was issued on the food. The President and his party would receive the same kind of meal as everyone else at the luncheon, but each selected at random from all the others. The whole crowd would have to be poisoned that way to ensure the death of the President.

Employees of the Trade Mart and other personnel who were to be on hand in a working capacity on Friday were given the once-over as were those in the official greeting party at Love Field.

PRESS PASSES were issued Thursday according to three lists provided by news media executives. The passes are

See SECRET SERVICE on Page 19-A

TIME

THE WEEKLY NEWS MAGAZINE

E PLURIBUS UNUM

Bernard Safran

**PRESIDENT
JOHNSON**

VOL. 82 NO. 22
(REG. U.S. PAT. OFF.)

The first issue of Time *after the assassination featured President Lyndon Johnson. The magazine had a policy of not using images of deceased individuals on its cover.*

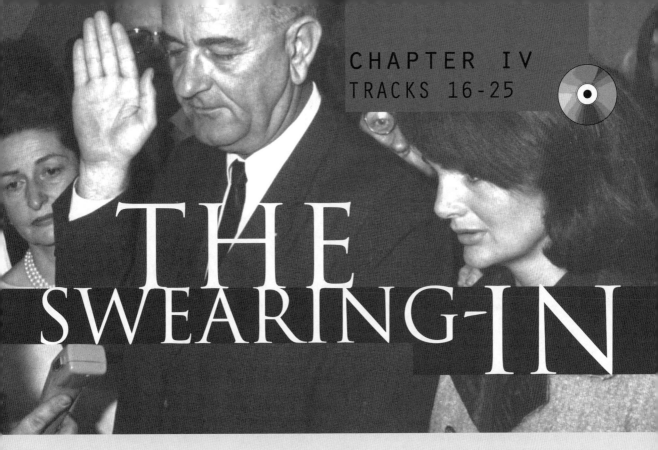

THE SWEARING-IN

NOVEMBER 22   2:30 PM – 5:05 PM (CST)

PRESIDENT JOHNSON AND his wife, Lady Bird, wait on Air Force One for Jacqueline Kennedy and the casket to arrive, then wait for the press pool to board the plane. Federal Judge Sarah T. Hughes is asked to administer the oath of office. Concerned about the possibility of a plot to bring down the government, aides recommend that Johnson be sworn in immediately. No one knows the exact words to the oath of office, and a call is made to Deputy Attorney General Nicholas Katzenbach, who dictates the oath.

Johnson takes the oath of office with his wife and Mrs. Kennedy at his side. Air Force One lifts off less than ten minutes later, bound for Andrews Air Force Base outside Washington, D.C.

Mrs. Johnson tries to comfort Mrs. Kennedy. Mrs. Kennedy tells her, "Oh, what if I had not been there. I'm so glad I was there." Mrs. Johnson notices that Mrs. Kennedy's dress is stained with blood—one leg almost entirely covered, and her right glove caked with it. Mrs. Johnson asks if she would like some help changing clothes, and Mrs. Kennedy responds fiercely, "I want them to see what they have done to Jack."

On the long flight back to Washington, President Johnson makes several calls using the airplane's air-to-ground communications system, including one to Rose Kennedy, the president's mother, and another to Nellie Connally, wife of the wounded governor. Air Force One touches down at Andrews shortly after 6:00 p.m. Eastern Standard Time. A lift truck extracts the heavy bronze casket bearing the body of the fallen president and places it into an ambulance. President Johnson makes a brief public statement in front of microphones and television cameras, then goes to the White House.

2:30 P.M. (CST)
ABOARD AIR FORCE ONE AT LOVE FIELD

MALCOLM KILDUFF
assistant White House press secretary

As soon as I got to the plane, Jim Swindal, the president's pilot, said, "The president has been looking for you." I walked in and I talked to the president. He said, "Mac, I've got to get sworn in here.... They feel I should be sworn in here in Dallas. We're trying to get hold of the judge." He said, "Do we have to allow some of the press in here?" I said, "Yes, we do."

SID DAVIS
White House correspondent, Westinghouse Broadcasting Company

We raced to the airport and got there just as they were putting the casket into the airplane. They had moved Air Force One to a rather secluded part of the field—to a more secure area. The Oneal Funeral Home hearse was parked at the rear of this Boeing 707. They'd lowered the rear stairs and put the casket in there—it was a huge bronze casket, must have weighed a ton.

CHARLES ROBERTS
White House correspondent, Newsweek

All the curtains were drawn. They had gotten the president's casket aboard by removing some seats from the back of the airplane. They were waiting for the press—the president, I later learned, had insisted on some press witnesses to his swearing-in—and for Judge Sarah Hughes, the woman judge who administered the oath. She arrived and was taken aboard. Then Kilduff gave us the signal to come aboard. I can remember Smitty [UPI correspondent Merriman Smith] as we crowded aboard the plane. We went up the forward ramp and were pushing back toward the midsection of the plane. Smitty looked down at his right hand and said, "My God, I've lost my typewriter."

The casket of John F. Kennedy is carried aboard Air Force One at Love Field for the flight to Washington, D.C.

MERRIMAN SMITH
White House correspondent,
United Press International

Aboard Air Force One...all of the shades of the larger main cabin were drawn. The interior was hot and dimly lighted. Kilduff propelled us toward the president's suite two-thirds of the way back in the plane. I wedged inside the door and began counting. There were twenty-seven people in the compartment. Johnson stood in the center with his wife, Lady Bird. U.S. District Judge Sarah T. Hughes, a kindly faced woman, stood with a small black Bible in her hands, waiting to give the oath.

The compartment became hotter and hotter. It developed that Johnson was waiting for Mrs. Kennedy, who was composing herself in a small bedroom in the rear of the plane. She appeared alone, dressed in the same pink wool suit she had worn in the morning when she appeared so happy shaking hands with airport crowds at the side of her husband. She was white-faced but dry-eyed. Friendly hands stretched toward her as she stumbled slightly. Johnson took both of her hands in his and motioned her to his left side.

SID DAVIS
Westinghouse

It was just a matter of minutes until Mrs. Kennedy appeared. I was startled when I saw her because I had never seen her with a hair out of place. Even in the most casual clothes, she was always beautiful and well-dressed. Obviously, she was just in a state of shock, I guess, but she just seemed bewildered. My notes say her right stocking was saturated with blood from her husband's head wound. By that time it was caked on her right leg. I saw some blood on her skirt and on her right wrist. She had said at the time she didn't change her dress because she wanted the people of Dallas to see what they had done.

CHARLES ROBERTS
Newsweek

[Kennedy aide] Larry O'Brien had found a Bible in the president's sleeping compartment and brought it up. They had the oath read over the phone from Washington on a secretary-to-secretary basis and then it occurred to someone—how do we know that this is *the* presidential oath? [Johnson aide Jack] Valenti got Deputy Attorney General [Nicholas] Katzenbach

Lyndon B. Johnson, aboard Air Force One at Love Field, prepares to take the oath of office. At left is Judge Sarah Hughes, who administers the oath.

and made sure that this was word-for-word *the* oath, and it was typed out on a little Air Force One memo pad. The judge had that and the Bible. Mac Kilduff found a Dictaphone machine and set that up.

2:32 P.M. (CST)
DALLAS

NBC NEWS:
ROBERT MACNEIL
(ON THE PHONE FROM DALLAS)

Dr. Malcolm Perry reported that the president arrived at Parkland Hospital in critical condition with neck and head injuries. Dr. William Kemp Clark, chief of neurosurgery, said the president was near death on arrival. A tracheotomy was performed, and the president was given blood transfusions, oxygen, and, after his heart failed, external massage. The president died at 1:00 P.M. Dallas time—about twenty minutes after arrival at Parkland Hospital.

2:38 P.M. (CST)
ABOARD AIR FORCE ONE

SID DAVIS
Westinghouse

Before [the judge] asked him to raise his right hand, Johnson said he wanted a glass of ice water. They brought a tumbler of ice water and I remember Johnson, he could swallow a whole glass of water at one time. He just gulped down this glass of ice water, and she proceeded with the oath.

MERRIMAN SMITH
UPI

"Hold up your right hand and repeat after me," the woman jurist said to Johnson.... Judge Hughes held out the Bible and Johnson covered it with his large left hand. His right arm went slowly into the air and the jurist began to intone the constitutional oath, "I do solemnly swear I will faithfully execute the office of president of the United States."

SID DAVIS
Westinghouse

I knew I was going to be in trouble if I didn't get this pool report perfect. This was one pool report that had to be right. There was a lot of anxiety on my part whether I was seeing everything I had to see—and writing down everything I had to see. I was wearing a chronograph and I hit the stopwatch on the thing as soon as [the judge] started to go—and when she finished the oath I stopped it. I clocked the oath at twenty-eight seconds.

CHARLES ROBERTS
Newsweek

Lady Bird stood on his right, and they faced the judge as she administered the oath. There was a minute or so of awkward silence and the president turned and kissed Lady Bird. He embraced Jackie, holding her by the elbows. The first words I remember immediately after the oath were Chief [Jesse] Curry of the Dallas police saying to Mrs. Kennedy, "You'd better go and lie down now, honey," or "little lady" or some diminutive affectionate like that. "You've had a real bad day." Whether Mrs. Kennedy heard him, I don't know. She didn't leave right away. There was handshaking all around, but a very solemn sort of handshaking. And then Mrs. Kennedy did go aft, and then the president turned and said, "Now, let's get airborne." That was eight minutes after he took the oath.

SID DAVIS
Westinghouse

[Malcolm] Kilduff came to Charles Roberts and myself and said, "There's only room for two reporters on the airplane going back to Washington. One of you has to get off. I want to flip a coin to see if Roberts stays or you stay, Sid." I said, "Mac, I'm going to get off; my company is waiting for me on the telephone, we're on the air live, they need me desperately. I'll do the pool report and file a story." Roberts worked for *Newsweek* and they had twenty-four hours before they went to press.

I clocked the oath-taking at 2:38 P.M. Central Standard Time. As I went down the ramp of the airplane with Judge Sarah Hughes, [Merriman Smith], who flew with the president so often he thought he owned Air Force One and everything on it, shouted down the stairs to me, "Would you call the UPI office and tell them the oath-taking took place at 2:37 P.M. Central Standard Time?"

I couldn't get anyone to lead me off the field. The airport was secured—they weren't certain if there were other killers around. I stood there and watched as Colonel Jim Swindal, who was the pilot of Air Force One, took that airplane—which was recently new and had fanjet engines that gave it more power—he took that plane down to the far end of the runway to my right. As he came roaring back down the runway, he had to come back in front of me and the judge. He took that airplane off the ground, and I thought he went almost vertically into the air. I'm assuming he did that because he may have been afraid there could have been somebody on the ground who would try to shoot at it.

It was really the most amazing thing. What you had was the new president of the United States on the airplane, the body of the fallen president in a casket in the back of the airplane, the widow of the fallen president, and the wife of the new president on this plane going back to Washington after such a glorious day in politics for John F. Kennedy. As I watched it disappear as a speck in the eastern sky—the four exhausts of its engines belching that stuff out behind it—it said something about the strength of this country, the fact that we had this thing happen, we didn't know who did it or why they did it, but the transition from one man to another was done in an orderly way.

MERRIMAN SMITH
UPI

The wheels of Air Force One cleared the runway. [Pilot James] Swindal roared the big ship up to an unusually high cruising altitude of forty-one thousand feet, where, at 625 miles an hour ground speed, the jet hurtled toward Andrews Air Force Base outside Washington. When the president's plane reached operating altitude, Mrs. Kennedy left the bedchamber and walked to the rear compartment of the plane. This was the so-called family living room, a private area where she and Kennedy, family and friends, had spent many happy airborne hours chatting and dining together. Kennedy's casket had been placed in this compartment, carried aboard by a group of Secret Service agents. Mrs. Kennedy went into the rear lounge and took a chair beside the coffin. There she remained throughout the flight.

2:47 P.M. (CST)
DALLAS

DALLAS POLICE DEPARTMENT RADIO TRANSMISSION (CHANNEL 2):

POLICE CHIEF JESSE CURRY:
Air Force One is airborne.

ABC NEWS:
IRV CHAPMAN

Here at the White House the American flag was lowered to half-staff above the Executive Mansion a short while ago. Church bells at St. John's across Lafayette Square were pealing. Several hundred people gathered on Pennsylvania Avenue. A major traffic jam, both cars and pedestrians. Washington police are trying to keep things moving. Extra security precautions are in force. White House guards are checking and double-checking credentials of those who enter. In the lobby of the executive wing, members of the White House staff and reporters are clustered about, looking stunned, awaiting developments.

DON GARDINER

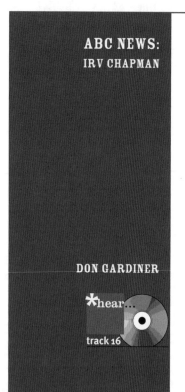

*hear...

track 16

The sudden news from Dallas came like a surgical shock. Doctors and nurses had to hurry to many a bedside to administer a sedative. In restaurants across the nation, the news broke amidst the luncheon-hour chatter. It stilled all conversation. Gloom fell on the tables. Some people got up from the table and walked away, others sat there in silence. The president is dead.

2:47 P.M. (CST)
LOVE FIELD

SID DAVIS
Westinghouse

I pleaded with the police to let me go back to downtown Dallas because I had these phones staring at me in the face, but you're not supposed to do your own broadcast story until you've given your pool report. They wouldn't let me off the field even then, but suddenly two press buses appeared out of nowhere, and the press corps was brought to the airport. Someone lifted me onto the top of a car and I stood on the trunk of this car and I gave the pool report. As soon as I gave the fact that Johnson was sworn in and the time, the broadcast reporters took off for the telephones.

JOE CARTER
overnight editor,
UPI, Dallas

The reporter for Westinghouse was pool man; he got off [Air Force One] and briefed us. When I had gone out to the airport that morning, I had quarters which I changed in for five dimes, and that became my supply of coins for pay telephones, which were my main lines of communication. I'd run out of my five dimes by now. There was a black woman at the airport trying to use the phone. I said, "Ma'am, I've got to call this in," and I grabbed the dime from her hand. I said, "Thank you." She sat there in utter amazement.

UPI WIRE:

```
FLASH
DALLAS—JOHNSON PRESIDENT.
BC352PES
```

2:47 P.M. (CST)
ABOARD AIR FORCE ONE
EN ROUTE TO ANDREWS AIR FORCE BASE, MARYLAND

CHARLES ROBERTS
Newsweek

We were really at the nerve center of the world in a way, but we didn't know that they had caught a suspect by then, and we didn't know that he was a loner. For all we knew, it was a worldwide conspiracy. We knew that about half the Cabinet was on its way to Tokyo. What had happened to them, we didn't know either. The uncertainty, the questions that arose—will the Russians do anything while we're in the air during this two-hour flight?—I'll never forget. [Merriman Smith], who won a Pulitzer Prize for his work that day, didn't have a typewriter. We had to get one of the White House typewriters, an electric typewriter, and find an outlet for him to plug into. Then we pooled our notes.

MERRIMAN SMITH
UPI

As the flight progressed, Johnson walked back into the main compartment. My portable typewriter was lost somewhere around the hospital and I was writing on an oversized electric typewriter which Kennedy's personal secretary, Mrs. Evelyn Lincoln, had used to type his speech texts. Johnson came up to the table where Roberts and I were trying to record the history we had just witnessed. "I'm going to make a short statement in a few minutes and give you copies of it," he said. "Then when I get on the ground, I'll do it over again."

The White House, code-named Crown, communicates by radio with Air Force One as it heads back to Washington. There is some confusion about whether the slain president's body will be flown by helicopter or transported by ambulance for an autopsy at the Naval Medical Center in Bethesda, Maryland. Arrangements are made for a forklift to remove the casket from the airplane and for a special ramp for Mrs. Kennedy to use to get off the plane. President Johnson also relays his intentions to meet with White House staff, congressional leadership, and Cabinet members as soon as he returns to Washington.

Westinghouse Broadcasting correspondent Sid Davis, seen in this television image, briefs other members of the press after he witnessed Lyndon B. Johnson take the oath of office aboard Air Force One.

GENERAL CHESTER CLIFTON:

Duplex, Duplex [Secret Service special agent Gerald Behn], this is Watchman. Over.

GERALD BEHN:

Go ahead, Watchman. This is Duplex. Over.

CLIFTON:

Duplex, this is Watchman. [Inaudible.]

BEHN:

Watchman, it's been arranged to helicopter—helicopter—the body to Bethesda.

CLIFTON:

This is Watchman. That's OK if it isn't after dark. What about the first lady?

BEHN:

Everybody else aboard, arrangements have been made to helicopter into the south grounds [of the White House].

CLIFTON:

[Inaudible]…if the helicopter operations will work when we have a very heavy casket. Over.

BEHN:

According to Witness [Captain Tazewell Shepard], yes.

CLIFTON:

This is Watchman. Don't take a chance on that. Also have a mortuary-type ambulance stand by in case helicopter doesn't work.

BEHN:

That's affirmative. I received.

CLIFTON:

Now some other instructions. Listen carefully. We need a ramp, a normal ramp [inaudible] in front of the aircraft on the right-hand side just behind the pilot's cabin in the galley. We are going to take the first lady off by that route. Over. Do you understand?

BEHN:

I receive. Affirmative.

CLIFTON:

Also, on the left rear of the aircraft where we usually dismount, debark, we may need a forklift rather than a ramp. [Inaudible] too awkward, maybe a platform to walk out on and a forklift to put it on, is that possible? Over.

BEHN:

Say again, Watchman. Say again.

CLIFTON:

I say again. The casket is in the rear compartment. [Inaudible] because it is so heavy that we have a forklift back there to remove the casket. If this is too awkward we can go along with the normal ramp and several men. Over.

BEHN:

Affirmative. We will try for the forklift.

CLIFTON:

Next item. Duplex. Next item…According to Mr. Johnson the press is to have its normal little fence at Andrews field and he is going [from] there by helicopter to the White House.

BEHN:

Say again Watchman, say again please. Watchman, this is Duplex. Say again.

CLIFTON:

The fence for the press, the normal little corral, it will have to be in front of the aircraft because that's where President Johnson will come off, OK?

BEHN:

*hear…

track 20

Watchman, should the secretary of defense and others be at Andrews on your arrival?

CLIFTON:

No, negative, President Johnson wants to meet…with White House staff, leadership of Congress and as many of the Cabinet members as possible at the White House as soon as we get there. At 18:30. 18:30. Over.

BEHN:

That is affirmative, Watchman, that is affirmative.

CLIFTON:

Read that to me.

BEHN:

All the leaders of Congress, as many Cabinet members as possible at the White House at 18:30. And the key members of the White House staff—[Presidential special counsel Theodore] Sorensen, [National Security Adviser McGeorge] Bundy, etc.

CLIFTON:

That is correct.

CBS NEWS:
CHARLES COLLINGWOOD

This is a special announcement by Frank Stanton, president of the Columbia Broadcasting System: "In respect for the feelings of a shocked nation, the CBS Television Network and the CBS Radio Network will carry no commercial announcements and no entertainment programs until after the president's funeral. CBS will continue to bring all the news relating to this tragic event, memorials, and special broadcasts and all other news of importance throughout this period."

BERNARD BIRNBAUM
associate producer,
CBS Evening News

As I was standing in the control room, suddenly [CBS executive producer] Les Midgley says, "How long can we stay on?" I'll never forget this. Standing in the back was Dr. Frank Stanton and—like the shot of a gun across the bow of a boat—he said, "Les, stay on as long as you want to." At the end of that program, we said we would stay on the air until the president was buried. So there weren't any commercials for four days.

3:23 P.M. (CST)
DALLAS

Networks identify Lee Harvey Oswald as the suspect.

ABC NEWS:

This from Dallas, Texas. The police department today arrested a twenty-four-year-old man, Lee H. Oswald, in connection with the slaying of a Dallas policeman shortly after President Kennedy was assassinated. He also is being questioned to see if he had any connection with the slaying of the president. Oswald was pulled screaming and yelling from the Texas Theatre in the Oak Cliff section of Dallas. He had a pistol; officers took it away from him after a fight. A police officer who was cut across the face in the fight quoted Oswald as saying after he was subdued, "Well, it's all over now."

A crowd gathers outside an electronics store in New York City to listen to news reports about the assassination of the president.

BOB SCHIEFFER
night police reporter,
Fort Worth Star-Telegram

I went back to the city room of the *Star-Telegram*. I had literally just walked in the door and every phone in the place was ringing. I answered a phone and a woman said, "Is there anyone there who can give me a ride to Dallas?" I said, "Madam, this is not a taxi service, and besides, the president has been shot." And she said, "Yes I know, I heard it on the radio. I think my son is the one they've arrested." It was Lee Harvey Oswald's mother. So I put aside those reservations about running a taxi service, and the city editor sent me and another reporter named Bill Foster out to pick her up. The reason the second reporter became involved was because I realized quickly I couldn't take her to Dallas in [my] open sports car, and so I went to Bill, who was the auto editor. As auto editor, he had this special perk. The local car dealers would give him a car to drive every week and a free tank of gas, and at the end of the week he'd write up what they called a "road test" report for the Sunday paper. You may not be surprised to know that it was generally a very good report. So Bill had a Cadillac that week, and the two of us went out to the west side of Fort Worth and there stood Marguerite Oswald. She had on a white practical nurse's uniform, she had a little blue travel bag, and she was standing on the lawn there wearing these huge black horn-rimmed glasses. She got in the car, I got in the back seat with her, and we proceeded on to the Dallas police station.

I interviewed her on the way and it was one of the most bizarre interviews I've ever had. She immediately began to talk not about this terrible thing that had happened to our president, but that people would not feel sorry for her and that she would starve to death and that they would feel sorry for [Oswald's] wife and give her money. It was so awful that some of those quotes I just couldn't bring myself to put them into the story that I wrote for the next day. I really learned a lesson as a reporter, and that is, you have to be very careful about censoring what people tell you because oftentimes they're telling you what they want you to know. As it turned out, she was obsessed about money.

District Attorney Henry Wade (far left, with microphone) speaks to reporters in the Dallas police lineup room after the assassination.

One of the odd things about this—she had actually worked as a governess for the publisher of the *Fort Worth Star-Telegram* shortly before the assassination took place. They had hired her, they had run a want ad in the *Star-Telegram* after they lost their housekeeper, but [Mrs. Oswald] worked for them only for a matter of days and the kids complained that she was just so mean. They demanded the parents get rid of her.

HUGH AYNESWORTH
science/aviation/space editor,
Dallas Morning News

So I went to the places that Oswald lived. Neely Street and Elsbeth, finally down to 1026 Beckley. But in this one place, I pounded on the door because I heard people in there and I just wanted to find out if they knew him, what he'd been doing. I knocked, and finally this man came to the door. He was naked. He didn't bother putting anything on. I looked back there and there was a woman back there. I had interrupted them. And he didn't speak very good English, and I kept saying, "Do you know this fellow here, this..."—we had two names then, we had Hidell and we had Oswald. I said, "I'm sorry," and I left there in a hurry.

DARWIN PAYNE
reporter,
Dallas Times Herald

I went to Oswald's rooming house. A large number of people were already there. There were TV cameras around, reporters, some police officers, and people who had rooms. I went in. You just went straight on in the house. I talked to some of the people who had rooms there and had them describe Oswald to me. They knew him as O.H. Lee. They told me that he occasionally would get on the telephone and talk in a foreign language. It sounded like an Eastern European language. It would have been Russian, of course, and he would have been talking to [his wife] Marina.

They said he was standoffish. He did not mix with them. Occasionally, he might sit down for a moment and watch a football game. I was shown his room, which was a very small room. The room had been totally cleaned out. The FBI and Secret Service had taken everything. There might have been a few pieces of furniture, a dresser, and a bed. There was a wastebasket there in which there was a banana peel. I wrote that down in my notes. I talked to the woman who managed the rooming house, and she told me about Oswald. She was a little bit tender about saying this. She said, "We described him as the butt-twister, because when he would get up to go to the telephone or maybe to get up to adjust the TV, he would twist his butt in a funny way. He had a funny walk." But they didn't particularly like him because he wasn't friendly to them.

From Darwin Payne's notebook, 11/22/63: 1026 North Beckley. Neat yard, Sign advertises rooms for tourists. A brick place. Oswald had been there six weeks.... Bobby Palmer, construction worker, says it's a bachelor place, a place where a lot of bachelors stay.... The housekeeper, Mrs. Earlene Roberts [says], He came here after the president was shot. I said, "You sure are in a hurry." He didn't answer. Oswald had a room off the dining room. He had been rooming here since October. His room, light blue color on the walls, single bed with sheets dumped and a blanket and a bedspread all wadded up.... There's an old pack of chewing gum in the wastebasket. Left some shaving cream. Dresser with a mirror on it. Mrs. Earlene Roberts [says], His hours were regular. He usually came in early. He'd make phone calls in a foreign language, German or Russian. I didn't pay much attention to him. He would shoot pool...he would hardly speak to you. He paid $8 a week for his room. There were plainclothesmen who came and stripped down his room. They found the holster to a .38 pistol here in his room. Four or five nights ago we all came in and George switched the TV over and it looked like it made him mad as fire. He never stayed up for the ten o'clock news. He'd come in and listen to the radio. He'd go to bed at nine or ten o'clock.... He was a loner. He was registered here as O.H. Lee. The police named him Lee Oswald. When he would go to the bathroom, he would twist. We called him the butt-twister. We called him that behind his back. He'd watch TV five or ten minutes, get up and be gone. He was fidgety.

3:23 P.M. (CST)
ABOARD THE STATE DEPARTMENT BOEING 707
SOMEWHERE OVER THE PACIFIC

PIERRE SALINGER
White House press secretary

There was a long flight ahead of us and little, if anything, that any of us could do. Finally, out of desperation, I suggested we play poker. Suddenly, there were half a dozen of us or more, all sitting down and pulling bills out of our pockets. It swiftly became a poker game out of Kafka or Ionesco—bizarre. We played for table stakes, and money flew back and forth across the table. But there was no bantering, no conversation, just low-voiced, dead-serious betting. From time to time, one or another of us would turn from the table, put his head in his hands, and sob. Time passed incredibly slowly.

Then, all of a sudden, the game was over, and all of the money was sitting in a pile in front of me. I counted it, and there was more than $800. I had won everyone's money. This was terrible. I shouldn't have won; I should have lost. I was appalled.

3:23 P.M. (CST)
ANDREWS AIR FORCE BASE

NANCY DICKERSON
correspondent,
NBC News

I was sent out to Andrews Air Force Base with instructions to try to get on the Kennedy family plane, which we understood was flying to Dallas with Robert Kennedy. The janitor was the only person available to take me to the base, and his car had no radio. The forty-five-minute drive was agony. There was no way of finding out anything. Arriving at Andrews, I still didn't know the outcome and was afraid to ask. I saw Mike O'Neill, [later] editor of the New York *Daily News*. He didn't need to say anything. I could tell by his face.

3:23 P.M. (CST)
ABOARD AIR FORCE ONE

Ground-to-air communications with the White House, code-named Crown, continue as President Johnson, code-named Volunteer, makes plans to meet with National Security Adviser McGeorge Bundy and Secretary of Defense Robert McNamara to get an immediate intelligence report upon his return. The new president and his wife, Lady Bird, code-named Victoria, also worry about their youngest daughter, Luci Baines Johnson, code-named Venus, and send instructions that she return to their home, code-named Valley, with her Secret Service agent.

WHITE HOUSE:

Dagger [Secret Service Agent Rufus Youngblood], Duplex [Secret Service special agent Gerald Behn] is on. Go ahead.

RUFUS YOUNGBLOOD:

Dagger to Duplex. This message is from Volunteer and Victoria relative to activities tonight.

GERALD BEHN:

Go ahead, Dagger. This is Duplex.

YOUNGBLOOD:

You are aware that we will go to Crown for meetings?

BEHN:

That is affirmative.

YOUNGBLOOD:

Volunteer will reside at Valley for an indefinite time—I repeat, Volunteer will reside at Valley for an indefinite time. Victoria requests that Venus [inaudible] to Valley with agent.

BEHN:

Will you say again?

[VOICE OFF-MIKE]:

Venus should go out to Valley with agent.

BEHN:

That is a roger.

YOUNGBLOOD:

Venus will go to Valley with agent. Victoria will go to Valley after first going to Crown. Do you understand?

BEHN:

That's affirmative.

MALCOLM KILDUFF
White House

All the way back [Lyndon Johnson] was planning on who he should meet with immediately, who he should call together immediately, to get [Secretary of State Dean] Rusk back immediately, who of course was on the plane to Japan. Immediately, he called Rose Kennedy from the aircraft; he called Governor Connally's wife from the aircraft; he wanted to get an immediate intelligence report from [National Security Adviser] McGeorge Bundy and [Secretary of Defense] Robert McNamara as soon as he hit the ground. His mind was working in a way that I think is extremely commendable because he was thinking in terms of this being, in effect, a national emergency, which of course it was.

MERRIMAN SMITH
UPI

When the plane was about forty-five minutes from Washington, the new president got on a special radiotelephone and placed a call to Mrs. Rose Kennedy, the late president's mother. "I wish to God there was something I could do," he told her. "I just wanted you to know that." Then Mrs. Johnson wanted to talk to the elder Mrs. Kennedy. "We feel like the heart has been cut out of us," Mrs. Johnson said. She broke down for a moment and began to sob.

4:20 P.M. (CST)

WHITE HOUSE:
Air Force One from Crown. Mrs. Kennedy on. Go ahead, please.

AIR FORCE ONE:
Hello, Mrs. Kennedy. Hello, Mrs. Kennedy. We're talking from the airplane. Can you hear us all right? Over.

ROSE KENNEDY:
Hello. Thank you. Thank you. Hello.

AIR FORCE ONE:
Yes, Mrs. Kennedy, I have Mr. Johnson for you here.

ROSE KENNEDY:
Thank you. Hello?

PRESIDENT JOHNSON:
Mrs. Kennedy?

ROSE KENNEDY:
Yes, Mr. President.

PRESIDENT JOHNSON:
I wish to God there was something that I could do and I wanted to tell you that we were grieving with you.

ROSE KENNEDY:
Yes, well thank you very much, thank you very much. I know. I know you loved Jack and he loved you.

LADY BIRD JOHNSON:
Mrs. Kennedy we feel like we've just had [inaudible].

ROSE KENNEDY:
Yes, all right.

LADY BIRD JOHNSON:

[Inaudible] son as long as you did.

ROSE KENNEDY:

Thank you for that, Lady Bird, thank you very much. Good-bye.

LADY BIRD JOHNSON:

Love and prayers to all of you.

ROSE KENNEDY:

Thank you very much. Goodbye. Goodbye. Goodbye.

4:32 P.M. (CST)

ABC NEWS:
ROBERT LINDLEY
IN BUENOS AIRES

Reaction to the assassination here could hardly be more profound. I saw a woman nearly faint when she read the news on the bulletin board of a newspaper. Crowds discussing the president's death make moving on the sidewalk impossible. On learning of the announcement, [the city's] two powerful newspapers blew the sirens they use only for the greatest catastrophes or developments. The last time they blew the sirens was on the death of Pope John XXIII earlier this year.

CHARLES ROBERTS
Newsweek

We were flying at absolutely flank speed, and I kept telling [Merriman Smith] we had an awful lot of work to do. We pooled our notes, and happily we agreed on just about everything. Two or three times the new president came to talk to us, once to tell us that he had called Mrs. Rose Kennedy; once to tell us that he had talked to Mrs. Connally, and then to read us, give us a copy of the statement he was going to read on arrival at Andrews. I think that probably this was the only time in my life that I ever felt like saying to a president of the United States, "Look, I know you want to talk, but I've got a lot of work to do."

MERRIMAN SMITH *UPI*	Thirty minutes out of Washington, Johnson put in a call for Nellie Connally, wife of the seriously wounded Texas governor. The new president said…"We are praying for you, darling, and I know that everything is going to be all right, isn't it? Give him a hug and a kiss for me."

4:35 P.M. (CST)

*hear…
track 23

WHITE HOUSE:

Stand by please. Air Force One from Crown, come in. [Inaudible] The Connally residence in Dallas is on the line. Mrs. Connally is available to speak with Mr. Johnson if he can get to the phone patch.

LADY BIRD JOHNSON:

[Inaudible] heard some reassuring news over the TV. We are up in the plane but the surgeon speaking about John sounded so reassuring. How about it?

NELLIE CONNALLY:

That was the surgeon who had just done the operation on him. John is going to be all right, we are almost certain, unless something unforeseen happens.

LADY BIRD JOHNSON:

I can't hear you too well, Nellie.

PRESIDENT JOHNSON:

Nellie, can you hear me? We are praying for you, darling, and I know that everything is going to be all right. Is it?

NELLIE CONNALLY:

Yes, it's going to be all right.

PRESIDENT JOHNSON:

God bless you, darling.

NELLIE CONNALLY:

The same to you.

From Air Force One, assistant White House press secretary Malcolm Kilduff, code-named Warrior, talks to associate White House press secretary Andrew Hatcher, code-named Winner, who is at the White House trying to answer news media questions and making arrangements for coverage of the arrival of Air Force One at Andrews Air Force Base in Maryland.

MALCOLM KILDUFF:

Winner, Winner, this is Warrior. Will you please advise that normal press coverage, including live TV, will be allowed at the base. Volunteer will make a statement on arrival. Did you read that? Over.

ANDREW HATCHER:

I read you clearly. My question is, is Mrs. Kennedy aboard Air Force One?

KILDUFF:

Warrior. That is a roger. Over.

HATCHER:

The other thing is, I'm setting up a press section on the South Lawn [of the White House] about fifty yards from the position of helicopter Number One. Will that meet Mrs. Kennedy's and the president's approval?

KILDUFF:

Winner, they are not returning to the house. For your own information, they're going someplace else I don't want to go in on the radio on that one. There will be an arrival there but it will be Volunteer. Over.

HATCHER:

Thank you. I will hold that information and we can say something after you arrive. Hold it just a second, let me look through my list of questions. Is it true that the body of President Kennedy will go to Bethesda Naval Hospital?

KILDUFF:

That is a roger, roger, but we are not saying that. Over.

HATCHER:

Well, we've already said it. I should have checked with you before doing, but I don't think it makes too much difference. It takes a lot off—we should know it—it takes a lot off us by doing it. I was in error.

KILDUFF:

So far as that press area on the South Lawn, there is no objection to that.

HATCHER:

Anything else I should know?

KILDUFF:

Yes, the pool on this aircraft is Chuck Roberts and [Merriman] Smith. We lost [AP correspondent Jack] Bell somewhere along the line. We don't have AP aboard but I have given them the statement of Volunteer on the death, which he will make at the airport.

HATCHER:

OK. Over and out.

4:35 P.M. (CST)

ANDREWS AIR FORCE BASE

NANCY DICKERSON
NBC News

I was told to wait for Air Force One to return. The hours dragged by.... Eunice Shriver [Kennedy's eldest surviving sister], arrived sobbing. She had been especially close to the president, and she had been chosen to go to Hyannis Port to break the news to her father. There was a sense of panic at Andrews, and security was understandably tight. Already a feeling of guilt was spreading through the Secret Service, which felt responsible for Dallas. As the news spread, the airport was closed and no one could get out or in, including the network camera crews. I negotiated the entrance of some of them so that they could begin setting up equipment to televise the return.

ABC NEWS:

*hear...

track 24

Down in Dallas, Texas, authorities are now questioning a twenty-four-year-old man to see if he has any connection with the slaying of President Kennedy. He is Lee Oswald. He is a definite suspect in the fatal shooting of a Dallas policeman and a definite suspect in the assassination of President Kennedy. Who is this Lee Oswald? His home is Fort Worth, Texas. He had been in the Marines. When he got out of the Marines, he said he wanted to go to Russia. He said he wanted to stay

ABC NEWS: 	there. He apparently became disillusioned with life under communist rule after working in a Soviet factory in Minsk, marrying a Russian woman, giving her a child. In the fall of 1962, he applied for a passport to return to the U.S. and bring his family back with him. The passport was issued.
CBS NEWS: **HARRY REASONER**	People will remember today as a date to date things in their lives from, in the same way that they did in the case of President Roosevelt. They would say, "Where were you when President Roosevelt died?" They will say the same thing about "Where were you when you first heard the news of President Kennedy's assassination?"

Lee Harvey Oswald sits in police custody after his arrest at the Texas Theatre in Dallas.

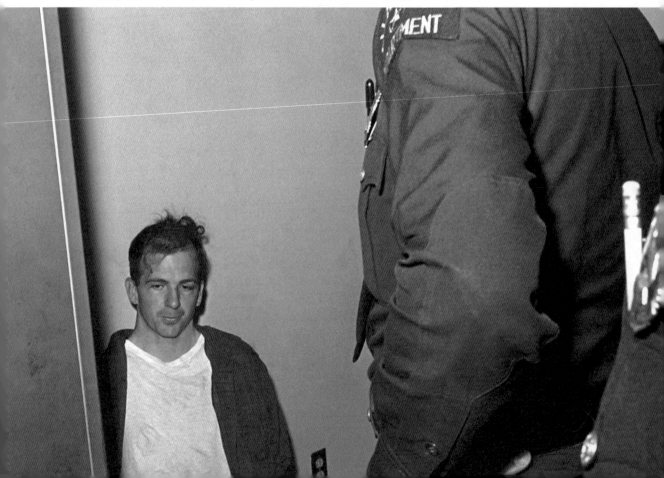

5:05 P.M. (CST)
ABOARD AIR FORCE ONE AT ANDREWS AIR FORCE BASE

CHARLES ROBERTS
Newsweek

We were representing the whole world press. Whatever was written, at least that day, about both the swearing-in of the new president and this unprecedented flight back with the dead president, the new president, the new first lady, and the widow of the late president aboard, had to be written in that time. Period. I was still typing as we taxied up to Andrews, and [Smith] was, too.

ABC NEWS:
DICK BATES

*hear...

track 25

The presidential jet has now landed. A truck arrangement has pulled up to the side of it. The back door of the jet is open. It would appear they are now pulling out the casket. It is a bronze casket. It is off the plane now accompanied by Secret Service men.... It is on a truck, the body of which rises up in the air on a hydraulic lift. The body of President Kennedy is back in Washington. A Navy ambulance is pulling up. The bronze casket carrying President Kennedy's body will be taken from here to Bethesda Naval Hospital. A Secret Service escort is now lifting the bronze casket off the truck. The casket is now being put into a gray Navy ambulance. Mrs. Kennedy is now coming down following the casket. With her are other members of the Kennedy family. Mrs. Jacqueline Kennedy and Attorney General Robert Kennedy will go with the body to Bethesda Naval Hospital.

CHARLES ROBERTS
Newsweek

We landed at Andrews at about six [P.M. EST] and the whole top layer of government that was not on that plane on the way to Tokyo was there, of course. We stood by while the president's casket was removed by a lift truck.

I remember looking at [McGeorge] Bundy because I was wondering if he had any word of what had happened in the world while we were in transit, whether this assassination was part of a plot. And he told me later that what he reported to the president during that flight back was that the whole world was stunned, but there was no evidence of a conspiracy at all.

MERRIMAN SMITH
UPI

[Charles] Roberts and I stood under a wing and watched the casket being lowered from the rear of the plane and borne by a complement of armed forces body-bearers into a waiting hearse. We watched Mrs. Kennedy and the president's brother, Attorney General Robert F. Kennedy, climb into the hearse beside the coffin.

The new president repeated his first public statement for broadcast and newsreel microphones, shook hands with some of the government and diplomatic leaders who turned out to meet the plane, and headed for his helicopter. Roberts and I were given seats on another 'copter bound for the White House lawn. In the compartment next to ours in one of the large chairs beside a window sat Theodore C. Sorensen, one of Kennedy's closest associates.... He had not gone to Texas with his chief but had come to the air base for his return. Sorensen sat wilted in the large chair, crying softly.

5:05 P.M. (CST)
ANDREWS AIR FORCE BASE

HELEN THOMAS
White House correspondent,
UPI

[My editors] told me to go to Andrews [Air Force Base] and be prepared to go to Dallas. We waited for what seemed like hours and everyone—from Capitol Hill, Bobby [Kennedy]—started converging. It was so somber. When Air Force One arrived, everyone just held their breath. [Merriman Smith] was coming down the back steps with a bundle of copy, not just on the assassination but on the swearing-in of the new president. I had a line open. I phoned in Merriman Smith's story from the plane. He had typed the full story and it was really good.

NANCY DICKERSON
NBC News

With no warning, Air Force One screamed to a stop and the network switched to us.... Bobby Kennedy rushed up the steps at the front. When Jackie came down the steps, she ran toward a government station wagon, but the door was locked and she had to run around to the other side. I forgot we were on the air and put my mike down thinking that I could help. With a blaze of sirens, the president's body and his widow took off for Bethesda Naval Hospital, where they began the long process of funeral preparation. A messenger was sent to the White House for the president's clothes. When they arrived, one of his friends there remembers thinking that his shoes weren't polished and how Jack would have hated that. The newly sworn President Johnson walked down the steps self-consciously, hat in hand, and with Lady Bird at his side, asked for our help and prayers.

An NBC crew at Andrews Air Force Base prepares to telecast the removal of the slain president's casket from Air Force One.

The president's brother, Robert, holds Jacqueline Kennedy's hand as her husband's casket is removed from Air Force One.

ROBERT ASMAN
senior producer,
NBC News

We had a little small mobile unit at that time; it was really a converted bread truck, but it had some electronic equipment in it. It happened to be out on the road, and we did have a walkie-talkie connection to it. We told them to get out to Andrews Air Force Base as quickly as they could. It turned out that we were the only network to arrive there, because we happened to have this truck on the road. We called the telephone company and told them we were going to need audio and video lines, so they met us out there, and we got the first signal.

The flight was due in at 6:00 P.M. At five minutes of six, we had the beginnings of flickerings of picture from Andrews, but we had no audio. We were sweating it out, because we knew the other [major] network [CBS] was depending on us for that picture. As the plane came in, suddenly audio came through and we had audio and video picture. It was a black-and-white picture, but it was there, and we got the first pictures of the body coming off Air Force One. After the ambulance had gone, the new president, President Johnson, came off the plane, and said his first words to the public as president. It was a very short statement, probably four or five paragraphs. But he was very reassuring, and I think for the country to hear the new president was a reassuring thing. It would be the beginning of the first live coverage of that four-day period when the Kennedy assassination had this impact on the whole world.

CBS NEWS:
HARRY REASONER

You have seen, live, from Andrews Air Force Base in Maryland, the arrival of the plane from Dallas, Texas, carrying the body of former president—the late President Kennedy—and also bringing Mrs. Kennedy and new President Lyndon Baines Johnson. The advances in technology which permit historic events like this to be seen by people as they happen also bring some of their own disadvantages. The ability to see President Johnson in his first public appearance since tragedy forced him into this office also meant that because of the noise in the place it was hard to hear his words.

President Lyndon B. Johnson, with Lady Bird Johnson at his side, speaks to the nation after arriving at Andrews Air Force Base.

5:05 P.M. (CST)
DALLAS POLICE DEPARTMENT

BOB SCHIEFFER
Fort Worth Star-Telegram

Things were so different in those days. For one thing, we never told people who we were as journalists. If people asked, we were instructed never to lie, but if they assumed we were a policeman or detective, we let them believe that, which is why I always wore a black, snap-brimmed hat when I worked at the police station because that's what the detectives wore. When I got to the Dallas police station, I took Mrs. Oswald in. To the first uniformed officer I found, I said, "I'm the one who brought Oswald's mother over from Fort Worth. Is there anyplace we can put her where these reporters won't be talking and bothering her?" He said, "Well, let me see what I can do." He actually found a little room off the burglary squad and he said, "Will this be all right?" and I said, "This will be fine." It had a phone which was a great advantage for me because I could then go out into the hall—by that time we had sixteen reporters on the scene and we were still putting out these extras—I could go out, get the information from our guys, go back, and phone it into the newspaper.

As the day wore on, [Oswald's mother] asked if she could see her son. So Captain Will Fritz, who was the chief of homicide, arranged to take her into a holding room just off the jail. I went right along. To this point—and I guess we'd been in the police station some hours now—no one had yet asked me who I was. Finally a man who turned out to be, I think, an FBI agent, said, "Now just who are you?" I said, "Well, who are you?" and he said, "Are you a newspaperman?" I said, "Well, aren't you?" At that point I guess I got the first legitimate death threat that I had ever received as an adult because he said, "I'm going to kill you if I ever see you again." I would think he didn't mean it, but he may have because he was really steamed. At any rate, I sort of apologized and said I didn't realize I wasn't supposed to be there and kind of blended on out into the crowd. I almost interviewed Oswald. As I tell people, it was the biggest interview I almost got but didn't.

Dallas nightclub owner Jack Ruby (in profile) mingles with reporters and police officers in a corridor of the Dallas police headquarters on the night of President Kennedy's assassination.

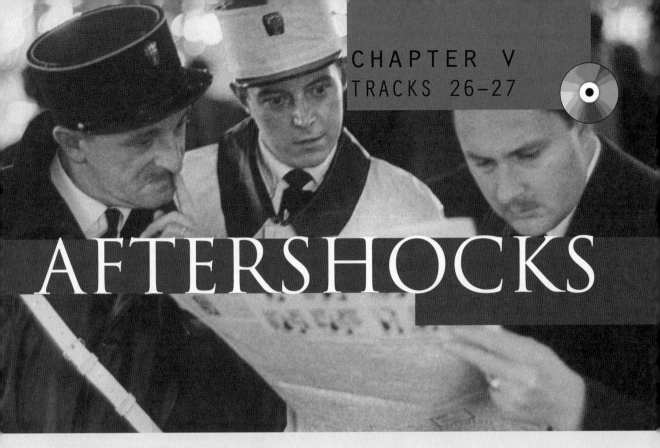

AFTERSHOCKS

NOVEMBER 22–23 5:10 PM – 2:00 AM (CST)

THE PRESIDENT'S CASKET is taken from Andrews Air Force Base to Bethesda Naval Hospital for the autopsy. In the District of Columbia, crowds gather along the streets as motorcycle police—sirens howling—escort family and friends from the White House to the hospital. Sirens and alarms blare from firehouses and passing police cruisers. At one point, after crossing the District of Columbia line and moving into Maryland, the motorcade is hurtling up Wisconsin Avenue at speeds of more than ninety miles per hour. President Johnson speaks with administration and congressional leaders before going home.

As the news flashes around the globe, people are stunned. Some weep openly on street corners. Schools are closed; the stock exchanges are shut down. College football games are canceled. Broadway goes dark. Television networks switch to continuous coverage as people gather in front of televisions and radios for the latest information.

Dallas police and other law enforcement officers question Lee Harvey Oswald, who is arraigned Friday night for the murder of police officer J.D. Tippit. Just before midnight Dallas time, Oswald is charged with the murder of the president.

BEN BRADLEE
Washington bureau chief,
Newsweek

We were asked to go out to Bethesda Naval Hospital to wait there for Jackie and the body and the apparatchiks to come back. I remember going out in a limousine with Steve Smith's wife, Jean [Kennedy Smith]. We had a motorcycle escort. One of the motorcycle cops came within an inch of being killed. He swerved terribly and it looked like he was going to be hit head-on. Somehow he miraculously escaped. That scared the shit out of everybody.

We got there. We waited for the plane to land and [Mrs. Kennedy and her party] to come to the suite. And then Jackie walked in. It was the most incredible sight—still with that pink dress on, still with that blood all over her. She went around to say hello to people. She was just on another planet. She greeted us, Tony Bradlee and I, and I remember her saying, "Do you want to hear what happened?" I didn't say, "Yes, yes," or anything like that. I just said, "Of course," or something. Then she felt constrained, as she always did, to say, "You know, this is all off the record." That made me feel like two cents. You are seeing somebody who is absolutely shattered. I was not ashamed of being a journalist, but I had no place there as a journalist. I mean I have eyes and I remembered things, but I wasn't really being a reporter there. Then she started describing it. But she was interrupted by other people coming up so she never completed a description. I know they tried to get her out of those clothes, and she wouldn't get out of them.

[Robert] McNamara was there, Kenny [O'Donnell], Larry [O'Brien], and Bobby [Kennedy] definitely came. One of the questions was where should the grave be. They asked everybody, as if we had given that any thought. I only remember that the idea of burying him in Boston—as a Bostonian myself—did not appeal at all. Then a bunch of them left. I think Bobby left with McNamara to go to the [Arlington National Cemetery] gravesite and came back saying it was wonderful. We finally got home to bed about six o'clock in the morning.

Members of a military honor guard line a hallway at Bethesda Naval Hospital while John F. Kennedy's body is prepared for burial.

6:15 P.M. (CST)

The principal exchanges, including the New York Stock Exchange, closed as soon as news of the presidential assassination reached them. On the New York Stock Exchange today, the Dow Jones closing averages showed thirty industrials at 711.49, down 21.16; twenty railroads at 166.41, down 3.28; fifteen utilities at 134.97, down 1.95. The 65 Dow Jones stock average down 6.15.

In Cambridge, Massachusetts, the Harvard–Yale football game will not be played tomorrow because of the president's death. Two of New Jersey's major universities have announced cancellation of football games scheduled for tomorrow, the Princeton–Dartmouth game and the Rutgers–Columbia match, both of those canceled. Horse racing at Aqueduct Track in New York canceled after the seventh race today. On Broadway, the bright lights of the Great White Way dimmed and flickered out in mourning for our president. Tonight's presentation at the Metropolitan Opera House has been canceled.

Under a portrait of President Kennedy bordered in black tape, an ABC News employee takes the latest news report on the assassination from a teletype.

6:15 P.M. (CST)
DALLAS MORNING NEWS

WALTER ROBERTSON
sports editor,
Dallas Morning News

We went through the motions of producing a sports section. We dug out a few old pictures of some of the many moments Jack Kennedy spent in sports—a shot of a very young JFK in football uniform, one of him absorbed in the action of an Army–Navy game, and another of him skippering his yacht off the New England coast. Much of our section for the issue of Saturday, November 23, was devoted to the memory of Jack Kennedy and to his mourning by a sports world he loved and which loved him. For us at the *News*, as in sports departments across the nation, it was many, many days before sports events again were more than just meaningless games.

**MARY ELIZABETH WOOD-
WARD**
*society section reporter,
Dallas Morning News*

In an almost deafening silence, everyone tried to do those things which had to be done—stories to be killed, pages to be made over, advance stories to be rewritten to coincide with this unexpected flow of history. [Asked by an editor to write a story,] I tried to remember that I was a reporter and that my job was merely to report what I had seen, not to dramatize, not to moralize, not to strike out in frustrated anger. For once there was no need to embroider. The naked facts were all that I needed.

BILL RIVES
*managing editor,
Dallas Morning News*

One of our society staff writers, Mary Elizabeth Woodward, an ardent admirer of the president and a devoted Democrat, was in a virtual state of collapse when I first arrived at the office after the shooting. She had been to the first-aid station a couple of times and taken some pills. I felt like Simon Legree, but I knew that Mary Elizabeth had a good story to tell and I wanted her to write it. She wrote a fine story, and I know that she did it while her feelings were in great turmoil.

In this television image, Dallas nightclub owner Jack Ruby (top right) stands among the reporters gathered at Dallas police headquarters for a press conference on the night of November 22, 1963.

6:15 P.M. (CST)
DALLAS TIMES HERALD

KEITH SHELTON
political writer,
Dallas Times Herald

There was an influx of journalists from all over the world. A lot of them made their headquarters at the *Times Herald*. That gave us an idea that this was really a worldwide story. They also stole clippings and pictures out of our library, charged phone calls to Paris. They generally were jerks.

JAMES CHAMBERS JR.
president,
Dallas Times Herald

[Out-of-town reporters] came in droves. One of them was Dorothy Kilgallen, who wrote that column, "Dallas: The City That Killed President Kennedy," which was a lie on the face of it. The city didn't kill Kennedy; Oswald killed Kennedy. But you know, that was the kind of reporting that really killed us as a city during that period.

ABC NEWS:
JOHN CASSERLY
IN ROME

It's already Saturday here, the early hours, but still a crowd outside the U.S. Embassy, men and women crying. Italian television simply shut down. In their words, we have nothing to say, but to mourn. Pope Paul VI went to the unprecedented length of inviting ABC into the papal apartments. He said, "I pray for President Kennedy, America, and the American people." Extra! Extra! The news vendors running through the streets of Rome. Everything is closing.

6:15 P.M. (CST)
NEW YORK CITY

WALTER CRONKITE
anchor,
CBS Evening News

I was finally relieved after being at the desk for seven or eight hours. Charles Collingwood came and they offered me relief for whatever time I wanted before going back on the air. I was a lot younger then and I managed to sit there for six hours without needing relief. When I got up, the first thing I noticed was that I was in shirtsleeves. My secretary had been

An NBC newsroom worker checks hanging teletype reports.

ordered to get my jacket, but I was busy talking when she got to the desk and they said, "Just put it over the back of the chair." They put it over the back of the chair and I never knew it was there.

I went into my little office. I was very anxious to talk to my wife. Betsy didn't watch daytime television and it was possible that nobody would have called her. I wanted to call her right away, not only to talk with her but to hear a friendly and sympathetic voice instead of [producer] Don Hewitt shouting into my ear all day. So I went in, and for the first time, I realized that the telephone lines all over the country were blocked with overuse with everybody calling everybody. I had twelve lines coming into my desk—two phones and six lines on each phone—and they were all lighted. Just then, one went dark and I grabbed it quickly and a woman was already on the phone, saying, "Hello, hello, hello," in this phony Park Avenue, phony British accent. I said, "Hello." She said,

"I'd like to speak to someone at CBS News. I'd like to speak to someone in control of CBS News." I said, "You're speaking to the CBS News Department." She said, "Well, I'd like to complain about CBS having on the air at this time that Walter Cronkite, crying his crocodile tears when we know he hated John Kennedy."

I never hated John Kennedy in the first place. In the second place, I disliked this tone. I said, "Madam, what is your name?" Naturally it was a hyphenated name, probably made up. Mrs. Parkhurst-Nolan or some such thing, and she gave an address on upper Park Avenue. I said, "Mrs. Parkhurst-Nolan, you're speaking to Walter Cronkite and you are a damn idiot," and I hung up the phone. I sat back and thought, well, Parkhurst-Nolan, Park Avenue, she's got to be a friend of [CBS Chairman] Bill Paley. This probably was the last phone call I'll make from CBS. I must say for three days I waited to hear from Paley's office that I had insulted one of his friends. But I never heard.

NBC NEWS:
SANDER VANOCUR

President Johnson left...for his home in Washington. Before leaving, he conferred with Defense Secretary [Robert] McNamara, Undersecretary of State George Ball, and FBI chief J. Edgar Hoover.

6:15 P.M. (CST)
DALLAS

Although one local Dallas reporter already has talked to a man named Abraham Zapruder, who filmed the assassination, other reporters are launching searches for someone who might have photographed the shooting. Details are disputed, with different recollections of who arranges for a nearby Kodak lab to prepare prints for projection.

DAN RATHER
New Orleans bureau chief,
CBS News

Nobody had any pictures, so [we said], let's try to find somebody who took pictures—in a crowd like that, plenty of people must have had cameras. Let's see if we can find some of them, and let's see if we can find particularly somebody who has pictures that wiggle—which is to say moving pictures.

Eddie Barker (left) of KRLD-TV in Dallas and Dan Rather of CBS News, shortly after the official announcement of the president's death.

Bob Clark of ABC News (left, back to camera), Peggy Simpson of the Associated Press, and Ike Pappas of WNEW Radio in a third-floor corridor of Dallas police headquarters the day after the assassination.

It wasn't I alone, but…a collection of three, four, five, maybe more people, all CBS people and our affiliate people [from] KRLD. My recollection is that Eddie [Barker] was key in this, helping. I don't recall specifically from where we got Zapruder's name. We were making calls, you know, [doing] what reporters do: "If you know anybody who had a camera there, if you hear of anybody who had a camera there, we'd sure like to talk to them." I remember that night discussing this with Eddie and some other people in his newsroom: "Damn, there must be somebody who's got pictures of this."

I remember that there was a conversation with Zapruder. He said he had taken home-movie pictures of it, but then we would question him about, "Well, are you sure you had the actual assassination?" He said, "Well, yes, I've got the whole thing." And while we might hope he had the whole thing, there was no way of knowing what he had. I talked to him and he said, "Well, you know, you will see once this gets processed." At that point I'm pretty sure I talked to Eddie or somebody to say, "Well, can we get somebody to process this stuff?" Pretty quickly, arrangements were made to have Mr. Zapruder get the film and have it processed on an expedited basis. We put him in touch with Kodak and said, "As soon as you get this stuff back, we'd sure like to have a look at it."

BERT SHIPP
assistant news director,
WFAA-TV

All of a sudden the suits come in, there were about four or five of them. They said they were FBI. They said, "We want you to process this." I looked at it. It's eight-millimeter film. I said, "I can't process this, we process sixteen [millimeter]. You've got to practically send this off to get this processed." So I told them, "Stay right there," and I called a guy at Kodak and said, "These FBI guys are fixing to ruin a very important piece of film." He said, "Well, tell them I'll meet them over by the lab at Love Field." It turned out to be the Zapruder film.

RICHARD STOLLEY
Los Angeles regional editor,
Life

[*Life* correspondent Tommy Thompson] had been a city editor of the Houston paper. He knew Texas. He said, "I'd like to go after the Oswald family," who lived in Irving, Texas. I think he said, "I know some cops in Irving." He took off with the photographer for Irving. I went into the Adolphus Hotel to set up a bureau, because other correspondents were coming in from elsewhere in the country. It was a suite, so we had about three phones in there. Suddenly, the phone rang. It was a Dallas stringer named Patsy Swank; she was calling from home. Another journalist, who was at the police department, had called her and said, "Patsy, I just got a tip from a cop that the assassination was photographed by a home-movie enthusiast." He had very few details, but he had a semblance of a name. He didn't know the name, but it sounded like "Zapruder."

7:19 P.M. (CST)
NEW YORK CITY

NBC NEWS:
BILL RYAN

Every candle is lit at St. Patrick's Cathedral. Saks Fifth Avenue has curtains drawn across all its display windows.

ROBERT PIERPOINT
White House correspondent,
CBS News

I went over to the Dallas Press Club, had five martinis and didn't feel a thing except continued shock.

DAN RATHER
CBS News

It was terrible—an almost constant struggle between your emotions as an American and as a human and your duties as a pro, as a professional. You reach a point—and it came very early in this because things were happening so quickly—of either you just lose it, you kind of go to pieces, or you're able to get focused with strong concentration and you just seal everything else out. Fortunately, all the reporters I knew that day were able to do the latter. I know that in my own case from time to time things that were deep inside oneself threatened to come up, volcanic-like, from within you and you just had to give yourself a quick lecture: "I can't think about that now, I can't deal with that now, I'll deal with that later." And that resulted in a delayed reaction about the time most other people in the country were beginning to go through what healing process they could. The full impact of those days—it was a delayed emotional reaction days later.

IKE PAPPAS
reporter,
WNEW Radio

It seemed like the whole world was descending on Dallas. Everyone was arriving about the same time. I went down to the police headquarters and I immediately filed a story. I worked all night picking up odds and ends. There was mounting pressure that night to bring Oswald to the press. They agreed finally to let us see Oswald. The agreement was that we would ask no questions. We're waiting in front of the door to the lineup room and in comes Oswald. They put him up on the platform, and we're all screaming, and of course, as he hit the door that agreement went through the window. People yelled, "Did you shoot the president?" He said, "That's what I'm accused of. I want to see a lawyer." In New York, we would have never got that close to a prisoner. They would never have produced him for us to ask questions of the assassin of the president of the United States.

He disappears, and everyone is running for telephones so they can file their stories. We didn't have cell phones in those days and there were very few phones there. I'm dying for a phone, thinking "I've got to file, I've got to file." Suddenly this guy comes up to me—he has a snap-brim fedora hat, a pinstriped dark suit. He looked to me like a vice cop. He said, "I'm not a detective. My name is Jack Ruby." He hands me his card and it says something like "Carousel Club—Girls! Girls! Cocktails! Dancing!" He says, "I run the Carousel Club. Get some of your friends and come on down to the club." I told him I needed a telephone. He walks over and interrupts Henry Wade, the district attorney, and says, "There's a reporter from New York and he needs a telephone and he wants to do an interview with you." Wade says, "Take him down to my office and let him use the phone." I wind up in Henry Wade's office feeding my live report.

Lee Harvey Oswald is presented to the news media at a press conference at Dallas police headquarters.

9:00 P.M. (CST)

ABC NEWS:
LES GRIFFITH
IN NEW YORK

Police say witnesses have identified Oswald as the murderer of the policeman. They say it has not been established that he murdered the president. However, police say it has been established that Oswald was in the building from which the president was shot when the shooting occurred. They say he has denied taking any part in the assassination of the president.

9:59 P.M. (CST)
WASHINGTON, D.C.
THE ELMS, THE JOHNSON RESIDENCE

NBC NEWS:
NANCY DICKERSON

President Johnson has arrived at his home. As he drove up, he acknowledged the greetings of the people waiting for him.... The Secret Service men who accompanied President Johnson carried their guns in the open. Mrs. Johnson said that the whole event is like a nightmare.

NANCY DICKERSON
correspondent,
NBC News

I was sent out to the Elms, the Johnson house, to report on his return. By then the neighborhood was swarming with security police, television floodlights were being installed, and the neighbors were out, quietly talking among themselves, just like everywhere else in the nation.... When LBJ's car arrived, he was surrounded by Secret Service men whose guns stuck out of every window, something I'd never seen before. He had the inside light on to read the paper, which seemed silly because it made him a lighted target.

WILBORN HAMPTON
reporter,
United Press International

[The press] would shout questions at him, "Why did you do it, Lee?" He reached over and looked at the press and said, "I demand my hygienic rights." He would make these comments apropos of absolutely nothing. Occasionally, he would say, "I didn't shoot anybody." It went on for hours.

CBS NEWS:
DAN RATHER

Now we'll take a closer look at the gun that police say was used to kill the president today. The gun is an Italian-made, high-powered rifle, 6.5 millimeter, which police tell us is roughly the equivalent of a thirty-caliber rifle. It's the rough equivalent to the kind of rifle that United States soldiers carry. It has a four-power telescopic sight on it. The shot which killed the president is believed to have been fired through that gun at one hundred yards, which is not a long range for this kind of weapon. The deer season is open in Texas and that kind of gun at a hundred yards would knock a full-sized deer completely off his feet.

HUGH AYNESWORTH
science/aviation/space editor,
Dallas Morning News

[My editors] said to me, "Nobody's interviewed the Tippits. Will you run on out there?" I thought, "My God, I've done more than I've ever done in a day in my life already, and now I have to do this unwelcome task." So I went out and I went up to the porch very meekly. There were all kinds of people there trying to talk to them. And I got one of these cops that I knew, and I called him aside and I said, "Look, I'll leave immediately. I don't have to bother Marie Tippit. I just want to get a little bit of what's going on and I'll leave, I promise you." So he filled me in with who the kids were, how long he'd been a cop and what he was like and that sort of thing. I went back and did a little piece on that. It was, I don't know, eleven o'clock, I guess, before I got out of there. But it was a pretty strident twelve hours.

Although by this time Abraham Zapruder, fatigued and distraught, already has made an appearance on WFAA-TV and apparently has spoken with other reporters, he tells Richard Stolley of *Life* magazine that Stolley is the first reporter to contact him.

A Dallas police official holds aloft a rifle that police say was used in the shooting of President Kennedy.

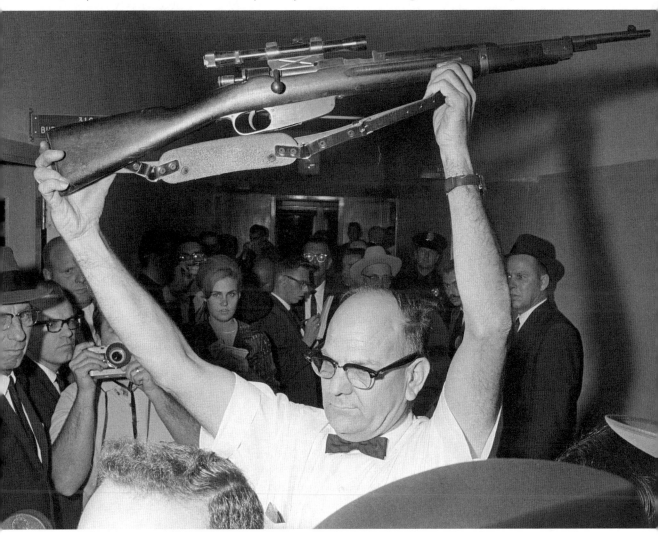

RICHARD STOLLEY
Life

I picked up the Dallas phone book and ran my finger down the Zs. Bingo! There it was—"Zapruder, Abraham." I called the number. No answer. I called that number every fifteen minutes for the next five hours. Finally, at about eleven, this weary voice answered. I identified myself. I said, "Is this Mr. Zapruder?" "Yes." I said, "Is it true, as I've been told, that you photographed the assassination?" "Yes." At that point I said, "Am I the first reporter to contact you?" He said, "Yes." Then I said—he was obviously very distraught—I said, "Did you manage to get the whole event?" I tried not to use the word assassination and that sort of thing. He said, "Yes." I said, "Have you seen the film?" He said, "I have. We had it processed." I thought, my God. He had answered yes to all these questions. I said, "Can I come out now and see it?" And he said, "No." Something just told me, "Lay off, lay off." I said, "Fine, I understand." This is a man who was a Kennedy fan, had just seen a murder committed. So I said, "Fine. When can I see it tomorrow?" He said, "Come to my office at nine."

11:30 P.M. (CST)
DALLAS

JACK FALLON
Southwest Division news manager, UPI

About 11:30 that night, the first call came that indicated what this story was going to do to the American psyche. It was the first nut call, the first conspiracy call. A man called and he talked in a very low voice. I could sense something was [odd]. He said, "I'm from headquarters." I said, "You are?" He said, "They sent me down to get to the bottom of this thing. We know you've got some information in the bureau." I said, "You're going to have a lot of digging to do, pal." He was shrieking into the phone, "You bastards! You killed him!"

I got another call as we were cleaning up loose ends from a man in Fort Worth who said, "I've got a story. The Secret Service had a big wild party the night before in The Cellar." I carried a story on that. It said they partied until the early hours and let it go at that. I gotta tell you, I had the Secret Service calling me and raising hell. Two FBI agents came in and I threw them out of the office.

NBC NEWS:
FRANK MCGEE

Sixty thousand Berliners gathered at Berlin City Hall to express their grief at the death of President Kennedy.

11:30 P.M. (CST)
WASHINGTON, D.C.

SID DAVIS
White House correspondent,
Westinghouse Broadcasting
Company

I rode the press plane back to Washington later that night. I went to the White House press room and Merriman Smith was waiting for me. I came in the door and he came running over to me and said, "You sonofabitch. I told you [the oath-taking] was at 2:37 P.M." I said, "My book said 2:38 P.M., Smitty." I rebelled. Smitty was upset because he had filed most of the story and his office used my time while he was on the airplane. It's a small detail but it's not a very small detail to reporters. It was a month or two before he forgave me.

MARIANNE MEANS
White House correspondent,
Hearst Newspapers

I cried on the plane all the way home. It was just a stunning story. I was very young at the time and my grandparents were alive. Nobody I knew well at all had died, and to have [the president] die in such an awful way was quite a shocking experience.

I went into the Hearst office and continued to flesh out things. At that point, of course, being journalists, our thoughts were turning to what kind of a president Lyndon Johnson was going to be. We're so coldhearted—we had to go on. I had to write the next day's story about what kind of president Johnson might make, even though I hadn't a clue, of course.

ROBERT PIERPOINT
CBS News

I caught a late plane back home to Washington that same night. I got in a little after midnight and was home by 1:00 A.M. I slept for maybe three or four hours and got up early. Our oldest daughter said, "It's pretty bad, Dad, isn't it?" I said, "Yes, it is, Kim." She said, "Then I guess that means we won't go down to Palm Beach this Christmas." The kids had been to Palm Beach two years in a row. I said, "No, I don't think so." She was probably about ten years old, and she knew enough to know it was tragic, but she didn't quite know yet the effect on everyone's lives, including ours.

HUGH SIDEY
White House correspondent,
Time

I went to the White House that night. There was something kind of wonderful about it. It was glowing. I remember standing there under those elm trees out front and being somewhat comforted, realizing that it had happened before and the old republic had gone on. It was a curious time in which the fragility of the system was apparent. I knew where Johnson's office was in the [Executive Office Building] and I could see the lights on and people scurrying in and out.

11:35 P.M. (CST)
ANDREWS AIR FORCE BASE

The plane carrying Secretary of State Dean Rusk and other Cabinet members lands at Andrews Air Force Base.

11:49 P.M. (CST)
DALLAS

ABC NEWS:
WALTER PORGES
*hear...
track 27

[We] just have word now from ABC affiliate WFAA in Dallas, Texas, that Lee Oswald has been charged with the murder of President John F. Kennedy.

EDDIE BARKER
news director,
KRLD-TV and Radio

Everything closed down. Dan Rather and I were doing something on into the evening. I hadn't eaten since breakfast. Neither had he. So we decided to go out. There was absolutely nothing open, so I called my wife and I said, "Do you mind getting up and fixing us a little supper?" And she did. We sat out on the floor in the living room rehashing the day. Hamburgers, big hamburgers. We may have had beer.

Secretary of State Dean Rusk, flanked by other members of President Kennedy's Cabinet, speaks to the news media after returning to Washington, D.C. At far left is press secretary Pierre Salinger.

IKE PAPPAS
WNEW Radio

I had to get ready for more broadcasts, so I went to the local independent radio station, which let me use their newsroom. I ground out pieces for the [morning] broadcast. At 2:00 A.M. the bell rings at the door. I'm still up from the dentist that morning, running on adrenaline. The station was playing funeral music, somber music. [The engineer] comes down and opens the door and in walks Jack Ruby! I think, "There's that weird guy again." He says, "Hi, fellas." He's got two bags of groceries in his hands. He says, "I saw your lights on and figured you might need some sandwiches." He was a police buff, a fire buff—a certain type who likes the excitement of hanging around police stations. I was very tired and I checked into a fleabag motel and fell asleep in the same clothes I left New York in.

ROBERT DONOVAN
Washington bureau chief,
Los Angeles Times

We worked for hours and hours. I didn't get back to the hotel until 2:00 A.M. The anguish of the thing really started to sink into me, that Jack Kennedy was dead. I hadn't eaten breakfast since that preceding morning in Fort Worth. We were able to send out for food and this old [black] waiter in a young bellboy's outfit, gray haired, old looking, we told him we were a bunch of newspapermen who'd been working for hours, we were dying, we gave him some money, couldn't he get us a jug? You couldn't buy liquor in Dallas. He said, "No, you couldn't do that because that would be breaking the law." Then he said in a voice I will never forget until my deathbed—he said, "There've been enough laws broken in Dallas today."

VIVIAN CASTLEBERRY
women's editor,
Dallas Times Herald

It was sometime after two o'clock in the morning before I pulled my car into our suburban driveway. My mother was waiting up for me. She said that [my daughter] had been greatly upset by the events of the day and that I must go and talk with her. I found her asleep, her face still swollen from sobbing. That night, as I had done in other critical times in our lives, I woke my sleeping child and our arms reached for each other.

I finally got to bed, and I may have been asleep for about an hour when I was suddenly jarred awake and said, "I do not have a story on the new first lady." I got up and put on my clothes and drove to the paper, before daylight, on Saturday morning, and started researching.

NBC NEWS:
DAVID BRINKLEY

It is one of the ugliest days in American history.

Dallas police department's homicide report for the assassination of President John F. Kennedy.

FORM OP HB-405

POLICE DEPARTMENT

HOMICIDE REPORT

CITY OF DALLA

Last Name of Person Killed	First Name	Middle Name	Race	Sex	Age	Residence of Person Killed	Offense Serial No.
KENNEDY, John F (PRESIDENT OF U. S.)			W	m	47	Washington, D. C. (White House)	F-859

Reported By — Title or Relationship — Race Sex Age — Address of Person Reporting — Phone of Person Reporting

Offense as Reported (Crime)
MURDER

After Investigation Changed to

Place of Occurrence — Street and Number or Intersection	Division	Platoon	Beat	Officers Making Report	I.D. No.	Name	I.D. No.
Elm St. (approx. 150' W of Houston)	H&R)	2	101	CN Dhority	476	HH Blessing 698	

Day of Week	Date of Occurrence	Time of Day	Date Reported	Time Reported	Report Received By	Received—Time—Typed
Fri	11/22/63	12:30PM	11/23/63	5:10PM	Mayo	5:10PM

DESCRIPTION OF DEAD PERSON

Age	Height	Weight	Eyes	Hair	Beard	Complexion	Identifying Marks, Scars, Etc.	Clothing

Coroner Notified
Joe B. Brown

Name of Coroner Attending—Time of Arrival   A.M. P.M.

Name of Prosecutor Attending—Time of Arrival

Pronounced Dead by Physician   Address   Person With Whom Accused Lived or Associated
Dr. Kemp Clark, 1PM, Parkland Hospital

DETAILS OF OFFENSE (Give Circumstances of Occurrence of Offense and Its Investigation) Use Both Sides of This Sheet.

The expired was riding in motorcade with wife and Governor John Connally, and his wife. Witness heard gun shot and saw the expired slump forward. More shots were heard and the expired fell in his wife's lap. Governor Connally was also shot at this time. Car in which they were riding was escorted to Parkland Hospital by Dallas Police Officers.

Witness Taken Into Custody   Address   Witness Taken Into Custody   Address
All witnesses affidavits are in Homicide Office.

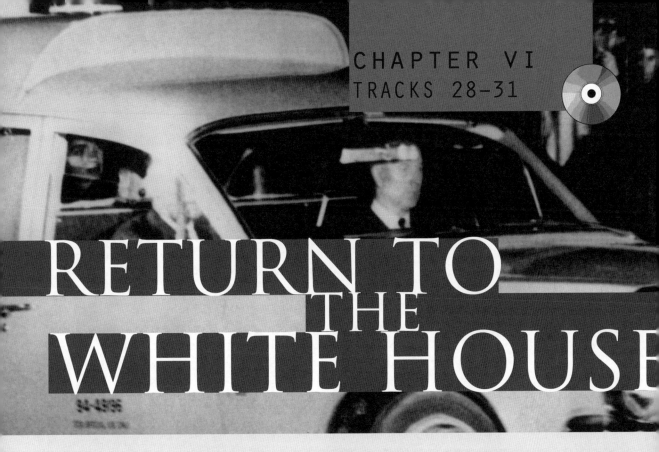

RETURN TO THE WHITE HOUSE

NOVEMBER 23–24   4:34 AM – 2:00 AM (EST)

BEFORE DAWN, AN ambulance delivers John F. Kennedy's casket to the White House. The body lies in state in a flag-draped coffin in the East Room on a catafalque similar to that used for President Lincoln. A military guard stands vigil in the room, and two priests are there as well. Kennedy family members and others come for private mourning.

In Dallas, Lee Harvey Oswald continues to deny that he shot the president, even though tests confirm that his fingerprints are on the rifle, paraffin tests for gunpowder on his hands are positive, and his handwriting has been linked to the purchase of the rifle from a mail-order house. Details about Oswald's life become known. He had traveled to Moscow a few years earlier and unsuccessfully tried to renounce his American citizenship, before returning to the United States with a Russian wife.

Millions of Americans stay in front of their television sets on a day when little happens except mass mourning. President Johnson meets with the secretary of state, secretary of defense, former Presidents Eisenhower and Truman, the Cabinet, and congressional leaders. One of the president's first official acts is to declare Monday a national day of mourning. John F. Kennedy's burial is planned for Arlington National Cemetery.

The ambulance carrying Kennedy's casket arrives at the White House and the casket is taken inside.

PIERRE SALINGER
White House press secretary

A black hearse drove through the northwest gate and past the squad of Marines standing at attention. Another honor guard stood at attention inside the North Portico of the White House and lined the corridors to the East Room. The casket of President Kennedy was carried by a group of men representing all of our military services. Following the casket came Mrs. Kennedy, Attorney General Robert F. Kennedy, other members of the family, and some of the president's closest associates—Ken O'Donnell, Larry O'Brien, and Arthur Schlesinger Jr. The casket was placed on a black-draped catafalque in the center of the room while four

A Marine Corps honor guard escorts the ambulance arriving at the White House with President Kennedy's casket.

guards took their places at the corners. Mrs. Kennedy walked forward slowly and knelt by the casket in silent prayer. She then leaned forward and kissed the casket and slowly walked out of the door of the East Room. Our chief was home.

SID DAVIS
White House correspondent,
Westinghouse Broadcasting
Company

track 28

It was a clear, very cold night. They had placed a string of these little oval-shaped kerosene lanterns they use on construction jobs on both sides of the driveway, so when the hearse came in, it drove through a row of flickering lanterns. It was an eerie scene. It was very funereal. There was black crepe over the North Portico and there were people outside the gates. I was amazed at the number of people who stayed up through the night waiting for the casket to come back to the White House.

I did something that broadcasters ought never to do. If you think you're going to break up, if you think something bad is going to happen to yourself and you're not going to get through it, you don't attempt it. I closed the broadcast with part of a Robert Frost poem that Kennedy used to use when he campaigned. He was always late in the '60 campaign, we were behind time at almost every stop we made, and the poem "Stopping by Woods on a Snowy Evening" became a hallmark of the campaign. I tried to get through "The woods are lovely, dark and deep, I have promises to keep and miles to go before I sleep, and miles to go before I sleep," and I got about three words into this thing and I broke up, I mean badly; I couldn't finish. It was just a powerful evening culminated by this very sad thing, considering he'd left two days before, a vibrant, healthy, energetic president looking ahead to the next election, and he came back in a casket.

7:00 A.M. (EST)

PIERRE SALINGER
White House

Finally, we went to sleep. [An hour later] the phone by my bed rang. I picked it up. The [White House] operator said, "Mr. Salinger, the president wants to talk to you." And for that instantaneous second, I thought to myself, it was all a dream, he wasn't really dead. Then a voice said, "Pierre, this is Lyndon Johnson. Pierre, I know how much President Kennedy meant to you, and I know how you must feel now. But I want you to stay on the job. I need you more than he ever did." I told him I would stay.

8:14 A.M. (EST)

NBC NEWS:
NANCY DICKERSON

The gates of the White House are closed now. Extreme security measures are being taken. President Johnson will go to the White House today to view the casket and pay his respects to Mrs. Kennedy.

A weary President Lyndon B. Johnson leaves his home on Saturday morning to go to the White House.

9:00 A.M. (EST)

ABC NEWS: President Lyndon Johnson arrived shortly after nine o'clock this morning, a few minutes ago, to begin his first full day as chief executive of the country.

CBS NEWS:
GEORGE HERMAN

President Johnson has already begun the kind of tight-packed and busy schedule which is going to be so very typical of his life from now on. At nine this morning, he arrived at the White House, and there are indications he went at once to the basement Situation Room, where, with the maps and charts and information constantly available there, he got his first intelligence briefing on the state of the nation and the state of the world.

9:00 A.M. (EST)
DALLAS

ABC NEWS:

There is new information just in from Dallas, Texas. Police Chief Jesse Curry says that Lee Harvey Oswald has readily admitted that he is a communist. Chief Curry says that he admitted to officers questioning him that he is a member of the Communist Party. Dallas police chief said apparently he was proud of being a communist. Said Chief Curry, he did not know if Oswald was a card-carrying member of the party.

BOB CLARK
Washington correspondent,
ABC News

Chief Curry came by two to three times to talk with reporters in the hallway. He was very responsive to questions about the case. And I finally put this to him, "Chief, do you have any concern for the safety of your prisoner in view of the high feeling among the people of Dallas over the assassination of the president?" He answered, quote, No. Precautions, the necessary precautions, will be taken, of course. But I don't think the people will try to take the prisoner away from us. Unquote.

A manacled Lee Harvey Oswald is led from the office of police captain Will Fritz by Dallas officer Elmer Boyd.

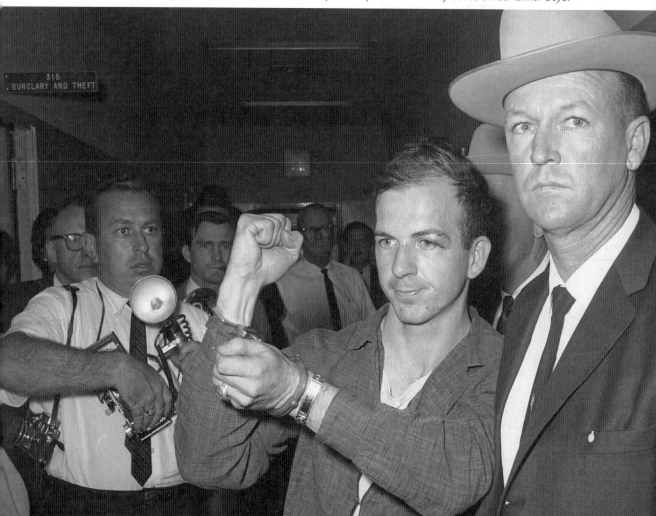

RICHARD STOLLEY

Los Angeles regional editor,
Life

[Abraham Zapruder] owned a garment factory only about a block and a half from Dealey Plaza. He said come at nine, I got there at eight. He looked slightly annoyed, but he let me in. And he said, "I'm about to show the film to two Secret Service agents," who hadn't seen it, and he said, "I guess you can come in and see it with them." We went into a little windowless room, no screen, he just projected it on the white wall. Eight-millimeter film, which is what it was, is about that big—*tiny*. You filmed it one side and then the other side, is how it worked with those eight-millimeter home-movie cameras. He had a projector, creaky projector, noisy, because there was no sound, of course. And he proceeded to show this few seconds of film to these two Secret Service agents who were about to see something pretty devastating, what is filmed evidence of their inability to perform their most important job, which is to protect the president.

It's become so familiar now, but seeing that for the first time is astonishing. You see the motorcade kind of snake around off Elm Street and then come around, and then turn again down toward Dealey Plaza. The limousine disappears behind a big road sign, and when it emerges, the president has both fists at his throat. He has been shot. [Texas Governor John] Connally was sitting on a jump seat in front of him, his mouth is starting to open wider and wider in this howl of pain, because the bullet that went through Kennedy then entered and badly wounded Connally.

You just kind of watch, transfixed, second after second. Connally finally goes down, falls off, and Nellie, his wife, is kind of cradling him as he goes down. The president is there with those hands, they're not clutching his neck, literally *fists* up there against his neck. And then suddenly we come to the famous, infamous, frame 313, and just, with no warning whatsoever, the whole right side of his head dissolves into this great mist of blood and bone, going forward, which shows there's no way the bullet could have come from *anywhere* but behind. He is sort of forward when that happens, and his body slams back against the seat, which you can see. Which gave rise to a lot of questions, including, "The bullet must have come from the front because it slammed him back." Physiologists say so much of the brain was destroyed that with some great galvanic response it just slammed, his muscles contracted, and he went back against the seat. Standing there with these two [Secret Service] agents, when it came to the head shot, everybody just went, "Ugh!" It was probably the most dramatic moment in my entire career in journalism, seeing the president murdered there, particularly being with two agents who were seeing it also. It really was a sickening visceral reaction.

And then he began falling over onto Jackie, who's looking around. She had been looking around kind of puzzled about why he was doing *this*. You have to understand, all this is six seconds, this all took place quickly. And she looks over there, and of course blood and brain matter is spilling on that famous pink suit of hers. And she watches this for a second or two, and then she turns around, puts her knees on the seat, and then climbs up on the trunk of the car, and you see her crawling along the trunk. Clearly, there are all kinds of interpretations, looking for help was the most charitable reason, I think. She wanted to get the hell out of there, as any other human being would have, because her husband's brains were in her lap. Connally was down there moaning, and God knows what was coming next.

The car behind the presidential limousine used to be called the Queen Mary. It's a great big open limo with wide running boards, and Secret Service agents stand on the boards and that's how they peruse. You could see all the guys looking backward, because that's where the shots were coming from. But Clint Hill saw what was happening to Mrs. Kennedy, jumped off the Queen Mary—cars are going probably five or six miles an hour at this point—and he sprinted ahead and jumped onto the bumper of the limousine and hauled himself up onto the trunk and pushed Mrs. Kennedy back into the seat. And about that point, the driver and the agent in the front of the limousine realized what was happening, looked around, and accelerated, and Clint just barely had gotten her in before it accelerated. He hung on and he managed to crawl into the back seat, and it went through the underpass to the hospital, Parkland Hospital.

9:00 A.M. (EST)

CBS NEWS:
WALTER CRONKITE

Meanwhile, these late reports—some people who had been spared for many hours the news of the death of the president have now been told. The ailing, seventy-five-year-old father of President Kennedy, Mr. Joseph P. Kennedy, has been told at his Hyannis Port home that his beloved son, the president of the United States, is dead. And Mrs. Rose Kennedy, the president's mother; his youngest brother, Senator Edward Kennedy; and his sister, Mrs. Eunice Shriver, were present when the president's father was told. Also standing attendance was a neurologist who stood by in case he was needed. There is no information at all as to whether or not the president's children have been told of the death of their father. Caroline, who was to celebrate her sixth birthday next week, and her young brother John, who was to celebrate his third birthday next week, were taken from the White House yesterday afternoon to an undisclosed destination.

10:49 A.M. (EST)
THE WHITE HOUSE

ABC NEWS:
EDWARD P. MORGAN

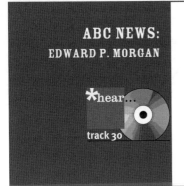

*hear...
track 30

Mrs. Kennedy took the two children—Caroline, who will be six next Wednesday, and John Jr., who will be three next Monday—into the East Room at 10:40 this morning. Mrs. Kennedy was heavily veiled, but she was composed. The two children were tearless, but they clung to her. They stayed in the room alone except for the priests and the honor guard for about ten or fifteen minutes until the rest of the Kennedy family came in.

People follow the news broadcast through the street-level window at the ABC News bureau in Washington D.C.

10:49 A.M. (EST)
DALLAS

NBC NEWS:
FRANK MCGEE

Oswald still insists he did not kill the president. The paraffin tests proved positive—Oswald did fire a gun during the last twenty-four hours.

10:49 A.M. (EST)
THE WHITE HOUSE

CBS NEWS:
GEORGE HERMAN

The members of the president's Cabinet, the members of the executive branch, holding presidential appointments, and close personal friends of the president are scheduled to arrive between 11:00 A.M. and 2:00 P.M. Associate justices of the Supreme Court are scheduled to arrive from two o'clock to 2:30 P.M. and also all the members of the federal judiciary who care to come. From two-thirty to five o'clock, the schedule calls for the members of the United States Senate, the House of Representatives, and the governors of the fifty states and territories, and the members of the diplomatic corps then between five and six o'clock.

BEN BRADLEE
Washington bureau chief,
Newsweek

We went back to the White House Saturday morning and there was some little memorial service. Oh, that "Navy Hymn." I can't hear it to this minute without just collapsing.

BARRY SCHWEID
writer,
Associated Press

On Saturday, Lyndon Johnson, at the outset, tried to do so many things quickly. He made a tremendous effort to cover all bases, be the president and relieve anxieties. We got a phone call about something that Johnson was going to do. He was going to visit Felix Frankfurter, the retired Supreme Court justice who was dying, seriously ill, at his mansion.

President John F. Kennedy lies in state in the East Room of the White House. Two priests kneel in prayer at left.

Could somebody go over and cover that? So they told me to run over to the house. It seems amazing now that Johnson found time on his first day as president to pay his respects to a retired Supreme Court justice. It was a different era, but the president had just been killed.

I go to the front of the building. All of a sudden, Johnson appears with some aides. He goes to the house. I walk in with him. No [Secret Service] agent, no nothing. Nobody knows me. I walk in with the president of the United States—alone. It seems like such an incredible story today. But there he was—I even remember his wearing an FDR kind of fedora. The building has this old-fashioned cage elevator. This cage was open, large, and had mirrors but very narrow, vertical top-to-bottom mirrors. Johnson looks at me a little bit quizzically. Then he takes a pocket comb out and begins to elaborately comb his hair, looking into the mirror. We go up to the residence, the elevator stops. He gets off. I get off. They open the door. By now I am so embarrassed, so nervous. I wanted to be thrown out. The maid made it clear that I could leave now. Johnson went in. I went downstairs and went back to the office. An editor said, "What the hell are you doing here?" He said, "You are supposed to stay with the president."

11:36 A.M. (EST)
DALLAS POLICE DEPARTMENT

Police take Lee Harvey Oswald from the elevator to the homicide bureau, and reporters rush to question the suspect.

JACK BEERS
photographer,
Dallas Morning News

The detectives led Oswald out and down the narrow passageway that uniformed officers managed to keep open. This is when I met the president's accused slayer head-on. I stepped out quickly raising my camera and we were looking right into each other's eyes. His defiant attitude was plain to see as I made his picture. As I stepped back, he came past me and looked first at my camera, then up into my face with a rather quizzical expression, and then his gaze darted to the man next to me. He had found what he was looking for—a microphone. He leaned toward Tom Pettit, a TV newsman who was holding the microphone, and said, "I want to get in touch with John Abt in New York." Pettit hollered, "Who?" and Oswald replied with the name and said he was a lawyer, then disappeared into the elevator room.

BOB HUFFAKER
reporter,
KRLD-TV

Every one of our television stations had received bomb threats by telephone. On Saturday, [CBS reporter] Nelson Benton and I were sitting on the floor on the third floor of police headquarters, leaning against the wall. Right in front of us were these elevator doors, several sets opening and closing. There had been so many bomb threats that one of us said, "What if somebody stepped out of those elevators and began to spray the crowd with automatic weapons?" We got up and moved. From that point on, we were aware there was the possibility of danger.

IKE PAPPAS
reporter,
WNEW Radio

It was chaos on the third floor of the Dallas police office. We were asked to stand behind a white-roped off area. They did not issue special press passes—anyone with a press pass was OK. I was stunned and amazed that we were permitted so close to the prisoner. Occasionally, out would walk Oswald and they'd escort him past us and we'd yell questions at him. You give reporters an inch and they're going to roll for a mile and a half. Later they brought in the rifle—a guy comes in with the thing, holding it over his head, saying, "This is the weapon."

11:36 A.M. (EST)
DALLAS

Though details are unclear, Abraham Zapruder apparently sells print rights to his film to *Life* magazine Saturday morning, and sells additional rights on Monday.

RICHARD STOLLEY
Life

While we were in there talking to Zapruder, other reporters were starting to come into the place. So I walked out and everybody looked at me, like, "Oh, God, *Life* magazine." So what I did is distance myself as far as possible from these guys. I didn't want to stick around. I didn't want to hang out with them. I didn't want to see the film when he was showing it to them. I actually walked into his office and discovered that this wonderful secretary was from downstate Illinois, which I am too, so we bonded about high school basketball and things like that, and later that became very important.

So then we all gathered out in the hall, and people said, "We want to talk to you, Mr. Zapruder, about this film." And he said, "Mr. Stolley here was the first one to contact me, so I'm going to talk to him first." And the others went berserk, just began screeching, shouting at him, said, "*Promise* you won't sign anything, you've *got* to promise you won't sign anything, Mr. Zapruder!" And he said, "I promise, I promise," and I thought, "In a pig's ass." We went into his office, and I thought, "There's no way in the world I'm going to walk out of this office without that film in my hand."

[Zapruder] was a very genial man. He'd been born in Russia and he came and he worked in the garment industry and then by the time when so many of those plants were moving south for cheaper labor, he went down to Dallas and set up this Jennifer [Juniors, Inc.]. I actually started by saying, "Mr. Zapruder, *Life* magazine has page rates for photographs, but when an interesting photograph comes along, sometimes we will pay more than space rates. That film that you have there, for instance, we might pay up to $5,000 for that." He looked at me and smiled, so that meant that he knew and I knew that he knew, so we could get real after that.

So we talked for a while, then I would throw in a new figure. He made very clear that he was doing this [because] the garment business was touch and go, so he wanted to secure the financial future of his family insofar as he could, but he also said that it was *very* important to him that the film *not* be exploited. He said that he had had a nightmare the night before, and he'd been passing through Times Square and there was a sleazy-looking guy standing out in front of a sleazy theater—this was pre-Disney Forty-second Street—saying, "Hey folks, come on in and see the president killed on the big screen." And he was visibly shaken by that dream and quite insistent that nothing like that happen. I said, "This is *Life* magazine, you know the reputation of *Life*, and I can guarantee you"—although there was no way in the world I could guarantee this, I was speaking for the New York editors, but I knew the reputation of the magazine—and I said, "We will be extremely careful with the use we make of this film," as indeed we turned out to be. So we were going up, and I'd go up $5,000, $10,000, and we'd chat. I finally got to $50,000.

I was authorized to go to $50,000, which was a hell of a lot of money back then. Now, what was happening while I was in there talking is that the reporters out in the hall were misbehaving badly. They were banging on the door, shouting, "Mr. Zapruder, you promised to talk to us!" And some of them were going out to a phone on the street and calling the office, and Mr. Zapruder was obviously getting more and more nervous and upset about this. And just about the time I reached $50,000, somebody kicked the door, I mean, something totally gratuitous like that. I said, "Mr. Zapruder, I'm being honest with you, this is as high as I'm authorized to go. If we're going to go beyond this, I'm going to have to call

New York." And then, "Bang!" And he looked at me and said, "Let's do it."

I went over to his typewriter in his office and typed out about a six-line contract, which we both signed, and he gave me the original and one copy of the film. And I said, "Do you have a back door to this place?" because I sure as hell didn't want to walk out. He showed me the back door, and I got the hell out of there, and poor Mr. Z then had to walk out into that hall, and [the reporters] were not nice to him.

11:36 A.M. (EST)
THE WHITE HOUSE

NANCY DICKERSON
correspondent,
NBC News

I spent Saturday standing in the rain across from the White House, trying to say something meaningful. JFK's famous rocking chair was carted across the street into storage, and I told a camera crew to get the picture. Friends and mourners started to arrive and I spent much of the day identifying men and women who had known JFK all their lives, their faces riveted with pain. Members of the Senate and House came, both those who supported him and those who did not, united by the tragedy of death.

GARY HAYNES
Atlanta bureau manager,
UPI News Pictures

On the airplane [from Atlanta], I was focused on what kind of picture you could get when the protagonist wasn't there—I was looking for symbolism. I had been in the Oval Office periodically and I knew the youngest [elected] president in history had a symbol of old age in his office—two rocking chairs. I thought, "If I can get the symbolic picture of the empty office and put the chair in the foreground, that would be a great photograph." When I got there, I immediately started figuring out how to get in there, and a porter said, "Hey pal, that stuff is gone. We're making room for the new guy and we're moving it across the street." I asked about the chairs and he said they were down in the hallway. I looked on the side, and there was the president's furniture. I asked him if he would give me a high sign when they got moved out, and he did. Instead of trying to attract attention, I left my cameras

NBC's Nancy Dickerson and Ray Scherer report in a light rain outside the White House the day after the president's assassination.

on the lawn near the front door and took only one camera and walked around casually in the rain to the other side.

The porter came out and gave me the high sign, and I followed him across the street and took the photograph of the chair, which was an exclusive. One of my UPI colleagues who worked in Washington was, for reasons never clear to me, screaming and carrying on, trying to alert [another UPI photographer]. In the process, he tipped off Eddie Adams, who worked for AP. He came running down the hallway and shot the picture of the chair in the front of the elevator—I could have killed him. The *Washington Post* ran my picture a full page.

1:52 P.M. (EST)

NBC NEWS:
FRANK MCGEE

It is raining in Washington, D.C.... So much history is taking place in so short a time.

1:52 P.M. (EST)
DALLAS

RICHARD STOLLEY
Life

Because *Life* normally closed on a Saturday night, the whole small editorial staff had flown to Chicago where the magazine was printed, which we occasionally did if there was a really late-breaking story. We got somebody from the Dallas bureau to fly the film to Chicago. Although it was in color, they ran a spread in that first issue, the memorial issue, in black and white. They omitted frame 313 in that first one, the grisly head shot picture, out of consideration for the family.

WES WISE
sports director,
KRLD-TV

I was assigned to come down and try to retrace the steps of Lee Harvey Oswald. I was sitting [near the Texas School Book Depository] in my KRLD station wagon when a man in a suit came over to the window and said, "Wasn't this a terrible thing?" It was Jack Ruby. You've got to remember that Jack Ruby knew every newsman in town. He made it a point to know every newsman in town. He was at every boxing match. He was at every fire. He was a real fixture. I was a witness at the Ruby trial. I testified that tears came to his eyes. He said, "Isn't this awful that Jackie is going to have to come back here and be a witness at a murder trial?" I said, "Jack, I don't think that will ever happen." Just in general conversation, I said, "You know, there is something that is really sad out there at the Trade Mart. They had two Western saddles for Caroline and John-John." I said I felt so sad that they would never see those saddles.

Two rocking chairs, favorites of President Kennedy, are removed from his White House office.

RICHARD STOLLEY
Life

Saturday afternoon I was back in the Adolphus Hotel. I get a phone call from [*Life* correspondent Tommy Thompson], who said, "I've got an exclusive with the family. I found the family; I've got them here. We've got to protect the story," which is to say we've got to get these people away from other reporters, because we both had been the first reporters to see these people. I said, "Bring them into the hotel." So I booked another room under a fictitious name. It was [Oswald's wife] Marina, with the little baby; crazy Marguerite, Lee's mother, with [Oswald's] other daughter, who was older; and Patricia McMillan, who was the interpreter. Marina at that point could speak almost no English. Bob, Lee's brother, also came with them. I gave him $40 for baby food and diapers for these two small children.

We put them up in this suite, told them to order anything they wanted to from room service, but for God's sake don't leave. When he came back with them, Tommy said, "I've got Oswald's trunk, and the family will give it to me for $10,000. They've got to have that money to hire a lawyer." I said, "What's in it, Tommy?" "Hell, I don't know," he said, "all his relics and artifacts from his Marine Corps and time in Russia." I said, "God almighty." So I called New York and I got the managing editor, an Iwo Jima Marine, named George Hunt. I told him what I had, and he said, "Absolutely not." I couldn't believe it. I said, "What?" He said, "You heard me. I'm not giving one f——g *dime* to that assassin." I said, "George, he is a *suspect* now, that's all he is, we don't know anything more." "I don't give a goddamn. I don't want you to give a dime to them." I started to argue with him and he hung up on me. So that's why we didn't pay the family. I mean, we paid for the food and the suite and all the rest, but we gave them no money at all.

HUGH AYNESWORTH
science/aviation/space editor,
Dallas Morning News

By Saturday, every newsman within three thousand miles was here, and many from farther than that. I remember they just stormed into the *[Dallas Morning] News* and sort of took over. I had one *New York Times* guy, I had to throw him out of my seat. He wouldn't give me my seat back and my own damn desk. And what was really horrible was, most of the media acted pretty nice, considering the verve and the excitement of the day and the pressures of competition, but some of them went into our library, and they stole all the clip files.

WES WISE
KRLD-TV

Everybody was on edge. There were some pretty hefty arguments up at the Press Club. We had a couple of fistfights between journalists. These were usually battles along political lines, Democrat versus Republican, conservative versus liberal. I was president of the Press Club and trying to keep peace.

RICHARD STOLLEY
Life

I got back to my suite. The phone rang. I picked it up, "Stolley, *Life*." This voice said, "OK, you sonofabitch, where are they?" I said, "Excuse me?" He said, "Don't pull that shit, you know what I'm talking about." And I said, "Sir? Who is this?" And he said, "This is agent so-and-so from the Secret Service. We know you've got the family and we want to know where they are." And I tried to play dumb again, and he finally said, "Look, we don't know what's going to happen to this family"—I mean, [the shooting] had caused tremendous emotion in Dallas—"and we want to make sure that that family is protected. We don't want to *not know* where they are. I'll make a deal: you tell me where they are, and I promise that I won't divulge that information to any other journalist." So I told him, and bless his heart, he kept his side of the bargain, too.

CBS NEWS:
WALTER CRONKITE

In the Dallas police station they're escorting out the mother and the wife of Lee Harvey Oswald, the man charged with the death of President Kennedy.

CBS NEWS:
NELSON BENTON

They are entering a door which leads to an elevator which goes up to the jail on the top floor of the building. The mother, the two children, the wife of Lee Oswald came out of the detective bureau, went into this door here on my left, and that door leads to an elevator which goes upstairs to the top floor of the Dallas Police Department building. The wife and the mother, who have been into and out of the detective bureau twice, have been quoted by the district attorney of Dallas County as saying they are trying to arrange counsel for Oswald. When they came out once before, the elder woman, his mother, would say only, "No comment." His wife would say only, "Go away."

JACK BEERS
Dallas Morning News

The next group I photographed were very much part of the story. It was Lee Harvey Oswald's wife, Marina, his two children, his mother, and brother. Marina had a very scared and lost look on her face, but the tension seemed to be broken when a detective took her to a private office where she could nurse the baby, and then he took the oldest child's bottle for a refill.

ABC NEWS:

*hear...

track 31

Now in Dallas, here is the voice of Police Captain Fritz of the Homicide Squad as he speaks to ABC's Paul Good.
Captain Will Fritz: I can tell you is that this case is cinched. This man killed the president. There's no question in my mind about it. I don't want to get into the basis. I don't want to get into the evidence. I just want to tell you that we are convinced beyond any doubt that he did the killing.

Marina Oswald, wife of Lee Harvey Oswald, is led into the office of Dallas police captain Will Fritz.

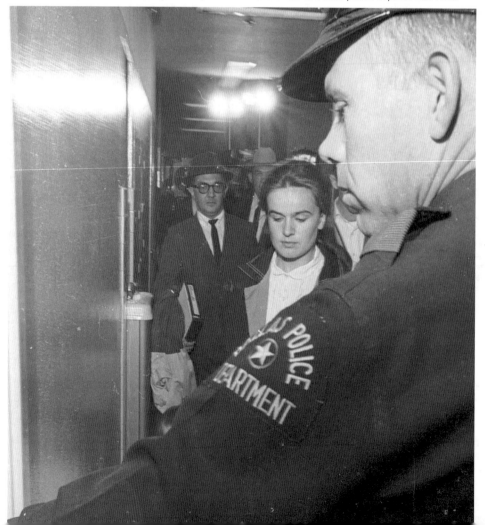

6:28 P.M. (EST)

6:28 P.M. (EST)
DALLAS POLICE DEPARTMENT

ABC NEWS: White House press secretary Pierre Salinger announced just a short time ago that the Kennedy family has decided that the assassinated President John F. Kennedy will be buried at Arlington National Cemetery. The interment will occur on Monday after a formal high requiem Mass.

DARWIN PAYNE
reporter,
Dallas Times Herald

Oswald was being interrogated that night. He was brought back and forth a couple of times into the homicide office. I could get a glimpse of him. I did not get to see his facial expressions because the mob was so great. When he would be brought out, everyone would rush to that area. Occasionally, the police chief, Jesse Curry, or homicide Captain Will Fritz would come out and make announcements. The press would rush to the scene. One reporter put his pad on the back of the police chief and took notes, using him as a brace. He was a pretty dignified individual. I remember a photographer got down on the floor and tried to take a shot up through the legs of the police chief.

Of course, it was all live on TV. You had live network television there. Every time a police officer would step out for an interview, the lights would go on this person. They would sort of wait until all the other cameras got in place, and then they would respond to the questions of the TV people, the network TV people primarily. The rest of us print reporters would stand just behind the TV people and take notes of what they were saying on TV. That was a first time as far as I'm concerned that the TV reporters took over on a major event. We had to rely on what they said on TV. Well everybody already saw it live on TV. What more could you do? You had to go for other angles, of course. Hometown reporters had a great advantage, though. We had a staff of thirty on the city side. We did cover a lot of details that the networks and the big newspapers didn't get.

ABC NEWS: The Soviet news agency, Tass, tonight accused the American police of trying to implicate the Communist Party in the assassination of President Kennedy and said the case against Lee Harvey Oswald is suspicious.

CBS NEWS:
WALTER CRONKITE

In Dallas, Texas, today there is another grief stricken family, not as well known, of course, as that family of President's Kennedy's, which is also racked by grief today, but their grief is as personal and as obviously deep to them. Mr. Tippit was the detective sergeant of the Dallas police force who was killed yesterday as he attempted to interrogate a man fleeing from the site of the shooting, a man the police say was Lee Harvey Oswald. We have some facts on Detective Tippit here. He was thirty-nine years old, he made $490 a month as a policeman. He had three children. They live in a neat suburban area of medium-priced brick homes on the southern edge of Dallas. The Tippits had no insurance. The police department in Dallas provides none.

6:28 P.M. (EST)
WASHINGTON, D.C.
THE ELMS, THE JOHNSON RESIDENCE

NANCY DICKERSON
NBC News

[The president asked my husband] and me to dinner, saying that he would send his car to pick us up. When we arrived at the Elms, we had to wait a long time to get by the guards. When we finally entered the house, the president had not yet arrived from the White House, Lady Bird was resting, and

Luci was in the living room barefoot in a green Chinese robe. I asked her how she would like living in the White House, and she said that she thought it would be awful: "How would you like to be sixteen years old and have Secret Service men chaperone you every minute of the day?" Even now, she said, she couldn't talk to any boy late at night because the phone light would go on in her parents' bedroom, and her father, seeing it, would either monitor the call or interrupt to tell her that she ought to be asleep. Then Lady Bird came down in a dressing gown and had a drink and some popcorn.

LBJ finally showed up.... It was the end of [his] first full day in office, and he carried on a running monologue throughout the evening. The television set was on, and he kept talking back to [Chet] Huntley and [David] Brinkley as they delivered the news. Right after the shots [in Dallas], LBJ had thought that the assassination might well be a conspiracy to take over the government, and he had ordered that House Speaker John McCormack be protected. Even at this point he was concerned about possible collaborators and about a conspiracy. He was going to keep the armed services on the alert for the moment because he still wasn't sure that the assassination was the work of one man and that there was no foreign involvement.

LBJ was also determined that there should be calm throughout the country, and whenever either Huntley or Brinkley said something that he thought might be inflammatory, he would talk back to the television set: "Keep talking like that and you'll bring on a revolution just as sure as I'm standing here."

LBJ was particularly concerned about the children involved. He said his first presidential letter had been to John and Caroline Kennedy.... As always, LBJ was obsessed with the telephones. He picked up the receiver, pushed a button and said, "Is this the White House? Sorry." Another button. "The White House? Oh, sorry." Then helplessly, "Bird," while unsuccessfully trying once more, and finally switching to commands, shouting, "Bird! Come over here and get me the White House."

Later we all trooped to the Johnson bedroom, where newspapers from all over were spread out on the bed and on tables, with the overflow on the floor. LBJ was fascinated by the headlines, and by the way newspapers were handling the story, and insisted on reading out loud and correcting the details of certain accounts.

Before [my husband] and I left the house, Lady Bird asked me what she should wear to the funeral, and I told her that she had no choice but to wear black. Since she didn't have anything in that color, I sent over some of my coats and dresses, then had Garfinckel's [department store] send her a couple of hats, and these were what she wore for most of the official mourning.

ABC NEWS: ABC News in Chicago has a late report on the rifle that is believed to have fired the shot that proved fatal to President Kennedy. [Here] is Frank Reynolds, ABC, in Chicago.

FRANK REYNOLDS The weapon used to kill President Kennedy was obtained from the Klein's Sporting Goods Company, a large retail and mail-order firm, located at 227 West Washington Street here in Chicago. According to Dallas police, the gun was purchased on March 20 by a person using the name of A. Hidell. Dallas police say the handwriting on the envelope used to order the gun matches the handwriting of Lee Harvey Oswald, the man in custody in Dallas charged with the murder of the president.

6:28 P.M. (EST)
DALLAS POLICE DEPARTMENT

CBS NEWS:
DAN RATHER Dallas Police Chief Jesse Curry came out just a few moments ago to tell us that unless there is something extra special, Dallas police are finished with their interrogation of Oswald for this evening. He indicated that Oswald would be transferred from the Dallas city jail, where he has been since his arrest yesterday afternoon, to the Dallas county jail—probably sometime tomorrow morning.

DARWIN PAYNE
Dallas Times Herald

As the evening drew on, the press kept pestering Chief Curry for information about when Oswald would be transferred the next day to the county jail. The city jail was a temporary holding facility. Once charges were filed, they would transfer the prisoner to the county jail. [Reporters] wanted to see Oswald and be able to ask questions of him when he was transferred. The pressure grew on the chief. Many of these reporters had been at the police station since Friday afternoon. They wanted to go get some rest. Chief Curry would not say anything. He didn't want to say when he was going to transfer him. Finally he did say, "Well, I'll tell you this. If you come here by ten o'clock tomorrow morning, nothing will have happened." So at that point the reporters took him at his word and by and large deserted the police station.

TERRANCE W. MCGARRY
reporter,
United Press International

Saturday night, we were going home. I was with [UPI reporter] Curt Gans and we were talking to [UPI manager Jack] Fallon. I said, "You know, there is this transfer tomorrow morning from the police station to the sheriff's jail. What if someone takes a shot at this guy Oswald?" Fallon said, "You guys go home and get some sleep."

Curt and I went to my apartment. As I recall, we drank an entire bottle of vodka, with orange juice. The more we talked about it, the more we were convinced that somebody would try to kill Oswald. We weren't thinking of the event in the way it happened. We were concerned about the Minutemen. They were similar to the militias. They were right-wing guys who had their own weapons. They thought they were going to have to form guerrilla bands against the Soviet occupiers or something. They were generally thought of as crazy and well armed. We also couldn't believe that anybody would be so stupid as to announce the real time [of the transfer] so we were sure the announced time was a phony time. We figured we would go several hours earlier. Then we went to sleep and set the alarm clock for five or six. And what had seemed such a brilliant idea after all the vodka the night before seemed like a really stupid idea when the alarm clock went off. Marlane, my wife, made me get up. She said, "If anyone shoots that guy and you knew ahead of time that it was going to happen, you will never forgive yourself."

DARWIN PAYNE
Dallas Times Herald

I got a call from the city desk. They had heard a report that police had in custody an eyewitness who could identify Oswald. I didn't know anything about that. Chief Curry had gone home. The police station was virtually deserted. I said I'd try to find out but I didn't have high hopes. I was panicking, considerably. We had an ace in the hole and that was to call the police chief at home. Gee, I hated to call him at home. Mrs. Curry answered the telephone, obviously sound asleep. You could tell she was just dead to the world. She got Chief Curry on the phone. He was obviously sound asleep. I could not make him comprehend what I was telling him, the question I had for him. He could not understand it. I believe [he]—and he probably should have—perhaps had taken sleeping pills or something. He could not wake up. He just sort of babbled as someone who was half-asleep. I finally had to give up and call the office and say, "I just don't have it." Of course, they did not have an eyewitness. It turned out to be not true.

Sheriff Bill Decker, who was a fabled lawman in Dallas County, called Chief Curry later on that night. An anonymous source had called the FBI, which called Decker saying death threats had been made on Oswald. Decker called Curry at home to tell him about that. He wanted to transfer him in the middle of the night, despite what Curry had told the reporters. As he told the Warren Commission later on, he could not reach the police chief because the telephone was out of order. So what had happened I feel certain is that after I called, the police chief took the telephone off [the hook]. If Decker had been terribly serious about it, I suppose he could have sent a car to his house. But the truth is he couldn't reach him on the telephone, I suspect, because I had called him at that hour. So I have often pondered about that.

EDDIE BARKER
news director,
KRLD-TV and Radio

Saturday night, I really kind of broke down. If you're working a story, you just don't think about yourself. You're trying to get the story. Saturday night late, it really hit me.

BILL RIVES
managing editor,
Dallas Morning News

Newspapermen may seem callous to some people because of their apparently calm decisiveness in covering tragedy. This is neither a fact nor a pose; it simply is an essential characteristic of persons in the business that they remain clear-headed. No one knew that I cracked up one night at home. I didn't know exactly why but I sobbed uncontrollably for hours. My wife sat up with me and did what she could to calm me down. Finally I managed to get about an hour's sleep. Then I dressed and went back to the office, where people thought that I— like other *News* staffers—was a nerveless human being who could become wrapped in a great tragedy without suffering any inner disturbance.

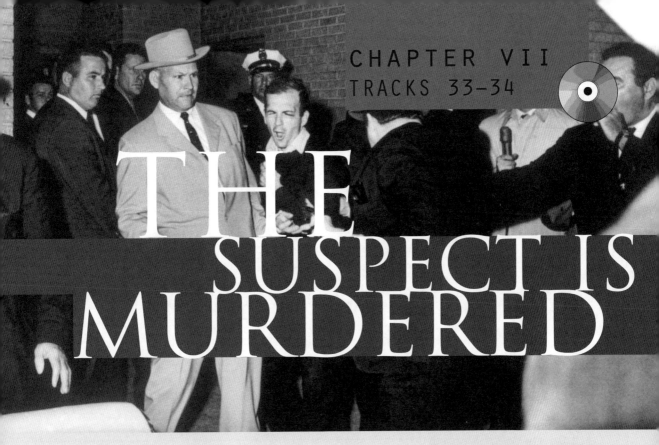

THE SUSPECT IS MURDERED

NOVEMBER 24   9:00 AM – 11:42 AM (CST)

DALLAS POLICE PLAN to transfer Lee Harvey Oswald from the city jail to the county jail on Sunday morning. A crowd of reporters gathers to cover the move, in the basement of the police building. As Oswald is being led out, a man suddenly lunges forward, points a pistol, and fires. Oswald grimaces and slumps as police wrestle the assailant to the floor. The shooting is broadcast live on network news to millions of American households. The gunman is identified as Jack Ruby, the owner of a Dallas nightclub.

CBS NEWS: **ROBERT PIERPOINT**	This is the day that John Fitzgerald Kennedy will leave the White House for the last time. His body has been lying in repose in the [East Room] of the White House. It'll be carried by caisson this afternoon up Pennsylvania Avenue to Capitol Hill and to the Rotunda where it will lie in state, and where people, great and small, from all over the world, can come during these next few hours to pay their last respects.

HUGH AYNESWORTH
science/aviation/space editor,
Dallas Morning News

I did expect some trouble because there were people that were *really* angry with [Oswald], because Dallas was already being berated and blamed, unfairly so in many instances. Oswald having been a man who defected to Russia was really something that in most people's minds meant something. So they'd say, "Somebody ought to kill that sonofabitch." When I woke up and saw that he had not been moved yet, I said to my wife, "I gotta go down there." She said, "I'm going with you," and she's three months pregnant with our first child. I didn't even shave, just went. Got down there and I saw all the people surrounding the City Hall and police department. We parked about two blocks away, and we tried to get in, and they stopped me three times. They wouldn't let her in at all.

ABC NEWS:

Additional news has come into us now. I would like to call in on the circuit Pierce Allman at WFAA in Dallas.

PIERCE ALLMAN

About four blocks from our studios a mob is beginning to gather just outside the county jail awaiting the transfer of Lee Harvey Oswald. At City Hall, police are beginning to worry and talk is now that he may be transferred the few blocks in an armored car. Just across the street is the spot where President Kennedy was killed and people are still bringing wreaths. But now there are a lot of grim faces and police are worried. They definitely don't want anything else to happen.

Reporters gather in the police department basement in anticipation of the transfer of Lee Harvey Oswald from the city jail to the county jail.

IKE PAPPAS
reporter,
WNEW Radio

It was going to be chaos. I said, "I think I'll go to the third floor and see if I can score an interview with Oswald on his way out." I was the only broadcast guy up there...the rest were [print]. Out comes Oswald a little late, surrounded by detectives. I went for my mike. "Do you have anything to say..." I got shoved up against the wall by a detective and I go crashing into the wall and they hustle him away.

HUGH AYNESWORTH
Dallas Morning News

The crowd got so bad. I remember one guy was searching on his hands and knees under one of the police cars that was parked there. I said, "What are you doing?" [He had] lost his teeth! Somebody hit him with his elbow and [he] lost his teeth!

TERRANCE W. MCGARRY
reporter,
United Press International

People all weekend had been yelling at Oswald, "Did you do it?" I was trying to think if I can get close to him and I can ask him a question—this is the kind of thing twenty-five-year-old reporters think about—I'll be a hero. If I can get close to him, what will I ask him? I thought yelling, "Did you do it?" was clearly unproductive. I remembered John Wilkes Booth, shooting Lincoln, he jumps to the stage in Ford's Theatre and by some accounts he yelled, "*Sic semper tyrannis!*" Thus ever to tyrants. I thought that's what motivates this guy. They want to be in the history books. They are little men who want to be big men. I figured I could jump the railing on the opposite ramp. That puts me behind him as he turns the corner. I can walk quickly up to him from behind. I figured I might have time enough to get in my "What do you think history will say of you?" question before some cop pushed me aside.

BOB HUFFAKER
reporter,
KRLD-TV

We were set up well in advance. Our plans were not to run the transfer [of Oswald] live. CBS was going to tape it in New York from our feed and run it later. They had other things on the air at the time. Channel 5, which was NBC, their van was broken and they had to tow it everywhere with a wrecker. [It was] a strange sort of van that looked like a bread truck. The NBC reporter was Tom Pettit. So it was Tom Pettit and me.... [CBS reporter Nelson Benton] and I decided he would sit in our van so he could see all of the monitors. He was going to narrate from there. They backed an armored car into the exit ramp and were unable to get it any farther down the ramp.

11:05 A.M. (CST)

NBC NEWS:
TOM PETTIT

We are standing in the basement corridor where Lee Oswald will pass through momentarily. Extraordinary security precautions have been taken for the prisoner.

As the time nears for the transfer, CBS television broadcasts a memorial service in Washington, D.C., and then an essay by Harry Reasoner. Dan Rather is in the studio of CBS affiliate KRLD-TV in Dallas, and CBS correspondent Nelson Benton is at the Dallas city jail along with KRLD-TV reporter Bob Huffaker.

DAN RATHER
New Orleans bureau chief,
CBS News

The agreement was that CBS coverage in New York would be thrown to us right on the eleven o'clock hour, or whatever time [Lee Harvey Oswald] was supposed to be moved. The plan was: go to the memorial service, come out, and Harry Reasoner would read the essay he had written, of which he was proud and rightly so. [CBS news executives] made a decision to go with the Reasoner essay before they came to us, and that was the problem.

Eleven o'clock came and went and [the network] was in [the middle of Reasoner's essay]. That's when the conversation got a bit heated. Nelson Benton—I give him credit—was just about apoplectic for fear that we wouldn't go live in time, and I reflected that to New York. We were alternately begging and demanding that they [switch to Dallas]. I remember that discussion well. "Let us have it" is the phrase I remember the most. Benton was literally shouting either, "Come to us," or "Take it," and then describing [Oswald and the detectives] being literally at the door. We told New York that, and they said, "Well, just hold on a minute," or "Hold on a second." We're saying, "Well, we're not in a position to hold anything. We can't hold this up. It's going [to happen]."

Lee Harvey Oswald is escorted from the city jail in Dallas for transport to the county jail. Moments later, he was shot and mortally wounded.

HUGH AYNESWORTH
Dallas Morning News

They had some threats that somebody was going to kill Oswald, so they decided to bring an armored car in. They got an armored car and backed it in the Commerce Street side, but in those days the armored cars had big turrets on top, so it could not back all the way down. They didn't want him to be exposed, to get him in to the armored car outside, so they decided to put a car behind the armored car, and they would take the armored car, with nobody in it, a very circuitous route to the county jail, where they had to be transferred. In the meantime, they would back a police car out on the Main Street side, with Oswald on the floorboard under a couple of cops' feet, and just take him straight down the eight to ten blocks, whatever it was. In backing that car out, that's when Ruby came from the Western Union, saw the crowd, walked up there, saw the cops. They saw him, but he walked right on in.

Jack Ruby (right foreground, in hat) watches as Lee Harvey Oswald is escorted from the Dallas city jail.

IKE PAPPAS
WNEW Radio

I used these New York City elbows pushing to get into position. I finally got to the point where I could see the door. I started talking into my mike. I didn't know at the time that I was pushing in right in front of Jack Ruby, who was waiting to shoot Lee Harvey Oswald. "Now the prisoner, wearing a black sweater, is being moved out toward an armored car, being led out by Captain Fritz. There's the prisoner—do you have anything to say in your defense?" I saw a black streak. Bang! There was a shot. I saw the flash on his sweater. I thought I was hit. At the moment of the firing and immediately afterwards, I thought there might be crossfire because the detectives had their guns out. I went down on one knee and then both knees and did that recording on my knees.

It was a crucial moment. I thought, what has happened? What am I seeing here? Is this really the assassin of the president of the United States himself being assassinated or was that a firecracker? I thought, if you never say anything ever again into a mike you must say it now.

WNEW RADIO:
IKE PAPPAS
hear...
track 33

There's a shot! Oswald has been shot! Oswald has been shot! A shot rang out. Mass confusion here. All the doors have been locked. A shot rang out as he was being led into his car.

NBC is the only television network to capture the scene live on the air when Oswald is shot.

Jack Beers of the Dallas Morning News *captured Jack Ruby lunging toward Oswald a fraction of a second before Ruby fired the fatal shot.*

NBC NEWS:
TOM PETTIT

*hear...
track 33

He's been shot! He's been shot! He's been shot! Lee Oswald has been shot! There's a man with a gun. There's absolute panic, absolute panic here in the basement of the Dallas police headquarters. Detectives have their guns drawn. Oswald has been shot. There's no question about it. Oswald has been shot. Pandemonium has broken loose here in the basement of the Dallas police headquarters.

DALLAS POLICE DEPARTMENT RADIO TRANSMISSION (CHANNEL 1):

DISPATCHER:
[Garbled] report to the Basement Code 3. [An emergency— use red lights and sirens.]
[A few moments of back-and-forth routine exchanges occur.]
UNIDENTIFIED SPEAKER:
What is the nature?
DISPATCHER:
It's a shooting.

11:21 A.M. (CST)
NEW YORK CITY

WALTER CRONKITE
anchor,
CBS Evening News

I was in the newsroom getting ready to go on the air a little bit later and had to watch the shooting on NBC. That was one of the bitter moments of coverage. We picked it up as fast as we could get on the air, which was a little time later.

11:21 A.M. (CST)
DALLAS POLICE DEPARTMENT

BOB HUFFAKER
KRLD-TV

Having played cops and robbers myself, I knew it was a .38. I had actually carried a Colt Cobra like the one that Ruby used. I had seen people who had been shot several times with

.38s and were not really seriously injured. When the shot was fired, I then of course turned my head and saw Oswald still standing, grimacing and beginning to fall. I couldn't make out anything much about the shooter because he was being mobbed by countless officers at the time. People were pointing guns at me and I was pointing a mike at them.

I was trying to be quiet so Nelson [Benton] could talk. Then I finally realized that Nelson couldn't have figured out with the melee of people. I had no communication with him at all.... It took me a little while to realize I should begin to talk.... For one thing, I knew we were on tape. NBC was live. [CBS] got me on immediately, live. I never had any communication. All I knew was to keep going and not stop.

CBS NEWS: **HARRY REASONER**	We are now switching to Dallas, where they are about to move Lee Oswald, and where there's a scuffle in the police station. Various voices:...has been shot...Lee Oswald...Oswald has been shot. [Many people shouting.]
CBS NEWS:	We are going to switch now to Bob Huffaker down in the basement of the courthouse, who is close to the scene. Go ahead, Bob.
BOB HUFFAKER	Lee Harold Oswald has been shot. We saw no—no one fire the shot, only a blast from some bullet here in the basement of Dallas police headquarters. Oswald fell to the concrete in front of our eyes, and immediately was covered by police officers who took him quickly, immediately, instantly from—from our sight.
BOB HUFFAKER *KRLD-TV*	I was the kid in the basement, saying Oswald has been shot. I was calling him Lee Harold Oswald. I got that direct from the police information officer.

Bob Jackson, a staff photographer for the *Dallas Times Herald*, captures the shooting in a picture that later wins a Pulitzer Prize and becomes one of the most famous photographs of all time. *Dallas Morning News* photographer Jack Beers shoots a dramatic photograph of the assailant, Jack Ruby, lunging toward Oswald, but he misses the moment of the bullet's impact by a fraction of a second.

BOB JACKSON
photographer,
Dallas Times Herald

My plan was to get a picture as soon as he stepped into an open spot and then try to get as many frames as I could as they walked up the ramp and put him in one of the vehicles. So finally they said, "Here he comes," and we could see him flanked by two police officers coming through the little crowd of people there. I had already prefocused on about a little over ten feet and I was looking through the camera. It was a pretty routine-type shot, and so it was very fortunate that I was looking through the camera when all this was unfolding. I was aware of somebody quickly stepping out from my right. It was very quick. And Ruby took maybe two steps or three and he fired, and I fired.

Bob Jackson of the Dallas Times Herald *snapped his camera shutter at exactly the moment the bullet struck Oswald.*

PEGGY SIMPSON
reporter,
Associated Press

I was fifteen feet away when Ruby came out of the crowd. I don't have a recollection of anything except sensing this movement to my right and then a shot being fired. It's hard to remember what you remember compared to the picture, which is still everywhere. I just was on automatic pilot and went straight ahead, past the body and the bedlam of cops jumping on Jack Ruby, and went out.... There was a phone there. I just picked it up and started dictating.

TERRANCE W. MCGARRY
UPI

[I was going to ask him] my "What do you think history will say of you?" question. As I was doing that, I heard a shot. I saw a guy leap out of the crowd. Short guy, little black over-coat. I couldn't see the gun.... I heard the shot. The whole crowd—Oswald, the guy who jumped out, a couple of the cops—they all went down in a pile on the floor. I ran up to the pile. Actually my secret strategy worked perfectly. I could run right up to them.... I looked down and a hand comes out of the pile with a gun. I was looking right down at the gun. I didn't even know whose gun it was. I didn't want to get shot so I backpedaled. For some reason I turned around and there was a cop who was guarding the entrance. He had his gun out and was tracking me with it. Although it sounds perfectly silly today, I looked at the guy and I said, "No, no, it's OK," like that should have made a difference.

UPI WIRE:

```
B U L L E T I N
    DALLAS (CQ)—LE (CQ) HARVEY OSWALD, ACCUSED
PRESIDENTIAL (CQ) ASSASSIN, WAS SHOT TODAY AS HE WAS
BEING TRANSFERRED TO ANOTHER (CQ) JAIL.
(MORE)
W1125ACS
U R G E N T
    POLICE HELD A SMALL ELDERLY MAN WITH A SMALL
CALIBER REVOLVER. THE SHOT RANG OUT IN THE BASEMENT
OF THE CITY HALL BUILDING AS OSWALD WAS BEING TAKEN
FROM THE POLICE BOOKING OFFICE TO TAKE A FEW STEPS TO
A CAR.
MORE
W1125 ACS
```

IKE PAPPAS
WNEW Radio

They dragged Oswald back inside and took whoever shot him away. A detective came out and was asked, "Who was it?" "That was Jack Ruby." Jack Ruby! I pulled out his card. He runs the Carousel Club. It was that same weird guy!

BERT SHIPP
assistant news director,
WFAA-TV

I left [reporter] Ron Ryland in charge of the [news] desk that morning. I told him, "Do this and this, and when you get everybody in place you can go down to the basement and shoot the transfer." [After Oswald was shot,] I rushed down to the station and [Ryland] was sitting there. He was an old Navy retiree. He says, "Chief, I got everything under control." I said, "Good, I'm glad you were down there in the basement when they transferred him." He said, "Chief, everything went well but I got one problem. I wasn't there." Well, I needed to go back to church after that. I painted the walls with words I didn't even know I knew. The network fouled up as bad as Ronald did. They had decided they wanted [film of] a church service in Fort Worth. We even sent our big truck over there.

PIERCE ALLMAN
manager of programming
and production,
WFAA-TV and Radio

I was in the control room that morning. I called ABC and said, "What do you want from Dallas?" They said, give us a church service. So on audio we were feeding that church service and on video we were feeding the coverage of the transfer. I had an eye on the monitor. The minute Ruby lunged forward, I grabbed the engineer. I said, "Flip it! Feed video! Feed the audio from the video!" At that time, it probably was one of the first instances where a national television audience witnessed a murder.

11:21 A.M. (CST)
THE WHITE HOUSE

ROBERT PIERPOINT
White House correspondent,
CBS News

We were on the front lawn of the White House and I was standing on a box with a view of the portico so we could show people coming in and out, personal friends and relatives of the Kennedys. I was talking as you try to do when you fill. All of a sudden I heard a commotion in my ears, commotion from the headquarters in New York over the fact they seemed to think Oswald had been shot. We had a reporter at the

scene who relayed the news. Then they went to me since I was live and asked, "Do you have any reaction from the White House?" I simply had no reaction except my own, which was once again shock.

11:27 A.M. (CST)
DALLAS POLICE DEPARTMENT

Oswald is taken by ambulance to Parkland Memorial Hospital.

DALLAS POLICE DEPARTMENT RADIO TRANSMISSION (CHANNEL 1):

OFFICER 18:
We will be Code 5 [en route] Parkland.
DISPATCHER:
10-4, 18.

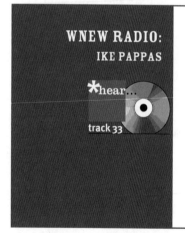

WNEW RADIO:
IKE PAPPAS

*hear...

track 33

Now the ambulance is being rushed in here. Here is the ambulance. Screaming red lights, people, policemen. The man rushed up, jammed a gun right into Oswald's stomach, and fired one shot.... That ambulance has arrived, they are rushing a mobile stretcher in. Oswald was carried back into the hallway.... Here is young Oswald now. He is being hustled in, he is lying flat. To me he appears dead. There is a gunshot wound in his lower abdomen. He is white...dangling, his head is dangling over the edge of the stretcher. And now the ambulance is moving out, flashing red lights.

TERRANCE W. MCGARRY
UPI

I could see Oswald was down. They pulled up his shirt. I could see the hole in his side. It was a neat, round, black hole. Ruby was close enough when he fired that the muzzle blast from the pistol cauterized the wound. There was no bleeding at all. There was just a perfect .38-caliber hole. As they were getting up off the floor, I heard cops say, "It's Jack! It's old Jack." I realized it sounds like the cops know the guy with the gun.

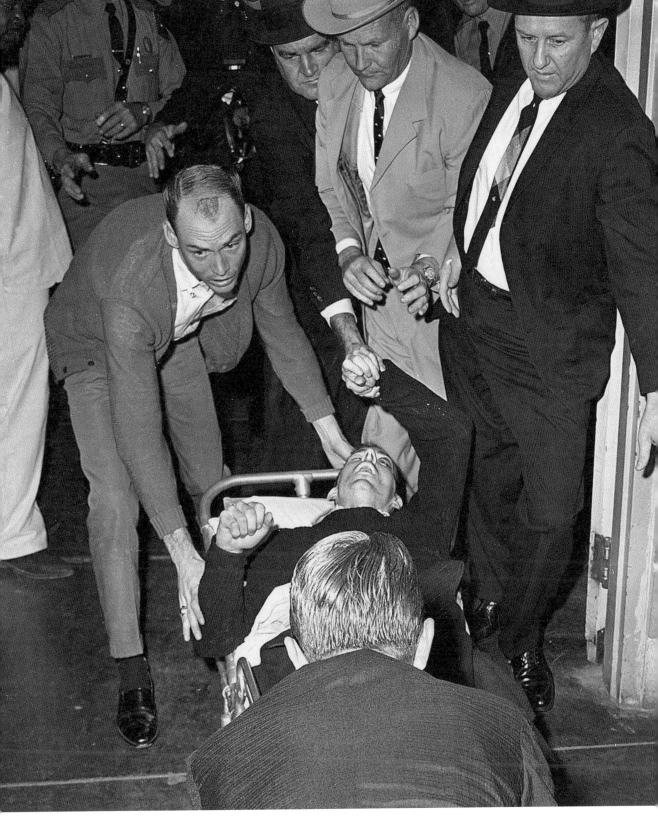

A mortally wounded Oswald on an ambulance stretcher.

My first reaction was that, in these circumstances, all cops, their instinct is to yell, "Lock the doors! Nobody move!" And my phone was on the other side of the swinging door. When I arrived [I had noticed] there were two phone booths. A guy from ABC Radio had staked out one of them. I got the other one. I got the UPI desk to call me back on that line so we tied up that line. I went through the door. Everybody else pretty much got sealed back on the other side.

I lucked out. They brought Oswald into the area where I was. It was great from a reportorial point of view. I think they put him on a stretcher right there. I got a better look at the wound. [UPI manager Jack] Fallon said, "Is this guy still alive or is he dead?" I said, "He's alive. His eyelids are fluttering. But this guy looks like he is really in serious condition. Staff the hospital." I was certainly no expert but he looked very pale. He was clearly barely conscious. His eyes were sort of rolled back. He wasn't saying anything.

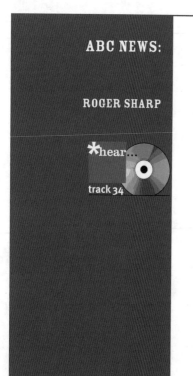

ABC NEWS:

ROGER SHARP

We are taking you to the county jail. Standing outside is Roger Sharp.

We're outside of the courthouse where a crowd of several hundred had gathered awaiting the arrival of Lee Harvey Oswald ten blocks away at City Hall, that arrival apparently stopped by a bullet. This crowd, when word flashed through the crowd that Oswald had been shot, broke out into a cheer. What's your reaction on hearing that Lee Harvey Oswald has been shot down?

Man: Well, I can't hardly say what right now, but I think people wanted a quick decision on his execution and get him put away. I think he should have been tried, but people sometimes take the law in their own hands on a thing like this.

Second man: I don't think anything can be too bad for him and maybe the trial wouldn't [have] done anything different—he would've been shot anyway.

Woman: Well, maybe the Lord wanted it this way. Maybe he didn't. Maybe this is the best thing for him, I guess. Maybe it's not, might be.

Second woman: I just feel like this is too good for him. I think he should have suffered more than what he suffered, and longer.

WES WISE
sports director,
KRLD-TV

I was stationed at the county jail for CBS. This was my big opportunity to get on the network. I was out in the middle of the street, and they had ropes because there were a lot of people there to watch his arrival. A blood-curdling thing happened. Sheriff Decker came out and said, "Lee Harvey Oswald has been taken by ambulance to the hospital. He's been shot." I said, "Sheriff, I think you ought to tell this crowd that." So he announced kind of loudly what had happened, and they applauded. There was such emotion against him that people applauded.

RICHARD STOLLEY
Los Angeles regional editor,
Life

[*Life* correspondent Tommy Thompson] and I went over to the county jail to wait, because we decided we wanted to see this guy. Suddenly we see a guy, a sound man for television, with earphones on, he said, "Jesus! Jesus!" I said, "What?" He pulls away and says, "Oswald's been shot in the basement of the city jail." We *ran* out of the county jail. The streets were clogged with cars. We banged on one door and the guy quickly locked it. Then there was a young guy with the window slightly open, and I threw a twenty-dollar bill in through the window and said, "We're reporters from *Life* magazine. Will you take us to the city jail? Oswald's just been shot." Well, fortunately, he thought that was an adventure, so we got in. Well, we got maybe three hundred or four hundred feet and got jammed up in traffic, so we jumped out of his car and ran back to the Adolphus Hotel, thinking, "What about our family?" And [we ran] into the Adolphus, up the elevator, down the hall. The door to their suite's wide open. The Secret Service, as soon as they heard Oswald was shot, they whisked in there and pulled them out, the whole family, out of that hotel.

11:27 A.M. (CST)
DALLAS

TRAVIS MAYO
amusements writer,
Dallas Morning News

My family had left church and just reached the car. Over the radio, we heard that Jack Ruby had shot Lee Harvey Oswald. As we drove from the parking lot, I yelled out the window to a man leaving the church, "Somebody just shot Lee Oswald!" "That's what the sonofabitch deserved," he replied.

11:42 A.M. (CST)

NBC NEWS:
FRANK MCGEE

The man has been identified as Jack Ruby, a nightclub owner in Dallas.

ABC NEWS:

Nick Robertson in Dallas, Texas, has some additional information.

NICK ROBERTSON

Oswald was brought down in the elevator to go out the basement door. Just as he stepped out of the elevator, Dallas nightclub owner Jack Ruby, who was dressed in a dark suit...pulled a small-caliber, snub-nose pistol, the caliber of which has not been completely identified, and fired at Oswald directly in the stomach from about six inches away. Oswald was hit; he was immediately dragged back into the elevator and taken upstairs. The man who shot him was taken into custody and also taken upstairs.... A few minutes later, an ambulance arrived, and he was taken [to] the ambulance covered by a blanket. At the time, his eyes were closed. It could not be determined by our reporter whether he was alive or not.

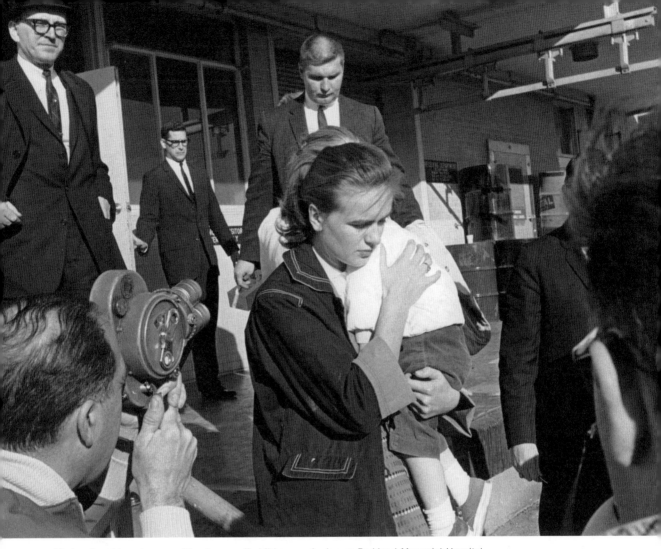

Marina Oswald carries one of her two small children as she leaves Parkland Memorial Hospital.

11:42 A.M. (CST)
NEW YORK CITY

OSBORN ELLIOTT
editor,
Newsweek

That Sunday morning I came back to the office just to look over everything and make sure we hadn't made some major goof, and I was pretty well satisfied with what we had done. *Newsweek*, in those days, was just a block away from St. Patrick's Cathedral. So I decided to stop in at St. Pat's on the way home, not for religious reasons, but out of curiosity to

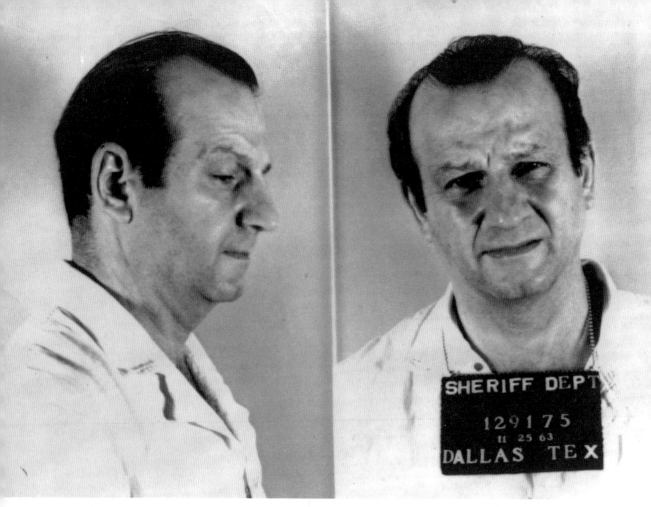

Jack Ruby is booked for the murder of Lee Harvey Oswald.

see if there was some priest up there talking about Kennedy, and sure enough there was. I stayed for a few minutes, then got in a cab, went home to Seventy-seventh Street, poured myself the stiffest hooker of scotch I've ever had, went upstairs to the little library, flicked on the television set, and "Bang-bang!"—Oswald was shot. So I threw on my hat and coat, got a cab, went back to the office, and of course we had to remake a major part of that story. I think we caught about two-thirds of the press run with the picture of Oswald being shot by Jack Ruby.

DARWIN PAYNE
reporter,
Dallas Times Herald

I went to [Ruby's] apartment. A lot of press people were there already. I started finding people who lived there and asked them questions about Ruby and got some information about how he would exercise in the pool, wear a bathing cap, about his dog, general information. I could not get into his apartment, because the police had sealed it off.

> **From Darwin Payne's notebook, 11/24/63:** Lowell Gaylor (a neighbor)—He was a regular old guy, the type of guy who would ask you to come down to his club. When we'd go down, everything would be free. He had two dachshunds, one named Sheba. He didn't interfere with anybody and nobody interfered with him. It shocked the heck out of me when I saw what he had done. He was a normal quiet guy. He was always sitting down and talking to everyone around the pool. He exercised a lot. He was concerned about his health because of his unusual and odd hours at the club. He was always telling me how he was going to get his hair to grow back. He even wore a ladies' bathing cap when he went in swimming. He took treatments for his hair too. He liked his dogs and was always afraid the owner or the manager would say something to him about getting rid of them. He'd talk to his dogs like they were kids. Jack Cole (who supplied acts for his club)—He is explosive. He has a tendency to be violent at times. He can be a close friend or a violent enemy. Physically he was a strong person. I knew he owned a pistol.

JACK FALLON
Southwest Division
news manager,
UPI

Jack Ruby had been in my office about five days before to buy photos from our [photo archive] of a stripper named Candy Barr. He owned a strip joint in Dallas. He was also a "Courthouse Charlie." He loved to hang around the media and the press.

WALTER CRONKITE
CBS News

I had a source in Dallas. My cousin, who was like a brother to me—we grew up together—was a vice president of the National Distillers out of Dallas for the southern area. As a whiskey salesman, he knew all the bars in Dallas. Even if he hadn't been a whiskey salesman, I suspect he would have known them. I called him right away and said the shooter, Jack Ruby, owned a bar. I said, "Do you know anything about Jack Ruby?" He said, "Oh, Jack Ruby, he's a nut. Why are you calling me?" It hadn't been on the air yet. I said, "He may have been the guy who killed Oswald." He said, "No kidding!" I said, "Well, tell me more about him." He said, "Well, he's kind of a nut. He's been around town a long time. He's owned several bars. He has always been a strange sort

NBC News' Tom Pettit (center) and Bob Huffaker of KRLD-TV in Dallas interview Dallas police sergeant Patrick Dean after Oswald was shot.

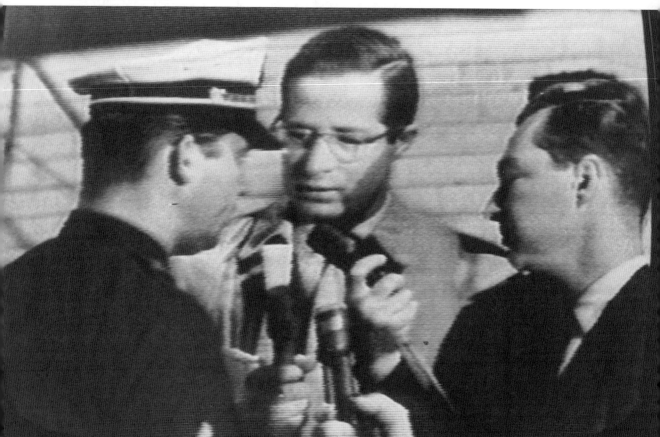

of character. I can't imagine why he would be shooting Oswald. He didn't strike me as the kind of patriot who would want to get rid of this assassin." He gave me a little word picture of what he thought Ruby was like. So we had a little inside story about Ruby. It turned out that Jack's version of him was pretty accurate.

11:42 A.M. (CST)
DALLAS TIMES HERALD

BOB JACKSON
Dallas Times Herald

As I got off the elevator and walked into the newsroom, everybody said, "Come over here to the wire machine," and there was Jack Beers' picture already on the wire. Jack Beers is the [Dallas] *Morning News* photographer. And somebody said, "Do you have anything like this?" and I said, "I'll let you know when I run my film."

CHARLIE DAMERON
assistant managing editor,
Dallas Times Herald

I said, "Jackson, what have you got? You got Oswald?" He said, "Yeah, I'm going to soup it out," but he was antsy. So he goes in and a little bit later I hear this war whoop, and he comes out with this film and he says, "I got it." So he got the epic picture of the half-century.

BOB JACKSON
Dallas Times Herald

I remember holding the wet film up to the light, and it looked sharp and good to me. I remember letting out a yell.

EDDIE BARKER
news director,
KRLD-TV and Radio

Bob Jackson at the *Times Herald* shot this Pulitzer picture, but he didn't know [at the time] what he had in the camera. [The *Morning News*] went with an early edition that had the picture that was shot just a second before his. The editor of the *Times Herald* called me and said, "God, we're in trouble. We don't have anything. Have you got some freeze frames we could use?" We gave them sixteen frames of film. About an hour later, [*Times Herald* managing editor] Felix McKnight calls back and says, "Barker, you can have your damn pictures back. We don't need that crappy film." Here they had this great Bob Jackson picture.

TERRANCE W. McGARRY
UPI

At one point, [UPI manager Jack] Fallon had said, "Well, describe this guy." I only got the briefest look at him. He said, "Tall, short, fat, skinny?" I said, "Short, pretty short." Fallon said, "Young, old, middle-aged?" I remember when Ruby's hat came off, he was bald in back. I was twenty-five. I said old. He looks pretty old. Fallon wrote something like, a small elderly man leaps from the crowd. We got a complaining letter from some client several days later. [UPI executive] Bill Payette, God bless him, showed me the reply he wrote back. "Dear Sir," he said, "The reporter covering this event is six feet tall and twenty-five years old. From his vantage point, Mr. Ruby was small and elderly."

Journalists, including Bert Shipp of WFAA-TV (holding microphone) gather in the office of Dallas County Sheriff Bill Decker, seated.

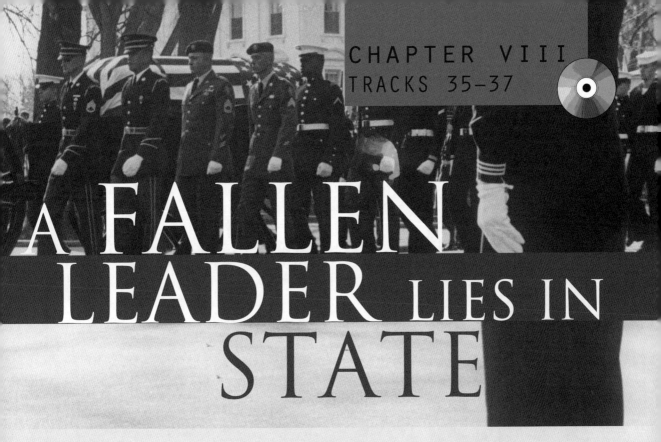

A FALLEN LEADER LIES IN STATE

NOVEMBER 24–25   12:00 PM – 1:03 AM (CST)

SHORTLY AFTER OSWALD is shot in Dallas, John F. Kennedy's casket is removed from the White House and escorted in a cortege to the Capitol, where the slain president will lie in state overnight in the Rotunda. Speakers eulogize the president, and Mrs. Kennedy and her daughter, Caroline, kneel beside the casket.

President Johnson and his wife ride to the Capitol in a car with Jacqueline Kennedy, Robert Kennedy, and Caroline and John Jr., the young Kennedy children. Mrs. Johnson recalls that inside the car, "the only note of levity was John-John, who bounced from the back to someone's lap to the front until finally the attorney general said, 'If you be good, we'll give you a flag afterwards and you can march with [Kennedy aide] Dave Powers.'"

In Dallas, Parkland Memorial Hospital doctors announce that Oswald has died. Back in Washington, world leaders from six continents arrive to attend Kennedy's funeral on Monday. The line of mourners waiting to get into the Rotunda grows to be several miles long. Shortly after 9:00 P.M. Sunday, Mrs. Kennedy appears in the Rotunda with Robert Kennedy. She kneels at the casket, and then silently departs.

12:00 P.M. (CST)
DALLAS

ABC NEWS:
BILL DOWNS

I have a late report from Parkland Memorial Hospital. Lee Oswald in the operating room at Parkland Memorial Hospital is reported to be in very critical condition. Don Gardiner, what's the latest word on Oswald?

DON GARDINER

This word we have...Lee Harvey Oswald is still alive. Reported alive by chief surgeon Dr. Tom Shires at Parkland Hospital just about ten minutes ago. However, it has been announced at the hospital that his heart motion did stop immediately. The doctors in attendance opened up the chest cavity to apply massage to the heart muscle to try to restore its beat. One of the doctors said a severe massive injury to the stomach and a major blood vessel injury is involved in the shooting by nightclub owner Jack Ruby of Lee Harvey Oswald.

12:08 P.M. (CST)
THE WHITE HOUSE

Kennedy's casket, borne on a horse-drawn caisson and accompanied by marching units and muffled drums, begins its journey from the White House to the Capitol. In the procession is a saddled but riderless horse; boots are turned backward in the stirrups to symbolize a fallen leader.

(right) NBC's Sander Vanocur is seen in this television image reporting from outside the White House the day that President Kennedy's casket is moved to the U.S. Capitol.

CBS NEWS:
ROBERT PIERPOINT

The funeral cortege has formed here at the White House, and the caisson is now rolling toward the North Portico, from where the casket containing the body of John Fitzgerald Kennedy, the thirty-fifth president of the United States, will be brought out through the North Portico and loaded into the caisson. President and Mrs. Johnson have arrived here to be with Mrs. Kennedy. She will be riding in a car directly behind the caisson. This sad day is a beautiful day here in Washington, bright, sunshiny, a little cold, but after the dismal rain of all day yesterday the ground is still wet, but the sky is bright and clear.

NANCY DICKERSON
correspondent,
NBC News

Sander Vanocur and I were assigned to the White House lawn to do the live commentary as the cortege left on its trip to Capitol Hill, where the slain president would lie in state. Before the procession started, a soldier led up Black Jack, the riderless horse, with…boots in reverse. Positioned right next to us, he was full of beans that cold morning, defiantly rearing up on his hind legs so that the soldier had trouble controlling him. I was a little scared of him, but I couldn't move away because our cameras and mikes were assigned to this specific spot.

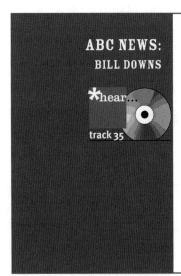

ABC NEWS:
BILL DOWNS

hear…

track 35

The cortege is turning past the Treasury Building up toward the Capitol, which is gleaming in the bright afternoon sunshine like a large confection, a cake. It's a beautiful sight, too beautiful to be so solemn and sad. The crowd has been very quiet, very attentive, as if Washington and the nation have been withholding their grief, as if it's unbelievable, and we have all felt that. It's as if we are waiting for something to make us weep because he was too young to die. Let's face it. But he is dead, the thirty-fifth president of the United States, and we have another. Washington is trying to get used to saying President Lyndon Johnson, President Lyndon Johnson.

1:02 P.M. (CST)
THE CAPITOL

Outside the Capitol, a twenty-one-gun salute is fired. The president's casket is taken inside the building, where Senate Majority Leader Mike Mansfield delivers a eulogy.

CBS NEWS: Mrs. Kennedy is still—oh—she's just about to turn. She's watching a wreath being carried in. It's the wreath of the vice president. He is accompanying it to the bier. President Johnson, in the utter silence here, is going to the bier with a huge wreath of—it looks to me like chrysanthemums. The president is going back to the stand behind Mrs. Johnson. Mrs. Jacqueline Kennedy is—and her daughter—are walking up to the casket. It will be her last goodbye for today. She kneels.

John F. Kennedy lies in state in the Capitol Rotunda surrounded by an honor guard of U.S. servicemen.

Hospital chief of surgery Tom Shires announces that Lee Harvey Oswald is dead.

UPI WIRE:

```
FLASH
OSWALD DEAD
VR125PCS11/24
```

ABC NEWS: DON GARDINER	We have a flash here that Oswald is dead. Oswald died at Parkland Hospital just moments ago from the gunshot wound inflicted as the police were moving Oswald from Dallas City Hall to the county jail.
CBS NEWS: WALTER CRONKITE	From our CBS newsroom in New York, a bulletin. Lee Harvey Oswald, the man who Dallas police say killed President Kennedy, himself is dead.
CBS NEWS: ROGER MUDD	Just as Walter Cronkite gave that bulletin from New York, it was coming in down here [at the Capitol] on the transistor radios that are held by members of the crowd, and we heard a cheer go up from the far side of the Capitol plaza.

The Capitol Rotunda is opened to the public and hundreds of thousands of mourners line up to view President Kennedy's casket.

NBC NEWS:
FRANK MCGEE

*hear...

track 36

Lee Harvey Oswald died forty-eight hours after the president—in the same hospital and the same emergency room. It is a bizarre story—utterly incredible.

PIERCE ALLMAN
manager of programming and production, WFAA-TV and Radio

I had already set up one feed the night before for the guys from BBC. They wanted to talk to some representatives from Dallas. Then the guys came back and wanted another feed. They said, "You know, Pierce, we were terribly dismayed at the death of Mr. Kennedy, but we were not at all surprised at what you did to Oswald." I said, "What do you mean?" They said, "It's frontier justice. You Texans are a violent lot. You carry guns. You don't discuss things, you just shoot it out. We never expected him to come to trial." I said, "Are you serious?" They said, "Oh, we see it all the time on the telly at home: Bat Masterson, Wyatt Earp, and Marshal Dillon." And they meant it. Of all the impressions of that weekend, that is one that has stayed with me because you realize then the enormous influence of modern media, in this case especially television.

RICHARD STOLLEY
Los Angeles regional editor, Life

I got a phone call from New York. The [Zapruder] film had been flown to New York to be shown to the editors there. They'd decided they wanted to buy all rights. For the $50,000 I had only bought print rights. So I got on the phone again with Mr. Z. He said, "Tomorrow morning, come to my lawyer's office. I have not sold movie or television rights to anybody."

2:45 P.M. (CST)
The Capitol

CBS NEWS:
WALTER CRONKITE

From around the world the dignitaries are converging on Washington for the funeral services tomorrow for President Kennedy. From Russia, First Deputy Premier of the Soviet Union Anastas Mikoyan is on the way. Prince Philip, Queen Elizabeth's husband, is on the way from England, along with Prime Minister Alec Douglas-Home and Labour Party Leader Harold Wilson. From France, President Charles de Gaulle had departed just a short while ago from Paris and will be in the United States shortly. From West Germany, Chancellor Erhard, and so the list goes. Ireland's President de Valera; Canada's Prime Minister Pearson; Greece's Queen Frederika; the Philippines' President Macapagal; the United Nations Secretary-General U Thant; South Korea's acting President Chung Hee Park; Israel's President Zalman Shazar; from the Netherlands, Crown Princess Beatrix; from Norway, Crown Prince Harald; from Luxembourg, the Grand Duke, Prince Jean; from Ethiopia, Emperor Haile Selassie; from Sweden, Prince Bertil; from India, Madame Pandit, the sister of Prime Minister Nehru; and from Belgium, King Baudouin.

2:45 P.M. (CST)
Dallas

EDDIE BARKER
news director,
KRLD-TV and Radio

As the afternoon went on, we were trying to develop who knew Ruby. I'll never forget it—I get a collect long-distance call. It was a stripper who had worked in his club Saturday night. She had fulfilled her engagement there and was on her way to another strip club in New Orleans. Her great line was: "If television needs me, I'll come back." I said, "Might as well. We need everybody we can get." Later, Tom Tierney, a big PR guy for Ford Motor Company, called me and asked, "Is there anything I can do? I'm going nuts." I said, "Yeah, get down here and I'll find a job for you." When [the stripper] got back into town she called and said she was at the Holiday Inn out on Central. I told old Tierney to pick her up. We were going to interview her. He came back in a little while. He looks at me and says, "You're not going to believe this. She opened the door, and she didn't have a damn thing on." So we had all kinds of characters in the deal. It turns out that Jack Ruby's sister, Eva, called Jim Underwood, who was our weather guy. He talked to her on the phone, and he went to get her to bring her down and interview her. By then the cops wanted her, so Underwood took her to the police station.

At Dulles International Airport outside Washington, a camera from NBC's affiliate records the arrival of foreign dignitaries for President Kennedy's funeral.

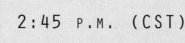
CBS NEWS:
WALTER CRONKITE

There has been a statement by Jack Ruby, the Dallas night-club operator who has been charged with the murder of Lee Harvey Oswald, the man police accused of assassinating President Kennedy. Jack Ruby's statement says simply, "I couldn't help it."

CBS NEWS:

Newsman Harold Walker of station WTOP here in Washington talked to Assistant Secretary of Labor [Daniel] Patrick Moynihan [and] asked him what lessons we might perhaps learn out of the depth of this tragic hour.

Daniel Patrick Moynihan: The French author Camus, where he came out at the end of his life, was that the world is absurd. A Christian shouldn't think that, but the—the utter senselessness—the meaninglessness—it—you know, we all of us down here know that politics was a tough game, and I don't think there is any point in being Irish if you don't know that the world is going to break your heart eventually. I guess we thought we had a little more time. So did he.

2:45 P.M. (CST)
FORT WORTH

MIKE COCHRAN
correspondent,
Associated Press

I wound up that night writing a story on Lee Harvey Oswald. I cleverly wrote something to the effect that he died as the most reviled man in, whatever. It was really clever because the AP in New York had to send a bulletin kill because it was so opinionated. Number one, he hadn't been convicted of anything. All he'd done is been murdered, and I'm decreeing him

Jacqueline Kennedy and her children Caroline and John Jr. leave the White House.

dying as one of the most reviled people, which was a great lesson. You learn a lot from an international bulletin kill!

That was shameful. It is interesting now, only in my defense, that I obviously let my own feeling about this creep in, but remember, this went through real editors and got on the wire, and then got killed. So there was maybe a universal feeling.

8:04 P.M. (CST)
THE CAPITOL

CBS NEWS:
ROGER MUDD

*hear...
track 37

Mrs. Jacqueline Kennedy made her first return visit to the Rotunda, accompanied by the attorney general. She came in right up to the main steps of the East Front and directly into the Rotunda. The policeman on guard stopped the moving lines just briefly. She went up to the catafalque, knelt, remained kneeling for two minutes, and then was escorted in full view of this mass of people back down the steps, and a limousine from the White House was waiting for her and she said, "No, no, I just want to walk." And she walked around the east face of the Capitol down the north side almost to the base of the Capitol Hill....

For the last eight hours, without surcease, mourning Americans have moved through this Rotunda, first in two rows, single file on each side, at the rate of perhaps six thousand an hour; and by mid-evening it became apparent that, at that rate, only very few of the assembled mass would be able to see. The line which formed here begins at the north end of the Senate and runs across the East Front of the plaza down Maryland Avenue, down Massachusetts Avenue, behind Lincoln Park, to the D.C. stadium on the Anacostia River, doubles back down East Capitol Street—forty blocks long, four abreast, estimated by police at five hundred thousand. The doors here will remain open until they must be closed at ten o'clock tomorrow.

The line to view Kennedy's casket in the Rotunda on Capitol Hill is at least three miles long.

BEN BRADLEE
Washington bureau chief,
Newsweek

I remember going down to the Capitol at two o'clock in the morning and there's still thousands of people stretched around there.

Mourners pay respects at the slain president's casket in the Capitol Rotunda.

TWO FUNERALS

NOVEMBER 25   8:57 AM – 6:00 PM (EST)

POLICE ESTIMATE THAT by Monday morning up to 250,000 people have passed through the Rotunda to mourn the fallen president. The casket is carried down the Capitol steps and placed in a processional that goes back to the White House, then St. Matthew's Cathedral, and finally to Arlington National Cemetery in Virginia.

At the White House, family members and dignitaries leave their cars to walk to the cathedral behind the casket.

After the funeral Mass is over, Mrs. Kennedy stands outside the cathedral with Caroline and John, who turns three this day. When pallbearers with the flag-draped casket pass, the widow whispers to her son, who then raises his hand in salute.

The cortege travels across the Arlington Memorial Bridge to the cemetery. At Mrs. Kennedy's request, a gas lamp—an "eternal flame"—has been installed at the grave site.

In Fort Worth, a far different funeral takes place. Lee Harvey Oswald is buried. Reporters are asked to carry Oswald's casket because there are no pallbearers.

MONDAY, NOVEMBER 25
8:57 A.M. (EST)
THE CAPITOL

The Capitol Rotunda, where Kennedy has been lying in state, is closed to visitors.

CBS NEWS:
ROGER MUDD

Police who were on duty all night say that mothers and fathers waited in line with babies in arms covered with swaddling blankets, the cold seeping in, but they stood, they waited, close to half a million people.

10:23 A.M. (EST)
THE WHITE HOUSE

CBS NEWS:
ROBERT PIERPOINT

A string of cars has come here to carry Mrs. Kennedy and the members of the family who will be going with her. Cold, clear air this morning. Still and quiet, no wind, as the members of the family and close friends move out of the White House. Slowly pulling away from the White House for the swift drive along Pennsylvania Avenue, retracing the procession of yesterday, the cortege moving on up to the Capitol and then to start the whole melancholy procession backwards again, back down here again to the White House.

President Kennedy's funeral procession crosses Memorial Bridge en route to Arlington National Cemetery.

10:36 A.M. (EST)
THE CAPITOL

NBC NEWS:
DAVID BRINKLEY

Mrs. Kennedy, flanked by Robert and Ted Kennedy, is getting out of the car. She is walking up the steps of the Capitol building. The stamina of this woman through these past three and four days has been indescribable. It has touched the entire nation.

10:45 A.M. (EST)

ABC NEWS:
NORM CRAFT
(WHISPERING)

*hear...

track 39

Mrs. Jacqueline Kennedy, the former first lady, has just come into the Rotunda. On her left, the attorney general, Robert Kennedy. On her right, Senator Ted Kennedy. They are now kneeling at the bier. They have arisen. They are now backing off from the casket. They have turned around and Mrs. Kennedy and Robert Kennedy are holding hands, just a simple, friendly gesture, and perhaps trying to help each other a little bit in their grief.

10:45 A.M. (EST)
DALLAS

IKE PAPPAS
reporter,
WNEW Radio

I got up in the morning to do a portrait of Dallas on the day of the funeral of the president. My concept was to go to the grassy knoll. I thought I would talk to people paying their respects there and put together a mood piece. There were hundreds of little handmade cards that children of Dallas had written, and handmade wreaths. I was practically in tears reading them. I did a walk-through, going from one to the other, doing ad-lib descriptions. It sort of brings tears to my eyes just remembering it today.

PIERCE ALLMAN
manager of programming and production, WFAA-TV and Radio

There were several [program directors] around the country, seven or eight of us, who had talked and said, "Let's leave our phone lines open during the funeral cortege." I was really uptight. All I could think of was that our early warning system was at best ninety or ninety-five percent effective and this was the only time that the leadership of the free world had been in one place at one time. All it would take would be one airplane. That's it. Is that part of the plan? Is this whole thing unfolding before our eyes? I realized they had security but I was tense until that procession was successfully complete.

10:45 A.M. (EST)
WASHINGTON, D.C.

OSBORN ELLIOTT
editor, Newsweek

I took my children down to Washington on that Monday and the security around the White House was almost nonexistent. There were huge television trucks, and we had some kind of passes that would have let us in to do something, but we didn't even use the passes. We went between two television trucks, with my two older daughters, who were then thirteen and ten, and we walked right up to the driveway by the portico, and we stood there and watched as [Charles] de Gaulle and all these characters came marching down, Bobby Kennedy, Jackie, etc. There's a picture that appeared in *National Geographic* a few months later and there you can see my little girls peering through the crowd as the caisson went by. That's how lousy the security was in those days.

There wasn't much room for any personal emotion until [that day]. I remember sitting in Kay Graham's office and watching the funeral and the burial on television in her office, and at that point, I just broke into tears. It got to me, finally.

Kennedy's funeral procession leaves Capitol Hill for the White House and St. Matthew's Cathedral.

GARY HAYNES
Atlanta bureau manager,
UPI News Pictures

You can't move around today the way you used to. I was alone at the Capitol and I came down the steps ahead of the coffin. You couldn't do that now because of security.

ABC NEWS:
DON GARDINER

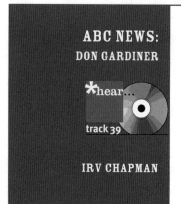
✱hear...
track 39

The mournful tolling of a church bell signifying the return of a president in a casket draped with the American flag back to the White House. Already, the lead units of the military procession are making their way toward St. Matthew's Cathedral where the funeral will be held. Here is Irv Chapman, ABC, at the White House.

IRV CHAPMAN

And now the caisson stands before us, flag-draped. Led by six horses, it will make its way to the edge of the driveway.

ABC NEWS:
DON GARDINER

The caisson stands to our left. A fractious horse, black horse, is being led by an Army enlisted man without rider, in tribute to a fallen warrior. And the hymns are sung and heads are bowed, and heads of state stand mournfully, prayerfully, as the contingent begins to move.... Striding vigorously forward is General Charles de Gaulle and other chiefs of state and governors who have honored our fallen leader, honored our country, by their presence here today.

CBS NEWS:	This is Dave Dugan at Connecticut Avenue. The solemn procession will go up Connecticut Avenue to St. Matthew's Cathedral. Mrs. Kennedy is walking the same route which she has taken many times on her way to Mass with President Kennedy. The heads of state are walking along behind. Not since the burial of the Unknown Soldier, forty years ago in Arlington Cemetery, has there been so many foreign dignitaries in Washington. Fifty-three countries are represented in all today.
NBC NEWS: **DAVID BRINKLEY**	No first lady has ever walked in her husband's funeral procession before.
CBS NEWS: **MARVIN KALB**	The casket now before the steps of St. Matthew's Cathedral. Mrs. Kennedy and her two children, Caroline and John Jr., the attorney general, Robert Kennedy, just behind her, being greeted now by Cardinal Cushing, the archbishop of Boston, an old friend of the Kennedy family. Inside the cathedral, President Johnson and the immediate family along with eleven hundred invited guests.

10:59 A.M. (EST)
St. Matthew's Cathedral

NANCY DICKERSON *correspondent,* *NBC News*	I've never been more cold than when I was standing on a ramp across from St. Matthew's Cathedral, identifying the family and friends arriving; old Mrs. [Alice Roosevelt] Longworth, who was much admired by the dead president; the politico who had been so helpful in the West Virginia primary; the old school friends.

Nancy Dickerson and Ellie Abel (standing) are positioned outside St. Matthew's Cathedral to cover President Kennedy's funeral.

ABC NEWS: Now, Richard Cardinal Cushing proceeds to the altar and the Mass begins.

BEN BRADLEE
Washington bureau chief,
Newsweek

[Kennedy's brother-in-law Sargent Shriver] called me to be an usher. That was strange. You were playing a role other than the role that you were on earth to fill. We had to go get fancy suits, I didn't own one of those. The church was unbelievable. Jesus Christ, seeing all those people there. About halfway up there was an aisle that goes out and I was stationed in the middle of one aisle on the left. I guess [*Time* correspondent] Hugh Sidey or somebody was on the other side. As the big shots came in, there was a terrible traffic jam and they'd stop right in front of you. I remember once [as he was leaving the church] Lyndon Johnson stopped five inches from my face.

ROBERT PIERPOINT
White House correspondent,
CBS News

I was invited to the funeral—Pierre Salinger had said those of us who wished to attend the funeral should do so. I had to make a decision to either broadcast or go to the funeral service, and I went to the service in the church. I was rather upset at the priest who used the text, "There is a time to live and a time to die." It was kind of fatalistic. Basically, I didn't care much for the service because I didn't think it was time for Mr. Kennedy to die.

1:21 P.M. (EST)

NBC NEWS:
DAVID BRINKLEY

Now the flag-draped coffin is being carried down the steps of the cathedral. The president's widow is standing with her children. She is whispering to John Jr. He is going forward. He salutes his father's coffin. Today is John Jr.'s third birthday.

HELEN THOMAS
White House correspondent,
United Press International

I was dictating. We had something that looked like a car battery for a phone. I was on the steps. I saw John-John start to raise his hand and I shouted to our photographer and we got the picture, got the photograph.

Jacqueline Kennedy, Caroline Kennedy, and John Kennedy Jr. outside St. Matthew's Cathedral after the requiem Mass for President Kennedy. When the president's casket passed in front of them, John Jr. saluted.

CBS NEWS:

Call to arms, as the caisson bearing the coffin of the late president is drawn slowly by six silver-white horses down Rhode Island Avenue toward Connecticut and the procession from St. Matthew's Cathedral, the solemn procession begins. Off to Arlington National Cemetery....

It will take at least an hour for the cortege to make the trip to Arlington National Cemetery across the Potomac River from Washington in Virginia.

GARY HAYNES
UPI News Pictures

I got into position at Arlington just below the Custis-Lee Mansion, and I used a telephoto lens to cover the procession coming down the avenue and the burial. Nobody knew what to do. It was a national outpouring of grief.

One of the most chilling souvenirs I have is the credential we needed at Arlington. It was like a paper tag at a garage sale and it simply said in big black letters, "ARLINGTON."

The press pass issued to UPI photographer Gary Haynes for the burial of President Kennedy at Arlington National Cemetery.

A crush of photographers and broadcast crews covers the burial at Arlington National Cemetery.

The funeral procession arrives at the cemetery.

ABC NEWS:
BILL DOWNS

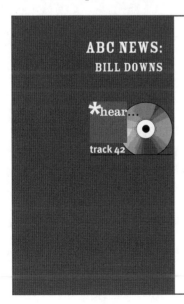

*hear...
track 42

And now, up Sheridan Drive, two limousines and the caisson is now coming into view. The leader on that dappled gray horse, the six other gray horses, the guard around the caisson, and we can see the brilliant white and red stripes of the flag. Army men are now lining the path of which the widow, Mrs. Kennedy, the president of the United States, and other dignitaries and members of the family will walk to the grave site. They have to walk up a slope towards the grave. An oak leaf—several of them seem to be floating down through this bright evening sun that is beginning to cast long, long shadows. The shadows already are reaching just to the far edge of the grave that will receive the assassinated president of the United States.

The Irish Guard salutes the casket. Fifty jet planes are flying over the grave site. Cardinal Cushing offers the benediction. A twenty-one-gun salute is sounded.

3:13 P.M. (EST)

Jacqueline Kennedy, Robert Kennedy, and Edward Kennedy light the eternal flame at the grave site.

French President Charles de Gaulle (saluting, light uniform) pays respects as a military honor guard holds the American flag over the casket of President Kennedy.

CBS NEWS: BILL LEONARD	The service is over. The sun has sunk behind the hill, overlooking President Kennedy's grave, but the flame at that grave is kindled and burns on.

3:13 P.M. (EST)
DALLAS

ROBERT MACNEIL
White House correspondent,
NBC News

While we were filming [people paying tribute at the grassy knoll], an old man sat down near us and turned on his transistor radio. Over it came the broadcast of the president's funeral in Washington. It was when I heard the lament played by the bagpipes of the [Scottish] Black Watch Regiment, marching in the funeral procession, that I really understood, with my feelings, what had happened. I sat there in

Along the funeral procession's route, mourners wept and took photographs.

the sunshine with the tears running out of my eyes, aware of how much the salt burned in them because crying was such an unaccustomed thing to do. Two weeks earlier, I had watched those same pipers playing on the South Lawn of the White House. It was a glorious autumn day, with President and Mrs. Kennedy watching from the balcony with Caroline and John-John. My own two children, a girl and a boy, were their same ages.

3:13 P.M. (EST)

CBS NEWS:
WALTER CRONKITE

Almost at the same hour, as the president was being laid to rest at Arlington National Cemetery, there were being held two other funerals. One a somewhat official one with a police honor guard in Dallas, Texas, for Detective Sergeant J.D. Tippit, the policeman who Lee Harvey Oswald was accused of shooting in his flight from the assassination scene. And there was another funeral with no ceremony in Fort Worth, Texas, this afternoon. Lee Harvey Oswald himself was taken to a bare plot under Secret Service guard.

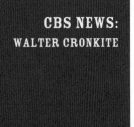

3:13 P.M. (EST)
FORT WORTH

MIKE COCHRAN
correspondent,
Associated Press

I got the tip that Oswald would be buried at Rose Hill Cemetery in Fort Worth. It turned out it wasn't much of a tip, because there were nothing but reporters and cops and federal agents there that morning, along with five members of the family, Marina and Marguerite, the two children, and Robert Oswald, Oswald's brother. It is true that Oswald's popularity that day was at an all-time low, so not only were there no pallbearers, but they had to recruit somebody to do the final rites thing because the preacher didn't even show up.

Journalists were pressed into service as pallbearers for Lee Harvey Oswald.

They got a guy on the staff or something to do it. Because I was with the Associated Press, I was among the first that they asked to be a pallbearer. I refused, and then Preston McGraw of UPI stepped up and said, "Certainly, I'll be a pallbearer." So then, if there's one thing I knew—stupid as I may have been, inexperienced as I may have been—if UPI was going to be a pallbearer, I was damn sure going to be pallbearer.

PRESTON MCGRAW
Dallas bureau manager,
UPI

I went over for the funeral. As I drove over, they were burying Kennedy in Washington. I listened to this thing on the way to Oswald's funeral. They had a lot of cops over there—I never saw so many cops. There were some [*Dallas*] *Times Herald* guys there, and [*Dallas*] *Morning News* and [*Fort Worth*] *Star-Telegram* [reporters]. As I went into the cemetery [the ex-Army officer who ran it] was reciting a poem that had this line: "If he was hanged over the highest hill, his mother would love him still." Of course he was talking about

Oswald. They had the body in a little shack out in the grassy area there. We got a report that it was somebody else's body. [Another reporter] went into the building and opened up the coffin and said, "Sure looks like Oswald's body to me."

The undertaker told us they would need pallbearers because there was a grassy space between this little building they had the coffin in and the hearse. He asked for volunteers. The officer told us, "You're not going to get any supper unless we get him buried!" Frankly, what I had in mind was to get up close to the family so I could ask Oswald's wife a couple of questions. So I stepped up and I told the AP man, "Come on up here," which he did. I got on the left side and he got on the right, then they got a lot of volunteers, and we put it in the hearse. Mrs. Oswald and her two young kids and his mother and his brother, who was a brick salesman, they were there. We had no sooner sat the thing down then the cops pushed us back and they formed a line. The head of the

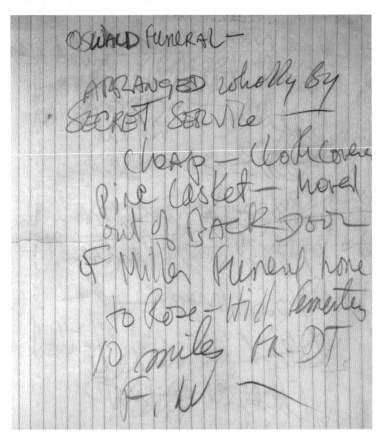

Notes about Oswald's funeral, made by Ike Pappas of WNEW Radio.

Dallas Council of Churches preached the sermon. He said the guy who was supposed to preach it didn't show up. As soon as the thing was over, Mrs. Oswald tried to put her ring on his finger but the ring wasn't quite big enough. In any case, Marina left the ring there. The Secret Service put her in a car and took her and the rest of them off. I went across the street and knocked on a woman's door and asked if I could use her phone, and I dictated a story to Dallas.

3:13 P.M. (EST)
DALLAS

CBS correspondent Dan Rather views the Zapruder film on Monday and tries to negotiate for rights, but first he vividly describes on the air what he has seen.

DAN RATHER
New Orleans bureau chief,
CBS News

The film was put up, it was shown—I was sickened, astonished, astounded. I knew the import of it and just blasted out of the room to go tell my superiors in New York what I had seen. I said, "I'll be back." There was never any discussion, in my presence, of broadcast rights or print rights—what was said to me was "You've got to look at this one time and one time only and then after you see it that one time we'll open a discussion about rights." I told my superiors, including the late Ernie Leiser Sr. and several other people who were on the phone. They said, "Listen, we've got to put this on the air." I agreed—we did [describe] it on the air—so that took a little while.

CBS NEWS:
DAN RATHER

We have just returned from seeing a complete motion picture of the moments preceding, and the moments of, President Kennedy's assassination and the shooting of Texas Governor John Connally. Here is what the motion picture shows...

CBS executives then authorize Rather to bid for the film. *Life* magazine's Richard Stolley also is bidding to obtain all rights to the film.

RICHARD STOLLEY *Los Angeles regional editor,* *Life*	I walked [into the office of Zapruder's lawyer] and there's Dan [Rather], sitting in a chair in the lobby. I knew Dan; I covered desegregation of schools for four years in the South, so we'd run across each other on racial stories, and we're good friends now. Zapruder had told him, "I'm going to show you this film, Mr. Rather, but you have to promise me that you will *not* describe this on television, on camera or on air, in any way." Zapruder was a very shrewd guy. And Dan of course said yes, but then, as I understand it, he described in exquisite detail what he had just seen on film. Mr. Zapruder was slightly annoyed at that.
DAN RATHER *CBS News*	That question [about not describing the film] never arose and was never discussed with me. It may have been with somebody, but not with me.
RICHARD STOLLEY *Life*	Dan left, and I went in. I met his lawyer, a wonderful man named Sam Passman, and I said, "It's a remarkable piece of film and we want to be able to control the whole thing." [Zapruder] said, "That's fine with me." I said, "We'll pay you an additional $100,000." He said, "That's fine with me." We didn't have to negotiate. He said, "We agreed, I don't want this figure, this amount, to be revealed." I said, "OK, that applies to both of us." He said, "Fine." Then his lawyer, Sam, said a very interesting thing. He said, "Abe, when it gets out—even though there's no figure—that you have sold your film to *Life* magazine, there's going to be hell to pay. Quite frankly, it's going to be 'Jew Garment Manufacturer Sells Film of President's Death to *Life* Magazine; Sum Not Revealed.' You know what this town is like." I mean, Dallas was a tough place then. And Sam said, "I suggest that we take the first year's payment"—[the money] was to be paid, $150,000, in $25,000 yearly installments—he said, "I suggest we take the first $25,000 and donate it to the J.D. Tippit fund." Tippit was the cop that Oswald shot before he went in the theater and was captured. Abe said, "Great idea," and I thought, "My God, there *is* a use for lawyers."
DAN RATHER *CBS News*	I remember that reluctantly, and pushing what they thought were the limits, [CBS executives] gave me a $10,000 limit to

bid for the film. When I went back to the office, I was told that the rights had been sold. I was surprised—shocked would not be too strong—and there was some discussion about how could this happen. It was said to me with a smile that *Life* magazine had made a preemptive bid. I protested a little—that wasn't exactly fair—but I did have in my mind that if they made a preemptive bid it was probably more than $10,000. At any rate, it was done.

6:00 P.M. (EST)

CBS NEWS:
WALTER CRONKITE

*hear...
track 42

Congress and the nation had reminders today that while the world seemed suspended by our tragedy, it really kept on its whirling way. In Vietnam, reports today of the bloodiest fighting in almost a year. Military sources report massive communist attacks have wiped out two strategic northern hamlets and more than a thousand mountain tribesmen defending them are now missing. Communist guerillas have stepped up their attacks against the hamlets ever since the overthrow of President Diem....

Terrorists took no break in Venezuela. Four persons were reported killed today in widespread outbreaks of pro-Castro terrorism. And six oil and gas pipelines were set afire.

In Lawrence, Massachusetts, police said today they're afraid a twenty-three-year-old single girl, whose body was discovered Sunday, is the tenth victim in seventeen months for Boston's mystery strangler.

In the world of finance, life must go on, too. Friday's tragic news sent stock exchange prices tumbling. The Dow Jones average dropped twenty-one points....

It is said that the human mind has a greater capacity for remembering the pleasant than the unpleasant, but today was a day that will live in memory, and in grief. Only history can write the importance of this day....

That's the way it is, Monday, November 25, 1963. This is Walter Cronkite. Good night.

CHAPTER X

REFLECTIONS...

FORTY YEARS LATER – 2003

ROBERT MACNEIL
White House correspondent,
NBC News

I have never run into anyone, in any country, who does not remember precisely where he was when he heard the news.

HELEN THOMAS
White House correspondent,
United Press International

Everybody remembers where they were. But for me, it was a transforming moment for America because we lost hope. Every president who succeeded Kennedy—they all had good points and bad points—but the legacy of hope died with him. You never had that same sense again that we were moving forward, that we could do things.

DAN RATHER
New Orleans bureau chief,
CBS News

I've never covered anything like it. Not before, not since, and I don't expect to in this lifetime, nor any lifetime beyond, to infinity and beyond.

ROBERT PIERPOINT
White House correspondent,
CBS News

Looking back over the last forty years since the assassination, it seems there has been a very, very bad effect on the country and the world. When Kennedy was in Texas, he was actually starting the beginning of the campaign to run for reelection. In the first three years of his time in office, his legislative agenda had largely been blocked by Southern Democrats who controlled the Congress and were extremely conservative and didn't like this young upstart from Massachusetts and didn't agree with most of his agenda. There were a lot of ideas that he could not get through. His political strategy was to wait and try to win a larger majority in Congress in the next election. That trip to Texas was the beginning of a campaign aimed at changing the tenor of Congress and getting rid of the old Southern Democrats and conservatives and trying to elect more progressive people. Some programs that Kennedy had thought about and tried to legislate through were actually enacted later because people wanted to honor the memory of JFK. Johnson was able to get though Congress some things that Kennedy could not, such as civil rights and Medicare, partly because he had liaison with the conservative Southern Democrats. If you look back, the changes that resulted from the assassination have been enormous in the area of foreign policy. Kennedy understood foreign policy, he had lived abroad, and I think he had a totally different vision than Johnson had. The result has been that since then and up to the war now with Iraq, the United States can and will prevail because of our power, anywhere in the world we want to. Johnson did not understand foreign policy, didn't care about it and really didn't follow through on some of the things that JFK tried to implement. I really believe that the world would have been much changed and much more peaceful if John Kennedy had not been assassinated.

JOE CARTER
overnight editor,
UPI

Those 6.2 seconds were a turning point in American history. Lee Harvey Oswald changed history in the United States and the world, and a different sort of man became president.

WILBORN HAMPTON
reporter,
UPI

It changed this country a great deal—the country became much more cynical. For those of us who were in their twenties in the '60s, and even for some of those who were in their twenties in the '70s, the young generation coming into

Bill Mauldin responded to news of the president's death with this editorial cartoon, which ran in the Chicago Sun-Times *on November 23, 1963.*

adulthood, it changed an outlook, it changed a trust, it created a bitterness and cynicism that we probably haven't shed yet. Whether you loved him or you hated him, something central had slipped out of this country.

BOB CLARK
Washington correspondent,
ABC News

(From a broadcast on the twenty-fifth anniversary of Kennedy's death) On this silver anniversary of the Kennedy assassination, Americans clearly have little taste for critical reexamination of their martyred president. Historians rank him at the bottom of the top third of all American presidents, below Lyndon Johnson and Dwight Eisenhower. But the American people, according to a recent poll by the Associated Press, rank him first, above Lincoln and Washington and FDR. Given the grim events in Dallas twenty-five years ago, this is understandable. John Fitzgerald Kennedy was struck down in his prime, as he was still striding buoyantly through the halls of Camelot. He had served his thousand days as America's leader with wit and charm and courage and grace. That is the way most Americans choose to remember him, and the brief, shining moments of his presidency.

KEITH SHELTON
political writer,
Dallas Times Herald

It caused Dallas to become a lot less extreme. I think it took some of the power away from the extreme positions and that a lot of people in Dallas became more moderate.

JAMES CHAMBERS JR.
president,
Dallas Times Herald

To show you the way that the minds of people were poisoned against the community, I went to Detroit about two months after the assassination for a meeting with the automotive people. I got in a cab and I said, "Take me to the Detroit Athletic Club, please." The cab driver said, "You must be from the South." And I said, "I am." He said, "Where are you from?" I said, "Texas." He said, "Where in Texas?" I said, "Dallas." He stopped the cab and said, "Get out. I ain't taking you anywhere."

PIERCE ALLMAN
manager of programming
and production,
WFAA-TV and Radio

I don't think any of us involved at the time recognized or accepted the enormity of the event. I was concerned with the day-to-day, with the details of what's unfolding, what's real and let's get it on the air. During that weekend, you had to be very conscious of all of the avenues that it could take. Was it a conspiracy? What would happen afterwards? There was

HE HAD THAT SPECIAL GRACE...

History will best judge John F. Kennedy in calmer days when time has made the tragic and the grotesque at least bearable. And surely history will judge him well—for his wisdom and his compassion and his grace.

John Kennedy was a wonderfully funny man, always gay and cheerful, never mean—but historians are prone to stifle laughter in formality. You could see a laugh coming in his eyes before you could hear it from his lips. His humor was often most appealing when he directed it against himself. One summer night in a Georgetown garden, candidate Kennedy was preparing for the first of many critically important appearances on "Meet the Press."

"You be Kennedy and I'll be Spivak," he suggested to his guest with relish, and the first question was already spilling forth: "All right, Horatio Alger, just what makes you think you ought to be President?"

Only days ago, his thoughts turned to the farewell party for a White House aide who had been memorialized in print as "coruscatingly" brilliant. "Those guys should never forget," he said with a smile, "50,000 votes the other way and we'd all be coruscatingly stupid."

John Kennedy was a forgiving man, far more forgiving than his friends. He forgave many the excesses of their ignorance—many men who hold high positions today because of this forgiving. He forgave quickly and for good, and soon found new quality in the forgiven.

An Appetite for Life: John Kennedy was a hungry man, ravenous sometimes for the nourishment he found in the life he led and the people he loved. This was both literally and figuratively true. He could eat ten bowls of specially prepared fish chowder without succumbing either to indigestion or embarrassment, and though he smoked only rarely, he could chain-smoke three cigars when the spirit moved him. His ability to devour the written word was legendary, and he could unwrap presents faster than a 5-year-old.

John Kennedy was a graceful man, physically graceful in his movements —walking, swimming, or swinging a golf club—and had that special grace of the intellect that is taste. He never told a dirty joke. He could not bring himself to be "corny" at a time when "corniness" is a hallmark of American politics. On his next to last trip, to the American wilderness, this compleat and urbane man was uncomfortable in the clothes of a conservationist; and he laughed loudest of all at the "Paul Bunyan" or "Johnny Appleseed" nicknames he quickly collected. During the 1960 campaign he used the phrase "Jackie and I" only once, and that was enough to embarrass him. He was a student of graceful expression, and had been since he started collecting rhetoric in a small, black leather book before the war.

A Palmer in Power: John Kennedy had a Walter Mitty streak in him, as wide as his smile. On the golf course, when he was winning, he reminded himself most of Arnold Palmer in raw power, or Julius Boros in finesse. When he was losing, he was "the old warrior" at the end of a brilliant career, asking only that his faithful caddy point him in the right direction, and let instinct take over.

John Kennedy was a restless, exuberant man, always looking forward to the next challenge. For a year now, it had been "Wait till '64" more and more often. And for a long time

UPI

he had wondered—at first in fun but increasingly in seriousness—what he would do after his second term. He wondered if he might become the editor of a newspaper. He had no real doubt that he would be re-elected—hopefully with the mandate that he missed so much after the 1960 election, the kind of mandate that would let him do what he thought the country needed done.

He wanted to run against Goldwater (though he liked Goldwater personally more than he liked Rockefeller), and settle forever the dangers he saw in standing still. John Kennedy was a blunt man, sometimes profane, when it came to assessing rivals. But in his judgment, no man was all bad who had run for political office, and by the same token, every man would be better if he ran for political office. He bore no man lasting grudge or envy, and his readiness to love was instinctive.

For John Kennedy was a loving man, lately come to lasting love. And historians are too far removed from love.

A Laugh With Love: John Kennedy reveled in love for the Irish patrimony that he had left so far behind. He laughed with love at the roguery of his grandfather, Honey Fitz, and his trip to Ireland was a pilgrimage to that love.

He loved his brothers and sisters with a tribal love. All Kennedys were born gregarious, but under siege it could be the Kennedys against the world.

John Kennedy loved his children with a light that lit up his world. He discovered his daughter when election brought them finally under the same roof, and he delighted in her pride and in her performance. His heart leapt up when he saw his son, careening through life as if there were no tomorrow, and he lit up the hearts of all who saw them enjoy each other.

And John Kennedy loved his wife, who served him so well. Their life together began as it ended—in a hospital—and through sickness and loneliness there grew the special love that lights up the soul of the lover and the loved alike.

John Kennedy is dead, and for that we are lesser people in a lesser land.

—BENJAMIN BRADLEE

An essay about John F. Kennedy, written by Ben Bradlee in Newsweek*'s December 2 issue.*

precious little time for reflection. Sometimes I marvel at having been there, having actually stood there, seen it and then had a hand in reporting it. I don't think about it that often, although when I do, it is as vivid as if it were yesterday.

DARWIN PAYNE
reporter,
Dallas Times Herald

I was historically aware that this was an earth-shaking event that I would never see the likes of again. I was very conscious of that and I was conscious that everything thereafter would seem small. I remember thinking specifically, What bigger story? The magnitude of everything seemed lessened after that.

GARY HAYNES
Atlanta bureau manager,
UPI News Pictures

I was really shaken up by the fact that we were all that vulnerable. You could be cut down no matter who you were. Life is really very fragile. I've tried to live it to its fullest since then.

BERT SHIPP
assistant news director,
WFAA-TV

Three or four of us got together about five days later. We went to a hotel room, got a bunch of strong beverages, served ourselves, sat there, and talked about it. It hit all of us that we had probably covered the most significant and important and far-reaching story we would ever cover in our lives.

But, jeez, everybody is always saying to me, "Forget about the assassination, tell us about interviewing the Beatles." In 1964, I slipped into the Beatles' dressing room when they were here for a concert. I sat in there for about ten minutes and we visited. They loved my accent so I got to stay. Well, I'd like to tell you about my time in Vietnam and the hurricanes I've covered and the big stuff.... Nah, my tombstone is going to read, "The guy who slipped into the Beatles' dressing room."

KEITH SHELTON
Dallas Times Herald

At the time, the [*Dallas*] *Times Herald* sold more papers in Dallas and Dallas County than the [*Dallas*] *Morning News* did. We were in a fierce battle for circulation. When they gave the Pulitzers, we were nominated for team effort. Bob Jackson was nominated for the photo. They gave Bob Jackson the photo Pulitzer and gave the *Morning News* the team effort, which we resented greatly because we were on deadline and they weren't. I think the Pulitzer committee just decided to give each paper one Pulitzer.

EDDIE BARKER
news director,
KRLD-TV and Radio

I've often said that the thing that changed Dallas back to a good image was the Dallas Cowboys. All of a sudden we had this great team. We became America's team. That really, I'm convinced, made the difference.

PIERCE ALLMAN
WFAA-TV and Radio

That was the first time I had seen the feeding frenzy. I guess it was the fine balance between trying to make news and to report news. I suspect it's the age-old problem: a lot of folks trying to make a name for themselves. You have to balance the right to know with how much can be accurately said. I thought the conduct of a lot of the reporters that we saw in action was inexcusable. I don't know if that's ever justifiable. For several of us [newsmen], it wasn't. We got pretty disenchanted with it. I left the station shortly after that and went to Southern Methodist University as director of alumni affairs.

BOB HUFFAKER
reporter,
KRLD-TV

I thought I was a hotshot. I was twenty-seven. I had driven a lot of fast cars. I prided myself on being the first guy on the scene. [The assassination story] was one of the things that ultimately caused me to change my career. I was not particularly proud of the behavior of many of these reporters that I saw. I also came to feel that perhaps broadcasting tragedy was not nearly as useful a thing as teaching children about literature. I left broadcasting a few years after that and got a Ph.D. and taught college English, then was editor with *Texas Monthly*. People asked me why I got out of broadcasting; I finally realized years later that I wanted the privilege of not speaking if I didn't want to speak.

ROBERT PIERPOINT
CBS News

We did three full days of day-and-night coverage of the assassination story. In those days, network news, particularly CBS News, was much more responsible, and I wasn't surprised they did away with commercials. CBS, at the time, was run by Bill Paley and Frank Stanton. It was a news-oriented administration that ran the company. Today, all the networks are owned by huge corporations, which are much more interested in profit and the bottom line than they are presenting the public with news and analysis. It was a chore, because going on the air on-and-off for three days without much sleep was wearing on all of us. But it was a different

Robert Goralski of NBC News (right) interviews UPI correspondent Merriman Smith, an eyewitness to many events surrounding the president's assassination.

era and the networks themselves were much more attuned to the public need to know.

WALTER CRONKITE
anchor,
CBS Evening News

It certainly was the first experience we had of that kind, that kind of coverage. I think we set a pattern that has been followed in emergencies ever since.

ROBERT ASMAN
senior producer,
NBC News

We never left the air for those four days. This was a remarkable breakthrough for the early '60s because we were all just beginning to use electronic equipment. I would say that that really started the whole recognition by the public and the industry that live television was something that could really bring a nation together. We had the ability now to do live coverage for a long, extended period.

ROBERT PIERPOINT
CBS News

Obviously, television came into its own during that period. Part of it was the inevitable result of technological changes, and part of it was the result perhaps that we could cover and did cover things live. People could see for themselves what was happening. Most of the television coverage that was done on the spot [in those days] was done with film, so you had to go and process and edit it—and that all took time. Nowadays you can do a lot more with videotape.... Nowadays, news can be seen as it happens. In those days, radio was still as important as television, if not more so. You were much more flexible with radio, but as technology developed, television technology went from film to videotape and now to small handheld cameras; and you can do so much more than we could in those days.

DAN RATHER
CBS News

I think television news came of age in public consciousness during those four days. One reason is that for the first time,

President Kennedy's grave site, marked with an "eternal flame," at Arlington National Cemetery.

print journalists acknowledged, gave respect for television news. Because of that—not just because of that, but it was helpful—I think the public sort of coalesced behind the idea that television news can be a very valuable part of American journalism. I would question before then whether public opinion really coalesced behind that thought. Certainly during some of [Edward R.] Murrow's broadcasts on [Senator Joseph] McCarthy and [other stories] there were moments, but there never had been a time like those four days.

WILBORN HAMPTON
UPI

Television became the source of news. You could see it—it was very moving—and you didn't have to wait until the next morning to read about who came to visit the president's casket. You saw the first lady and her beautiful two children come there, her head covered. You saw the famous walk down Pennsylvania Avenue with all the collected heads of state from around the world. Words couldn't quite convey the emotion that seeing it did.

OSBORN ELLIOTT
editor,
Newsweek

Whether we were aware of it at the time, it certainly came to be true that that week was an enormously important milestone in *Newsweek*'s history. I think that was the case because that week, many, many people were reading everything they could get their hands on. Many people, for the first time, were reading *Time* and *Newsweek* comparatively. And, while it sounds boastful and crass and commercial to say, all of which is true, I really do believe that we knocked the socks off *Time* that week. It really did mark *Newsweek*'s arrival into the grown-up world of newsmagazines.

HUGH SIDEY
White House correspondent,
Time

In the aftermath, it strikes me there wasn't any great change. I don't think *Newsweek* enjoyed a great surge or *Time* a great loss. We had huge newsstand sales, even with LBJ up there [on the cover].

There is no question that this changed the world as far as the media goes. The advent of the television world was suddenly kind of expanded so that everybody realized it was on us—television [now] being the principal news purveyor and not only giving us the breaking news but the emotions around it. The legend of Kennedy was born. Four days of continuous

Visitors flock to the late president's flower-bedecked grave site in the days following his burial.

television, I think, is really the foundation of the Kennedy mystique. What this did was focus the world's attention on the White House, on the presidency, like never before, and [led to] the realization that [the president of the United States] was not only the most powerful man but probably the most interesting man in the world.

JOE CARTER
UPI

Forty years later I can say this—I feel like what we reported that day was dead on target and we got it right. It was moved very rapidly and well written, it was professional. I'm proud to have been a small part of it.

PIERCE ALLMAN
WFAA-TV and Radio

I think a lot of us were aware that there was sort of a new phase of electronic journalism unfolding because some extraordinary percentage—ninety-seven or ninety-eight percent—of the TV sets in the U.S. were on and stayed on.

A.C. GREENE
editorial page editor,
Dallas Times Herald

Within a week after the assassination, everything that was sent to the editor or to the [*Dallas*] *Times Herald* came to me. We got literally thousands of letters from all over the world, especially from all over the United States, and a lot of them had money for Jacqueline Kennedy, but most of the money was for Officer Tippit's wife, and then Marina Oswald. From the *Times Herald* through me, from various readers all over the world, I sent Mrs. Tippit over $200,000. I sent Marina Oswald about the same amount. I got a thank-you letter from whoever was handling Marina Oswald's affairs at the time. You know, she didn't really speak very good English. It says, "Thank you. Mrs. Marina N. Oswald and children."

WES WISE
sports director,
KRLD-TV

I remember waking up the next morning—my birthday was the twenty-fifth—and I turned to my wife and I said, "This was a nightmare." She said, "If it was, we've had the same nightmare."

WALTER CRONKITE
CBS News

I never had any trouble sleeping after a day like that. Go to a bar and relax and go home and get some sleep. I guess that comes from the long experience, where you're up all night and have to be back the next day. At United Press, there were many of those times. If you got a story like Pearl Harbor for instance, you were there all night and until well into the next day. So I was used to that.

DAN RATHER
CBS News

After the worst of it had passed for most people, I had some very bad days and I know other reporters shared that. Tears, a sense of grief and anger, and just not wanting to think about anything else: nothing else is really important, this is the only thing that's important.

I did think about—in the weeks and months that followed—the responsibility of having a public trust as we do. It came into much sharper focus for me after those four days of what the responsibilities were and how hard one had to work to meet the responsibilities of that trust and the realization that no matter how hard you tried, no matter how hard you worked, that nobody could do it perfectly. I really think until that time I had the arrogance of youth believing that if God smiled and you were really lucky and worked hard that you

Newsweek

DECEMBER 2, 1963   25c

JOHN FITZGERALD KENNEDY

1917-1963

Newsweek's *December 2, 1963, issue featured John F. Kennedy on its cover.*

John F. Kennedy's grave at Arlington National Cemetery as it appears today, forty years after the assassination.

could do it perfectly. The difference before and after that time is I realized there's no way you could do it perfectly.

RICHARD STOLLEY
Los Angeles regional editor,
Life

A friend of ours had a traditional Thanksgiving Eve party. [A colleague] and I got there just in time for that, bursting with our experiences in Dallas, and nobody wanted to hear them. People were so grieving, so upset, so full of the horror of that week, they *did not* want to talk about it. A journalist, when you get into a very emotionally volatile situation, you really tend to shut everything down. And when we did want to talk about it, did want to vent, nobody wanted to hear it. It was very peculiar. Quite frankly, it wasn't until twenty years later when I did the special issue of *Life*, "Four Days That Stopped America," that I really understood what America had gone through.

WEATHER
Fair and warmer Sunday
with a high in the 40s. See
Page 46.

CHICAGO SUNDAY
SUN-TIMES

FINAL

© 1963 by Field Enterprises, Inc.

Vol. 17, No. 8   Phone 321-3000   SUNDAY, NOVEMBER 24, 1963   cc   9 Sections—20 Cents

Monday A National Day Of Mourning

1917   JOHN F. KENNEDY   1963

A Stillness For Chicago

Stories On Pages 5 and 11

FBI Traces Murder Rifle To Oswald

Chicago Firm Sold Weapon For $12.78

Stories And Photos, Page 2

Mauldin's Grieving Lincoln

Drawing Reprinted On Page 9

JACK FALLON
Southwest Division
news manager,
UPI

I never left the office. I just sacked out on a couch there. The kids brought me clean shirts. I finally got home Wednesday night about ten or eleven o'clock. Everybody was asleep. The next day was Thanksgiving. I walked in and poured myself a drink and I just sat down in the den for a minute. A neighbor had brought in a copy of the *Chicago Sun-Times* cartoon by Bill Mauldin. [The cartoon depicted the Lincoln Memorial statue weeping over President Kennedy's death.] I took a sip of my drink and threw [the rest of it] in the fire. That was my human reaction.

PETER LISAGOR
Washington bureau chief,
Chicago Daily News

The press, under circumstances like that, is not some kind of institutional monster or automaton or a robot. It's really a bunch of people. It's guys like you and me. We operate as kind of proud of a profession in which we are trained, but in situations like that, really, the story gets too big. You do your little piece of it and hope you've done the best job you can.

WHERE ARE THEY NOW?

COVERING THE ASSASSINATION of President John F. Kennedy was a defining moment for most of the journalists interviewed for this book. Some went on to become well-known through national publications and high-profile television careers; others excelled in Texas journalism. A few left journalism because of the impact of the assassination and its aftermath.

Walter Cronkite became known as the "most trusted man in America" during his nineteen-year tenure as anchor of the *CBS Evening News*. He was succeeded by **Dan Rather** who has been anchor and managing editor of the *CBS Evening News* since 1981.

Ben Bradlee spent twenty-three years as executive editor of the *Washington Post* and was in charge of news coverage during the *Post*'s Watergate revelations and the publication of the *Pentagon Papers*. He retired in 1991 and currently serves as vice president at large of the newspaper. Bradlee wrote two books on Kennedy, *That Special Grace* and *Conversations with Kennedy*.

Robert MacNeil, until his retirement in 1995, was executive editor and co-anchor of *The MacNeil-Lehrer NewsHour*, a nightly news program with Jim Lehrer on PBS.

Helen Thomas, who became one of the most recognized White House correspondents, worked for United Press International for fifty-seven years. She resigned in 2000 at the age of eighty to become a columnist for Hearst News Service.

Bob Schieffer joined CBS News and has spent more than thirty years covering the White House, Pentagon, State Department, and Capitol Hill. He currently is chief Washington correspondent and anchor of *Face the Nation* for CBS.

White House correspondents **Bob Clark, Robert Pierpoint, Sid Davis**, and **John Bennett** had long careers in Washington journalism. **Tom Wicker** covered the White House, Congress, and national politics for the *New York Times*, headed the newspaper's Washington bureau, and wrote "In the Nation," an opinion column, before his retirement in 1991. **Marianne Means**, longtime White House correspondent for Hearst Newspapers, remains a syndicated political columnist and Hearst's Washington columnist. **Hugh Sidey**, now Washington contributing editor for *Time*, has written about the American presidency for more than thirty years.

Richard Stolley covered events and personalities for *Life* magazine for nineteen years and in 1974 was founding editor of *People* magazine. He later served as managing editor of *Life*, editorial director of all Time Inc. magazines, and currently is senior editorial adviser to Time Inc.

Ike Pappas spent four decades as a television and radio news correspondent, producer, and executive. As a correspondent for CBS, he covered wars in Vietnam and the Middle East, the civil rights movement, and other major news stories.

Hugh Aynesworth has spent fifty years in journalism as a reporter, editor, publisher, and author. He now is Southwest bureau chief for the *Washington Times*. **Jack Fallon** became foreign editor for UPI before leaving journalism, and **Terrance W. McGarry** became UPI news manager in Mexico, Central America, and Canada and worked for the *Los Angeles Times* before retiring. **Joe Carter** later worked for the administrations of Lyndon B. Johnson and Jimmy Carter and became director of the Will Rogers Memorial Commission of Oklahoma.

Eddie Barker remained a journalist in Texas, working for more than fifty years in broadcasting, and currently works at both KPLT-AM in Paris, Texas, and KRLD 1080 in the Dallas area. **Bert Shipp** spent almost four decades in Texas journalism, retiring from WFAA-TV in 1999, though he still works several days a month for the station. **Vivian Castleberry** became known as the "grandmother of women in journalism in Dallas," working as women's editor of the *Dallas Times Herald* for twenty-eight years.

Several Dallas reporters left journalism after covering the slaying of the president. **Wes Wise** turned to politics and was elected to three terms as mayor of Dallas. **Pierce Allman** left journalism shortly after the assassination to become director of alumni affairs for Southern Methodist University. **Bob Huffaker** earned his Ph.D. and taught English before becoming an editor of *Texas Monthly*. **Darwin Payne** also left journalism for academia, joining the faculty of Southern Methodist University in 1971. He has written several books and was co-editor of *Reporting the Kennedy Assassination: Journalists Who Were There Recall Their Experiences*.

IN MEMORIAM

Robert Baskin, who was Washington bureau chief for the *Dallas Morning News* from 1958 to 1972, died in 1983 at the age of sixty-five. He worked briefly for the *Fort Worth Star-Telegram* after serving in the Army in World War II, joining the Dallas newspaper in 1947. He retired in the late 1970s.

Jack Bell died at age seventy-one in 1974. After retiring as chief political writer for the Associated Press, he was a columnist for Gannett News Service. The author of several books on the presidency, he served as president of the Gridiron Club in Washington, D.C., for the 1971–1972 term.

Network television news pioneer **David Brinkley** died in 2003. He was eighty-two. His fifty-five-year career in journalism began with UPI in 1942. In 1951 he became Washington correspondent for NBC-TV's *Camel News Caravan*. He made his mark on broadcast journalism from 1956 to 1970: teaming with Chet Huntley in New York, he helped define television news on the nightly *Huntley-Brinkley Report*. Brinkley left NBC in 1981, moving to ABC, where he moderated *This Week with David Brinkley* on Sunday mornings until 1997.

Nancy Dickerson, CBS News' first female correspondent, died at age seventy in 1997. She worked for CBS from 1954 to 1963, when she moved to NBC News. She later became an independent producer. Her syndicated news program, *Inside Washington*, aired daily from 1971 to 1974. She also produced documentaries and was a commentator for Fox TV News and PBS.

Tom Dillard, who died in 2002 at age eighty-seven, started in the news business as a copyboy in Fort Worth at age fourteen. He took up news photography at age twenty and in the early 1950s developed a camera set-up that could take photographs in rapid succession. He joined the *Dallas Morning News* in 1947 and soon became head of the newspaper's photo department. He retired in 1978.

Robert Donovan, longtime Washington bureau chief for the *Los Angeles Times*, died in 2003 at age ninety. He began working in Washington in 1947 and joined the *Times* bureau in 1963. Although he covered President Kennedy's assassination and many other major stories, he probably is best known as the author of the 1961 best-seller *PT 109*, the story of Kennedy's wartime heroics that was the basis for a feature film.

Texas historian, author and newspaper columnist **A.C. Greene** died in 2002 at the age of seventy-eight. He joined the *Dallas Times Herald* in 1960 and worked there as a reporter and editor until 1968. An avid student of Texas history, he wrote more than twenty books and for several years was a university professor. His popular "Texas Sketches" column was a regular feature in the *Dallas Morning News* from 1983 until his death.

Remembered as a fearless and independent photojournalist, **Doris Jacoby** died in 2002 at age seventy-five. She joined the staff of the *Dallas Morning News* in 1953. Known especially for her fashion photography, she was assigned to take pictures of Jacqueline Kennedy when the president and his wife visited Dallas on November 22, 1963. She left the newspaper in 1965 to start her own photography business.

Malcolm Kilduff, the assistant White House press secretary who accompanied President Kennedy to Dallas and made the official announcement of Kennedy's death, died in 2003 at age seventy-five. Kilduff continued to work in the White House press office until 1965. He afterward held several newspaper jobs, including a stint as editor of the *Beattyville Enterprise* in Kentucky.

Chicago Daily News political writer and Washington bureau chief **Peter Lisagor** died at sixty-one in 1976. Lisagor wrote a syndicated column and was a widely known radio and television commentator. He was a regular panelist in the early days of the PBS public affairs program *Washington Week in Review* and appeared frequently on NBC's *Meet the Press*.

Bill Rives died in 1983 at age seventy-two. The one-time sportswriter began his journalism career in the Dallas bureau of the Associated Press in 1935. He joined the *Dallas Morning News* after World War II and rose to the position of managing editor in 1961. He left the *Morning News* for other newspaper work in 1964 and retired in 1976.

Charles Roberts, a longtime *Newsweek* correspondent, died at seventy-five in 1992. He worked for several Chicago newspapers before joining *Newsweek* and was the author of two books. He retired in 1982. Thomas Heggen, author of the novel *Mr. Roberts*, said the main character of his book was modeled largely on Charles Roberts, with whom he had served in the Navy during World War II.

Merriman Smith, whose coverage of the assassination for UPI earned him a Pulitzer Prize, died in 1970 at age fifty-seven. In the course of thirty years in Washington, Smith covered six presidents and authored five books, all the while building a reputation for independence, tirelessness, and aggressive reporting. He was awarded the Presidential Medal of Freedom in 1968.

Forty years after the assassination of President Kennedy, most people we interviewed had remarkably detailed memories of what happened that November weekend. Though individuals' recollections differ on some events, there were no major divergences.

We conducted in-person and telephone interviews with thirty-three journalists in Texas, Washington, D.C., New York, Virginia, Oklahoma, Maryland, Illinois, and California. Of course, more journalists than those we interviewed were eyewitnesses to some part of that historic weekend. But for sake of clarity we chose to feature those who had the most prominent roles or those whose compelling stories have received little previous exposure.

We also relied on a number of secondary sources to flesh out the story. Oral history collections were a rich source of material. In particular, the Sixth Floor Museum at Dealey Plaza's ongoing oral history project, parts of which can be viewed online at www.jfk.org, was a valuable resource. The *Dallas Morning News* has a collection of personal recollections with vivid details, written by staff reporters, editors and photographers not long after the assassination. Many of those are available on the newspaper's CD-ROM, called "JFK Assassination: The Story Behind the Story, Dallas, November 22, 1963." The John F. Kennedy Library and Museum made available several oral histories from journalists who covered the assassination.

We also relied on the memoirs of several journalists, some of them now deceased, who were eyewitnesses to parts of the weekend's events. Personal details of the events on the airplane carrying Cabinet members to Japan were culled from two of White House press secretary Pierre Salinger's memoirs.

Particularly valuable was a roundtable session with journalists that was recorded in December 1963 for a Group W broadcast called "Dialogue on Dallas." The recording contains, among others, the extensive recollections of assistant White House press secretary Malcolm Kilduff, who died in March 2003, shortly before we hoped to interview him.

Also helpful were oral histories recorded by the Newseum's broadcasting division.

The timeline that details the chronology of events is based on information from several sources. As far as we know, no official timeline exists, and often there are different times recorded for different events—although those times in many cases are just a few seconds or minutes apart. Of necessity, some events that were not officially timed, but that are known to have taken place, are placed in those general time frames.

We decided to rely principally on the timeline used by William Manchester in *The Death of a President*, published in 1967. Additional elements came from the Dallas Police Department radio transmissions from November 22 to 24, 1963, as excerpted in the *Warren Commission Hearings*; a timeline account of NBC news coverage called *Seventy Hours and Thirty Minutes: As Broadcast on the NBC Television Network by NBC News*, published in 1966; the times that UPI bulletins were sent, as documented in the bulletins themselves; the times for certain broadcasts noted in *November 22, 1963*, a two-LP recording of ABC Radio Network news coverage; and, in a few cases, the explicit written recollections of some of the participants.

We were fortunate to get access to the complete written transcript of CBS Television Network broadcast coverage from Friday, November 22, through Monday, November 25, 1963.

Michael Dolan, a freelance researcher, provided extensive audio research for the book, obtaining copies of the archival recordings featured in the book and on the CD, and providing valuable assistance in sorting out the timetable of the first day's broadcast news coverage.

He clocked videotape of the first four hours of CBS television news coverage on November 22, and audiotape of CBS radio for part of the day, to determine times that various news reports were made. Those times were used in Chapter III to track CBS coverage during the interval leading to the official announcement that the president was dead. Though other researchers have clocked times that are slightly different than these—by a minute or so—the differences are not significant, and we believe this is an accurate timetable.

Rarely heard vintage audio recordings of radio communications between the White House Situation Room and Air Force One and the plane carrying Cabinet members on November 22, 1963, were obtained from the National Archives, the Lyndon Baines Johnson Library and Museum, and other sources. Also obtained from the LBJ Library were "Mrs. Johnson's Diary Tapes, November 22–24, 1963," poignant recollections by Lady Bird Johnson that she recorded after the assassination, as well as audio recordings of telephone conversations President Johnson had with a variety of people in the hours and days after the assassination.

Transcripts of WNEW Radio reporter Ike Pappas' live report from the Dallas jail were made from an audio tape provided by Pappas. A transcript of WFAA-TV's interview with Abraham Zapruder on November 22, 1963, came from the Sixth Floor Museum.

We conducted no investigations and made no determinations as to theories about conspiracies involving the death of President Kennedy. Our sole intention was to provide the best and most vivid recollection of history as seen through the eyes and ears of the journalists who witnessed it.

ACKNOWLEDGMENTS

Many journalists who covered the story of the assassination and its aftermath generously contributed their memories, photographs, and reflections to this book. We thank them all. We extend special appreciation to the journalists of Dallas and Fort Worth for their wonderful stories and warm hospitality.

Our research efforts were helped enormously by the staff of the Sixth Floor Museum at Dealey Plaza, which chronicles the life and death of President Kennedy through innovative exhibits, and preserves the site where the sniper's nest and rifle were found after the assassination. Executive Director Jeff West, Director of Interpretation Ruth Ann Rugg, Archivist Gary Mack, and Oral History Coordinator Stephen Fagin granted access to countless oral history files, did special research, and answered relentless questions while providing us space to work and conduct interviews. The Sixth Floor Museum staff helped us find rare photographs and broadcast transcripts, and assisted us in locating local journalists who played key roles in news coverage of the assassination.

We were aided by freelance researcher Michael Dolan, who provided extensive audio research for the book and assistance in compiling the companion audio CD. Elizabeth Hamlin helped locate oral histories and other materials at the John F. Kennedy Library and Museum.

Many of the journalists we interviewed shared private photographs and archival broadcast materials. In particular, we thank Bob Schieffer, Hugh Sidey, Gary Haynes, Sid Davis, Mike Cochran, Ben Bradlee, Joe Carter, Andy Hanson, and Tom Alyea for making available to us rare photographs, broadcast tapes, original notes, and press passes.

Literary agent Raphael Sagalyn was integral to this project, helping to shape it as well as sell it. Alex Lubertozzi had contagious enthusiasm for the project from the beginning and was our able editor. Tara Utsey's project management and Todd Stocke's editorial direction smoothed the production process, and designer Megan Dempster brought the many visual elements together gracefully. Special thanks to publicist Vicky Brown and designer Jenna Jakubowski for their dedicated efforts, as well.

This book is the product of the hard work of many people at the Newseum, who provided hours of editing, photo research, and fact-checking. They include Karen Wyatt, Don Ross, Ann Rauscher, Indira Williams, Julia Wyatt, Jerrie Bethel, Rick Mastroianni, Mary Glendinning, and Kristi Conkle. Andrea Shepard provided technical assistance.

Our special appreciation goes to the Newseum's Gene Mater, who worked tirelessly to arrange interviews with key broadcasters who once were his colleagues at CBS News. We also thank former CBS producer Sandy Socolow for providing us valuable research assistance.

From beginning to end, the book would not have been possible without the vision of Freedom Forum Chairman and Chief Executive Officer Charles L. Overby, Newseum President Peter S. Prichard, Executive Director and Senior Vice President Joe Urschel, and Managing Editor Margaret Engel.

Every effort has been made to attribute all the materials that have been used in this book and audio CD. If any errors have been made, we will gladly make corrections in future editions.

INTERVIEW SOURCES

Allman, Pierce. Interview by the authors. Dallas, Texas, February 18, 2003.

Alyea, Tom. Telephone and e-mail interviews by the authors. March 14 and April 27, 2003.

Asman, Robert. Interview by Ken Crawford. Arlington, Virginia, December 17, 2001. Video recording, Newseum, Arlington, Virginia.

Aynesworth, Hugh. Interview by the authors. Dallas, Texas, February 17, 2003.

Barker, Eddie. Interview by the authors. Dallas, Texas, February 17, 2003.

Baskin, Robert. First-person written account, 1964. The Dallas Morning News, Dallas, Texas.

Beers, Jack. First-person written account, 1964. The Dallas Morning News, Dallas, Texas.

Bell, Jack. Interview, April 19, 1966. Transcript, John F. Kennedy Library and Museum, Boston, Massachusetts.

Bennett, John. Telephone interview by the authors. March 20, 2003.

Biffle, Kent. First-person written account, 1964. The Dallas Morning News, Dallas, Texas.

Birnbaum, Bernard. Telephone interview by the authors. July 11, 2003.

Bradlee, Ben. Interview by the authors. Washington, D.C., March 6, 2003.

Brinkley, David. Excerpted from his book *David Brinkley: A Memoir* (New York: Ballantine Books, 1995).

Carter, Joe. Telephone interviews by the authors. March 14 and 19, 2003.

Castleberry, Vivian. Interview, October 14, 1991. Oral History Program of the Sixth Floor Museum at Dealey Plaza, Dallas, Texas.

Chambers, James. Interview, June 10, 1994. Oral History Program of the Sixth Floor Museum at Dealey Plaza, Dallas, Texas.

Clark, Bob. Interview by the authors. Arlington, Virginia, March 4, 2003. Additional excerpts from interview by Jerry Grossman, Arlington, Virginia, September 19, 2001. Video recording, Newseum, Arlington, Virginia.

Cochran, Mike. Interview by the authors. Fort Worth, Texas, February 18, 2003.

Couch, Malcolm. Interview, c. 1989. Oral History Program of the Sixth Floor Museum at Dealey Plaza, Dallas, Texas.

Cronkite, Walter. Interview by the authors. New York, New York, April 3, 2003.

Dameron, Charles. Interview, January 12, 1995. Oral History Program of the Sixth Floor Museum at Dealey Plaza, Dallas, Texas.

Davis, Sid. Interview by the authors. Bethesda, Maryland, March 17, 2003.

Dickerson, Nancy. Excerpted from her book *Among Those Present: A Reporter's View of Twenty-Five Years in Washington* (New York: Random House, 1976).

Dillard, Tom. First-person written account, 1964. The *Dallas Morning News*, Dallas, Texas.

Donovan, Robert. Excerpted from "Dialogue on Dallas," Group W, December 1963. Audio recording, National Archives: Assassination Records Review Board. RG 541.

Elliott, Osborn. Interview by the authors. New York, New York, April 2, 2003.

Fallon, Jack. Telephone interview by the authors. April 4, 2003.

Greene, A.C. Interview, June 18, 1992. Oral History Program of the Sixth Floor Museum at Dealey Plaza, Dallas, Texas.

Grunwald, Henry A. Excerpted from his book *One Man's America: A Journalist's Search for the Heart of His Country* (New York: Doubleday, 1997).

Hampton, Wilborn. Interview by the authors. New York, New York, April 2, 2003.

Haynes, Gary. Telephone interview by the authors. February 3, 2003.

Huffaker, Bob. Telephone interview by the authors. April 30, 2003.

Imm (Bashour), Val. Interview, September 20, 1995. Oral History Program of the Sixth Floor Museum at Dealey Plaza, Dallas, Texas.

Jackson, Bob. Interview by Ken Crawford. Colorado Springs, Colorado, April 1, 2003. Video recording, Newseum, Arlington, Virginia. Additional excerpts from interview, November 22, 1993. Oral History Program of the Sixth Floor Museum at Dealey Plaza, Dallas, Texas.

Jacoby, Doris. First-person written account, 1964. The Dallas Morning News, Dallas, Texas.

Kilduff, Malcolm. Excerpted from "Dialogue on Dallas," Group W, December 1963. Audio recording, National Archives: Assassination Records Review Board. RG 541.

Lisagor, Peter. Interview, 1966. Transcript, John F. Kennedy Library and Museum, Boston, Massachusetts.

MacNeil, Robert. Interview by the authors. New York, New York, April 2, 2003.

Mayo, Travis. First-person written account, March 25, 1964. The Dallas Morning News, Dallas, Texas.

McGarry, Terrance W. Interview by the authors. Bristow, Virginia, April 14, 2003.

McGraw, Preston. Interview, October 9, 2001. Oral History Program of the Sixth Floor Museum at Dealey Plaza, Dallas, Texas.

Means, Marianne. Interview by the authors. Washington, D.C., March 6, 2003.

Pappas, Ike. Interview by the authors. Arlington, Virginia, March 3, 2003.

Payne, Darwin. Interview by the authors. Dallas, Texas, February 15, 2003.

Pierpoint, Robert. Telephone interview by the authors. March 20, 2003.

Quinn, Mike. First-person written account, 1964. The Dallas Morning News, Dallas, Texas.

Rather, Dan. Telephone interview by the authors. May 22, 2003.

Rives, Bill. First-person written account, 1964. The Dallas Morning News, Dallas, Texas.

Roberts, Charles. Interview, April 11, 1966. Transcript, John F. Kennedy Library and Museum, Boston, Massachusetts.

Robertson, Walter. First-person written account, 1964. The Dallas Morning News, Dallas, Texas.

Salinger, Pierre. Excerpted from his books *P.S.: A Memoir* (New York: St. Martin's Press, 1995) and *With Kennedy* (Garden City, N.J.: Doubleday, 1966).

Schieffer, Bob. Interview by the authors. Washington, D.C., March 10, 2003.

Schweid, Barry. Telephone interview by the authors. April 28, 2003.

Shelton, Keith. Interview by the authors. Frisco, Texas, February 16, 2003.

Shipp, Bert. Interview by the authors. Dallas, Texas, February 17, 2003.

Sidey, Hugh. Telephone interview by the authors. April 9, 2003.

Simpson, Peggy. Interview by the authors. Arlington, Virginia, March 5, 2003.

Skedgell, Robert. Excerpted from *Now the News: The Story of Broadcast Journalism* by Edward Bliss Jr. (New York: Columbia University, 1991).

Smith, Merriman. Excerpted from his November 23, 1963, UPI dispatch, published in his book *Merriman Smith's Book of Presidents: A White House Memoir*, edited by G. Timothy Smith (New York: Norton, 1972).

Stolley, Richard. Interview by the authors. New York, New York, April 2, 2003.

Thomas, Helen. Interview by the authors. Washington, D.C., March 3, 2003.

Wicker, Tom. Excerpted from *The Working Press: Special to the New York Times*, edited by Ruth Adler (New York: Arno Press, 1981).

Wise, Wes. Interview by the authors. Dallas, Texas, February 15, 2003.

Woodward, Mary Elizabeth. First-person written account, 1964. The Dallas Morning News, Dallas, Texas.

SOURCES FOR AUDIO TRANSCRIPTS

ABC Radio Network. *November 22, 1963*. Excerpts from news coverage aired November 22 through November 25, 1963. New York: American Broadcasting Company, n.d. Two LPs.

CBS Television Network. "The Assassination of President John F. Kennedy as Broadcast on the CBS Television Network." November 22 through November 25, 1963. New York: Columbia Broadcasting System, 1963. Unpublished transcript.

Dallas Police Department radio transmissions, November 22 through November 24, 1963. Excerpted from *Warren Commission Hearings: Investigation of the Assassination of President John F. Kennedy*. Vol. 23. Washington, D.C.: U.S. Government Printing Office, 1964.

Johnson, Lady Bird. "Mrs. Johnson's Diary Tapes, November 22–24, 1963." Audio recordings. Serial no. SRT 9201. Lyndon Baines Johnson Library and Museum, Austin, Texas.

NBC Television Network. *Seventy Hours and Thirty Minutes: As Broadcast on the NBC Television Network by NBC News*. New York: Random House, 1966.

Pappas, Ike. Live WNEW Radio news report of the murder of Lee Harvey Oswald. November 24, 1963. From *Four Days That Shocked the World*. Colpix CXX608. LP.

"Recording of Radio Communications with Air Force One." November 22, 1963. Includes calls made by Lyndon B. Johnson and Lady Bird Johnson from Air Force One and radio transmissions between the White House Situation Room and the plane carrying Cabinet members. Audio recordings. Serial nos. SRT 969-1, 969-2, and 969-3. Lyndon Baines Johnson Library and Museum, Austin, Texas.

Zapruder, Abraham. Live WFAA-TV interview by Jay Watson. November 22, 1963. Transcript, Sixth Floor Museum at Dealey Plaza, Dallas, Texas.

SUGGESTED READING

Belo Interactive, Inc., *JFK Assassination: The Story Behind the Story, Dallas, November 22, 1963.* 2002. CD-ROM.

Bishop, Jim. *The Day Kennedy Was Shot.* New York: Funk & Wagnalls, 1968.

Bliss, Edward. *Now the News: The Story of Broadcast Journalism.* New York: Columbia University Press, 1991.

Bradlee, Ben. *A Good Life: Newspapering and Other Adventures.* New York: Simon & Schuster, 1995.

Brinkley, David. *David Brinkley: A Memoir.* New York: Ballantine Books, 1996.

Cronkite, Walter. *A Reporter's Life.* New York: Alfred A. Knopf, 1996.

The Dallas Morning News. *November 22: The Day Remembered.* Dallas: Taylor Publishing Company, 1990.

Dickerson, Nancy. *Among Those Present: A Reporter's View of Twenty-Five Years in Washington.* New York: Random House, 1976.

Elliott, Osborn. *The World of Oz.* New York: Viking Press, 1980.

Gordon, Gregory, and Ronald E. Cohen. *Down to the Wire: UPI's Fight for Survival.* New York: McGraw-Hill, 1990.

Grunwald, Henry A. *One Man's America: A Journalist's Search for the Heart of His Country.* New York: Doubleday, 1997.

Hampton, Wilborn. *Kennedy Assassinated! The World Mourns: A Reporter's Story.* Cambridge, Mass.: Candlewick Press, 1997.

Hlavach, Laura, and Darwin Payne, eds. *Reporting the Kennedy Assassination: Journalists Who Were There Recall Their Experiences.* Dallas: Three Forks Press, 1996.

Johnson, Lady Bird. *A White House Diary.* New York: Holt, Rinehart and Winston, 1970.

MacNeil, Robert. *The Right Place at the Right Time.* Boston: Little, Brown and Company, 1982.

MacNeil, Robert, ed. *The Way We Were: 1963, the Year Kennedy Was Shot.* New York: Carroll & Graf, 1988.

Manchester, William. *The Death of a President.* New York: Harper & Row, 1967.

Pett, Saul, Sid Moody, Hugh Mulligan, and Tom Henshaw. *The Torch Is Passed: The Associated Press Story of the Death of a President*. New York: Associated Press, 1963.

Rather, Dan, with Mickey Herskowitz. *The Camera Never Blinks: Adventures of a TV Journalist*. New York: William Morrow and Company, 1977.

Report of the Warren Commission on the Assassination of President Kennedy. New York: McGraw-Hill, 1964.

Salinger, Pierre. *P.S.: A Memoir*. New York: St. Martin's Press, 1995.

———. *With Kennedy*. Garden City, N.Y.: Doubleday, 1966.

Schieffer, Bob. *This Just In: What I Couldn't Tell You on TV*. New York: G.P. Putnam's Sons, 2003.

Schlesinger, Arthur M. *A Thousand Days: John F. Kennedy in the White House*. Boston: Houghton Miffin, 1965.

Sidey, Hugh. *John F. Kennedy, President*. New York: Atheneum, 1964.

Slater, Robert. *This ... Is CBS: A Chronicle of 60 Years*. Englewood Cliffs, N.J.: Prentice Hall, 1988.

Smith, A. Merriman. *Merriman Smith's Book of Presidents: A White House Memoir*. Edited by Timothy G. Smith. New York: Norton, 1972.

Trask, Richard B. *Pictures of the Pain: Photography and the Assassination of President Kennedy*. Danvers, Mass.: Yeoman Press, 1994.

United Press International and American Heritage Magazine, comp. *Four Days: The Historical Record of the Death of President Kennedy*. New York: American Heritage Publishing Company, 1964.

Zelizer, Barbie. *Covering the Body: The Kennedy Assassination, the Media, and the Shaping of the Collective Memory*. Chicago: University of Chicago Press, 1992.

AUDIO AND PHOTO CREDITS

Some audio segments have been edited for time and content. While we have attempted to achieve the best possible quality on the archival audio, some audio quality is the result of source limitations. Archival audio research by Michael Dolan. Audio editing by Tara Utsey and Todd Stocke. Audio recording, engineering and mastering by Christian Pawola at Music & Sound Company, DeKalb, Illinois.

Archival audio provided by and copyright of: ABC Radio; CBS News Archives; NBC News Archives; National Archives and Records Administration; The Sixth Floor Museum at Dealey Plaza; Lyndon Baines Johnson Library and Museum; Sid Davis; Westwood One, Inc.; Colpix Records; and Ledford Enterprises.

Photographs are used by permission: Page 1, ART RICKERBY/Time Life Pictures/Getty Images; 2, 5, Courtesy Andy Hanson; 9, Joe McAuley/Fort Worth Star-Telegram Photograph Collection, Special Collections, University of Texas at Arlington Libraries; 10, Newseum collection; 11, 12, 13, Cecil W. Stoughton/John F. Kennedy Library; 14, Newseum collection; 15, Courtesy The Sixth Floor Museum at Dealey Plaza/Tom Dillard Collection; 16, Cecil W. Stoughton/John F. Kennedy Library; 17, Courtesy Hugh Sidey; 18, ART RICKERBY/Time Life Pictures/Getty Images; 20, Courtesy The Sixth Floor Museum at Dealey Plaza/Darryl Heikes, Dallas Times Herald Collection; 22, Courtesy The Sixth Floor Museum at Dealey Plaza/William Beal, Dallas Times Herald Collection; 23, Bettmann/CORBIS; 26–27, Courtesy The Sixth Floor Museum at Dealey Plaza. Photographer Abraham Zapruder, Zapruder Collection. © 1967 (Renewed 1995) The Sixth Floor Museum at Dealey Plaza. All Rights Reserved.; 28, Courtesy The Sixth Floor Museum at Dealey Plaza/Jay Skaggs, Jay Skaggs Collection; 29, Courtesy The Sixth Floor Museum at Dealey Plaza/ Phil Willis, Phil Willis Collection; 31, James W. Altgens/The Associated Press; 32, Photo by Tom Dillard/Courtesy Richard B. Trask; 34, UPI/Library of Congress/Prints and Photographs Division/New York World-Telegram and Sun Collection; 36, The Associated Press, courtesy John F. Kennedy Library; 38, Courtesy The Sixth Floor Museum at Dealey Plaza/William Allen, Dallas Times Herald Collection; 41, Cecil W. Stoughton/John F. Kennedy Library; 43, 47, CBS Photo Archive; 51, The Associated Press/KRLD-TV; 54, NBC/Globe Photos, Inc.; 58, CBS Photo Archive; 59, Newseum collection; 61, CBS Photo Archive; 63, Courtesy The Sixth Floor Museum at Dealey Plaza/Andy Hanson, Dallas Times Herald Collection; 65, Courtesy Andy Hanson; 77, The Associated Press; 79, Courtesy Sid Davis; 83, George Smith/Fort Worth Star-Telegram Collection, Special Collections Division, University of Texas at Arlington Libraries; 83, Photo by Jim Murray, © 1999 Richard B. Trask; 83, Courtesy The Sixth Floor Museum at Dealey Plaza/WFAA Collection; 85, CBS Photo Archive; 92, Hulton Archive/Getty Images; 94, Courtesy Ben Bradlee; 99, CARL MYDANS/Time Life Pictures/Getty Images; 104, Courtesy Andy Hanson; 106, Courtesy Tom Alyea; 109, Courtesy Ike Pappas Collection; 111, Courtesy Sid Davis; 112, Newseum collection; 113, Newseum collection/gift of Gary Stevens; 115, Cecil W. Stoughton/LBJ Library; 117, Cecil W. Stoughton/John F. Kennedy Library; 118, Cecil W. Stoughton/LBJ Library; 124, National Archives and Records Administration; 128, O. Fernandez/Library of Congress/ Prints and Photographs Division/New York World-Telegram and Sun Collection; 130, Bill Sauro/New York Herald Tribune/Library of Congress/Prints and Photographs Division/New York World-Telegram and Sun Collection; 140, The Associated Press; 143, NBC/ Globe Photos, Inc.; 144, Wally McNamee/UPI/Library of Congress/Prints and Photographs Division/New York World-Telegram and Sun Collection; 146, Martin Luther King, Jr. Library/Washington Star Collection; 147, The Associated Press/courtesy Library of Congress/Prints and Photographs Division/New York World-Telegram and Sun Collection; 149, Ralph Crane/Time Life Pictures/Getty Images; 151, Robert Philips/Time Life Pictures/Getty Images; 152, ABC Photography Archives; 153, Library of Congress/Prints and Photographs Division/New York World-Telegram and Sun Collection; 155, NBC/Globe Photos, Inc.; 157, Courtesy The Sixth Floor Museum at Dealey Plaza/KDFW Collection; 160, CORBIS; 163, 167, Bettmann/CORBIS; 169, UPI/Library of Congress/Prints and Photographs Division/New York World-Telegram and Sun Collection; 171, 172, 174, UPI/Library of Congress/Prints and Photographs Division/New York World-Telegram and Sun Collection; 176, Courtesy The Sixth Floor Museum at Dealey Plaza/Bill Winfrey, Tom Dillard Collection; 180, ABC Photography Archives; 182, Robert Knudsen/John F. Kennedy Library; 187, NBC/Globe Photos, Inc.; 189, CORBIS; 192, Courtesy The Sixth Floor Museum at Dealey Plaza/Dallas Times Herald Collection; 201, Bob Jackson/Dallas Times Herald; 205, 206, CORBIS; 208, Jack Beers/The Associated Press; 211, Bob Jackson/Dallas Times Herald; 215, Ted Powers/The Associated Press; 219, Courtesy Andy Hanson; 220, UPI/Library of Congress/Prints and Photographs Division/New York World-Telegram and Sun Collection; 222, NBC/Globe Photos, Inc.; 225, Courtesy Andy Hanson; 227, Douglas Chevalier/The Washington Post; 229, NBC/Globe Photos, Inc.; 231, Casamento/The Washington Post; 235, NBC/Globe Photos, Inc.; 237, Paul M. Schmick/Martin Luther King, Jr. Library/Washington Star Collection; 239, Special Collections & Archives George Mason University Libraries/Ollie Atkins Collection; 241, UPI/Library of Congress/Prints and Photographs Division/New York World-Telegram and Sun Collection; 243, Wally McNamee/The Washington Post; 248, NBC/Globe Photos, Inc.; 249, UPI/Library of Congress/Prints and Photographs Division/New York World-Telegram and Sun Collection; 250, Courtesy Gary Haynes; 251, Cecil W. Stoughton/John F. Kennedy Library; 252, Courtesy Ben Bradlee; 253, Martin Luther King, Jr. Library; 255, Courtesy Gene Gordon; 256, Courtesy Ike Pappas Collection; 261, The Associated Press; 263, Bill Mauldin/The Associated Press/Chicago Sun-Times; 265, Newseum collection; 268, NBC/Globe Photos, Inc.; 269, Special Collections & Archives George Mason University Libraries/Ollie Atkins Collection; 271, The Associated Press; 273, Newseum collection; 274, James P. Blair/CORBIS; 275, Newseum collection; 277, CORBIS.

The Newseum, the world's first interactive museum of news, takes visitors behind the scenes to show how and why news is made. It strives to help the public and news media understand one another better. The Newseum is funded by the Freedom Forum, a non-profit, non-partisan foundation. Visit www.newseum.org. The Newseum's *President Kennedy Has Been Shot* is co-authored by award-winning journalists Cathy Trost and Susan Bennett.

Cathy Trost, a former reporter for the *Wall Street Journal* and UPI, is the co-author of the critically acclaimed *Running Toward Danger: Stories Behind the Breaking News of 9/11.* She was the founding director of the Casey Journalism Center on Children and Families at the Philip Merrill College of Journalism at the University of Maryland.

Susan Bennett, director of International Exhibits at the Newseum, is a veteran editor and reporter who covered foreign affairs, national politics, and Congress in Washington. She was previously an editor and writer on *USA TODAY*'s editorial page, national correspondent for Knight-Ridder newspapers, and a bureau chief and state editor for UPI.

About the Narrator

Dan Rather has been anchor and managing editor of the *CBS Evening News* since 1981. In 1962, he joined CBS, and on November 22, 1963, in Dallas, was one of the first journalists to confirm the death of President Kennedy. He has served as a CBS News bureau chief in London and Saigon and as a correspondent for *60 Minutes, 60 Minutes II,* and *48 Hours.* He is the author of *The American Dream, Deadlines & Datelines, I Remember,* and *The Camera Never Blinks.*